Images of Modern America

OLD COWTOWN MUSEUM

Keith Wondra and Barb Myers

ARCADIA PUBLISHING

ISBN 978-1-4671-1743-2

Published by Arcadia Publishing
Charleston, South Carolina

Printed in the United States of America

Library of Congress Control Number: 2016937020

For all general information, please contact Arcadia Publishing:
Telephone 843-853-2070
Fax 843-853-0044
E-mail sales@arcadiapublishing.com
For customer service and orders:
Toll-Free 1-888-313-2665

Visit us on the Internet at www.arcadiapublishing.com

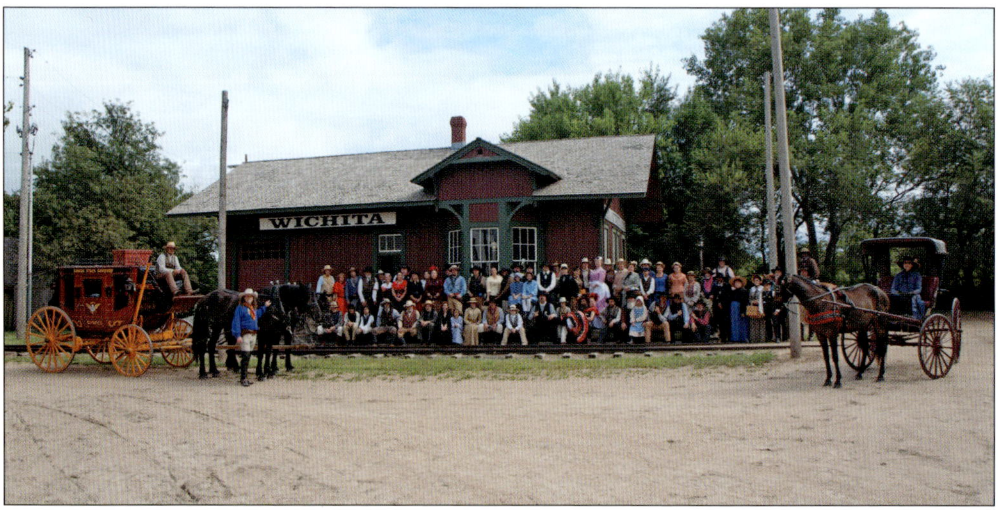

The book is dedicated to the volunteers at Old Cowtown Museum, who make the institution into a regional attraction and outdoor museum. (Courtesy Keith Wondra.)

Images of Modern America

OLD COWTOWN MUSEUM

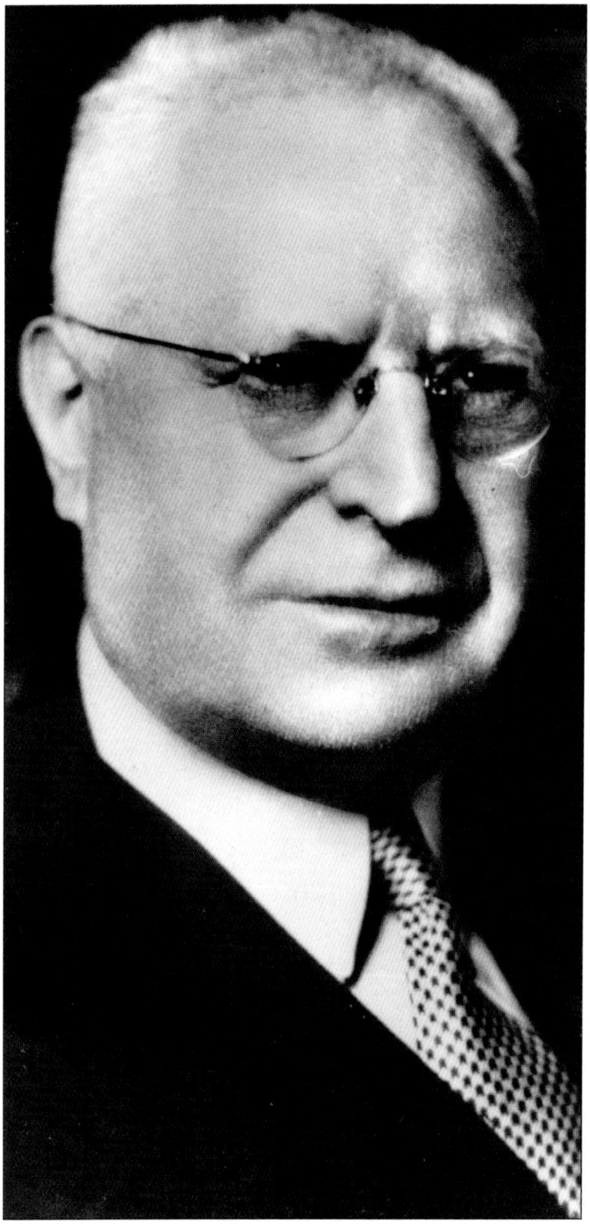

The idea of a museum to preserve Wichita's past, including the preservation of Wichita's first permanent church building as a historical monument, began in the mind of Victor Murdock, son of *Wichita Eagle* founder Marshall Murdock. Victor passed away in 1945, five years before his idea became reality in the founding of Old Cowtown Museum. (Courtesy Old Cowtown Museum and the Wichita-Sedgwick County Historical Museum.)

On the Front Cover: Cattle drive during "Rails & Trails" (Courtesy Charlayne Talley and Old Cowtown Museum)

On the Upper Back Cover: Dixie Lee Saloon Girls (Courtesy Old Cowtown Museum)

On the Lower Back Cover: (from left to right) Steampunk Day (Courtesy Keith Wondra), Bon-Ton Drug Store (Courtesy Treva Mathur), and Old Sedgwick County Fair (Courtesy Old Cowtown Museum)

Contents

Acknowledgments 6
Introduction 7
1. Foundation 9
2. Living History 25
3. Events and Groups 41
4. Myth and Reality 65
5. Decline and Resurgence 89
Bibliography 95

Acknowledgments

Writing a book about an institution that has a long history in Wichita, like Old Cowtown Museum, could not be done without help from the community. Unless otherwise noted, all photographs presented here are from Old Cowtown Museum's collections. For the first 30 years, the museum was known as Historic Wichita Cow Town. From 1981 to the present day, it has been known as Old Cowtown Museum. For the sake of consistency, Old Cowtown Museum will be used throughout, except for in direct quotations.

The authors, therefore, are grateful to director David Flask for making this project possible. Particular thanks go to Teddie Barlow and Kelly Fay, who answered questions about and gave access to the museum's archives.

Even though Old Cowtown Museum has many pictures covering its 66 years of existence, other institutions and persons contributed photographs to complete the book, including Howard Eastwood; Orin Friesen; Coleen Dyson and Shirley Mosher of Girl Scouts of Kansas Heartland; Bob Garrett; Lauren Pope and Ken Spurgeon of Lone Chimney Films; Treva Mathur; Doug McGovern; Jim Powell; Charlayne Talley; Lela Meadow-Conner of Tallgrass Film Association; Chris Teufel; Linda Thom; Brian Corn of the *Wichita Eagle*; Teri Mott of Wichita Festivals, Inc.; Jami Frazier-Tracy of Wichita-Sedgwick County Historical Museum; and Mary Nelson of Wichita State University Libraries, Special Collections and University Archives.

Thanks also go to Bob Garrett, Jim Grimes, Steve Grimes, Stan Harder, Gary Huffman, Dennis Kennedy, Elizabeth Kennedy, Phil Lovechik, Mary Manlove, Dr. Jay Price, and Francene Sharp.

INTRODUCTION

"Relive yesterday at historic Cowtown. Walk down the wooden sidewalks of the Old West. Take an excursion into the past. Walk down the wooden sidewalks of Wichita's Cowtown. The hollow echoes of your boots will bring back memories of Jessie Chisholm and 'Buffalo Bill' Mathewson, who walked this way so long ago. Here is the Old West living on in these old frame buildings, bright and fresh with 20th-century paint but alive with old memories." So reads *Relive Yesterday at Historic Cowtown*, a brochure from the early 1960s about Wichita's Old Cowtown Museum. The end of the brochure proclaims that there is fun at Cowtown as well as history, a theme that holds true in the museum's promotional literature today.

Richard "Dick" Long, manager of the *Wichita Eagle* morning edition, started in the 1940s writing the "Wichita Historical Panels," articles on the city's early history that appear in the *Wichita Eagle* with illustrations by Ben Hammond. Long's articles coincided with several pieces of writing on Wichita's history from Victor Murdock, son of the *Wichita Eagle* founder Marshall Murdock. Murdock's and Long's writings started an effort to preserve buildings from Wichita's early history that would later become Old Cowtown Museum.

It was at this same time that Long turned in an article on Wichita's first church building being used as a boardinghouse in the 600 block of North Main Street. Murdock confirmed the story's accuracy and contacted the owner, but due to wartime housing shortages, the building was not for sale. He predicted that once the war was over, the structure would be a fire hazard and be condemned. Long then made a promise to Murdock that if Victor was gone he would see that the building be restored. Victor Murdock died July 8, 1945.

Long received word, a few years after Murdock's death, that the former boardinghouse was being condemned due to a recent fire and that a salvage operator acquired the building. Long bought the building for $400 and included was the Hodge House, mistaken for years as the Parsonage. With their two new buildings, Long and others formed Historic Wichita, Inc. on April 28, 1950.

Later, Historic Wichita, Inc. started looking for suitable locations for its two structures. It asked for help from the Wichita Park Board, which passed the decision on to Emery Cox, director of Wichita parks. Historic Wichita's first choice was Central Riverside Park which was unattainable. The staff then drove to Oak Park, believing that they had worn the director down, but Cox explained that the city had put thousands of dollars into the area. A parking lot and historic buildings would ruin the atmosphere of the natural woodland. Director Cox suggested 23 acres of undeveloped sandhills by the Big Arkansas River owned by the Wichita Water Department. With the help of Cox, Historic Wichita, Inc. leased the land for 99 years at a dollar a year. Once the site had been chosen, preservation of the buildings could start.

The restoration of the church and parsonage was barely complete when Historic Wichita, Inc. acquired two more buildings to preserve: the Munger House and Wichita's first jail. The Eunice Sterling Chapter of the Daughters of the American Revolution saved the Munger House. It donated it to Historic Wichita, Inc. in hopes that the new organization could preserve it. When the Wichita School Board purchased land for a school expansion, it discovered the city's first jail at Twelfth and Main Streets in 1951. The school board would not donate it, so it sold the deteriorating structure to Historic Wichita for $1. These four buildings became the foundation for a cow town village that would later become Old Cowtown Museum.

From 1953 to 1955, Historic Wichita, Inc. relocated or erected six buildings to/on the site, including a depot from Anness, Kansas; a building from North Main that became interpreted as a drugstore; a replica of Wichita's first school; the Cow Town Fire Station No. 1; a barbershop, built from the second story of the structure from North Main; and the Wichita Township Hall, which became a post office exhibit. With the 10 buildings, Historic Wichita, Inc. decided to open a frontier village and called it Historic Wichita Cow Town.

Old Cowtown Museum coincided its opening with the world premiere of *Wichita*, starring Joel McCrea and Wichita's own Vera Miles, at the city's Miller Theatre. Even though Old Cowtown Museum started out as a shrine to the founders of Wichita, the connection of the museum's opening to the *Wichita* world premiere meant that Cowtown was no longer just a shrine to the founders of Wichita. Instead, it became a place to celebrate the image of the Wild West. Even the promotional material helped promote this new image by glorifying Wyatt Earp and Billy the Kid and their roles in Wichita history.

After its opening, Old Cowtown Museum became an afterthought to many in Wichita. Through the years, city support of the struggling museum was inconsistent, and by 1958, rumors spread that Old Cowtown Museum might have to close. In 1958, members of Historic Wichita, Inc. asked the Wichita Area Girl Scouts to assist with interpretation during the busy summer months. Marge Kirby, a teacher at Wichita East High School, served as the site director of the Girl Scouts at Old Cowtown. The Girl Scouts at Cowtown created a bond with the museum that lasted generations, with many fondly remembering their time at Old Cowtown Museum.

The biggest growth of Old Cowtown Museum came from the celebration of Kansas's centennial in 1961. In preparation for the centennial, 15 buildings were added to the museum, bringing the total to 27. By the end of 1961, Cowtown continued promoting itself as an authentic frontier village. But the "authenticity" was based on Hollywood's version of the Old West—not Wichita's history. The claim of authenticity would continue until the mid-1970s.

With the demise of Westerns, Old Cowtown Museum reinvented itself around telling the stories of Victorian Wichita and the role of agriculture in the development of Sedgwick County. The 1990s saw the continuation of the interpretation of the role of agriculture and the addition of the roles of women and minorities to the museum's interpretation.

In 2000, Old Cowtown Museum started to have financial problems. Things came to a head in 2006 when the museum's attendance and debt became front-page news in the *Wichita Eagle*. After a year of negotiations with Historic Wichita-Sedgwick County Inc., the museum's board and the City of Wichita came to an agreement and the city took over day-to-day operations.

The story of Cowtown chronicles an evolution from being a shrine to a tourist attraction, then a living history museum, and, finally, a western-themed museum. A product of 1950s Old West nostalgia, Cowtown has, in spite of its problems, outlasted many of its peer institutions such as Old Abilene Town in Abilene, Texas, and Burketown in Greensburg, Kansas. Cowtown has had to adapt to survive; gone are the days of interpreting just the Old West version of history. With new events such as Steampunk Day, Old Cowtown Museum has lived up to its founder's expectations. Richard "Dick" Long and Victor Murdock would be surprised and proud of what their dream has become.

One

FOUNDATION

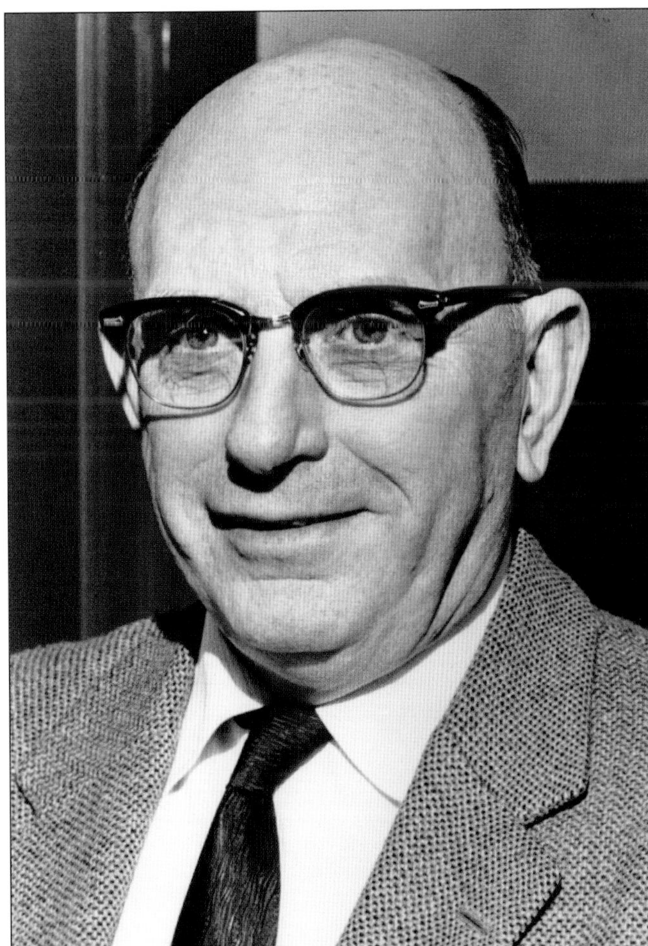

Dick Long was editor of the *Wichita Eagle* morning edition in the 1940s and the primary force behind the formation of Historic Wichita, Inc. in 1950. The nonprofit was responsible for the purchase, remodeling, reconstruction, and upkeep of the buildings "deemed to have historic merit" to the city's history. Long was the president of Historic Wichita, Inc. from 1950 to 1961. (Courtesy Old Cowtown Museum and the Wichita-Sedgwick County Historical Museum.)

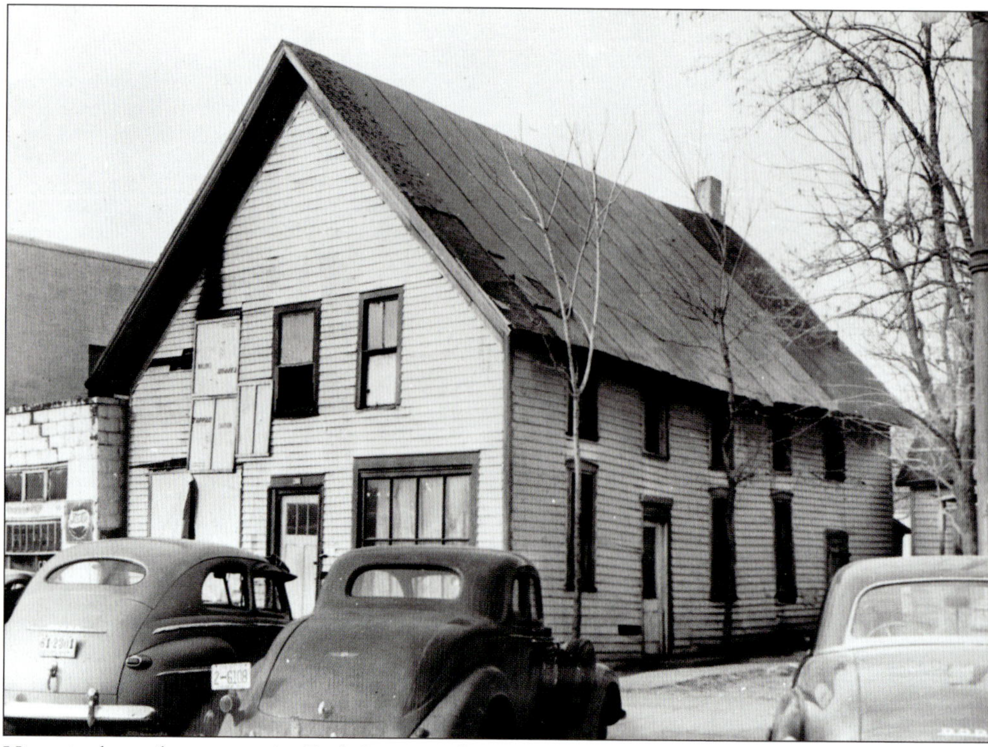

Historical articles written by Dick Long in the 1940s led to a bid by Victor Murdock to buy the first permanent church building, located at 605 North Main Street. This was the First Presbyterian Church, originally built in 1870. It had been sold to the Catholic Church in 1875 and was purchased in 1886 by Millie and Wesley Hodge. By World War II, the building was utilized as a boardinghouse, and Millie Hodge declined Murdock's offer. However, in 1948, Dick Long heard that the building had been condemned, and he was able to purchase it and the building next door for $400 in 1952. (Above, courtesy *Wichita Eagle*; below, courtesy Keith Wondra)

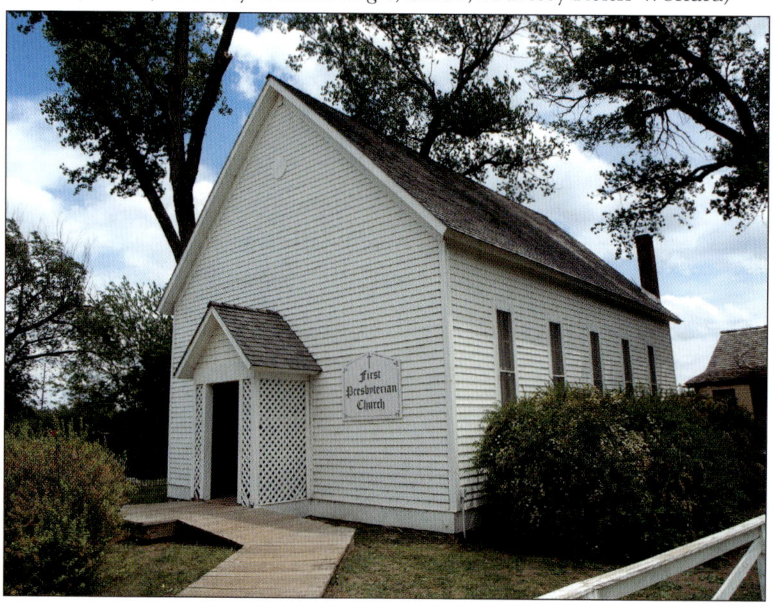

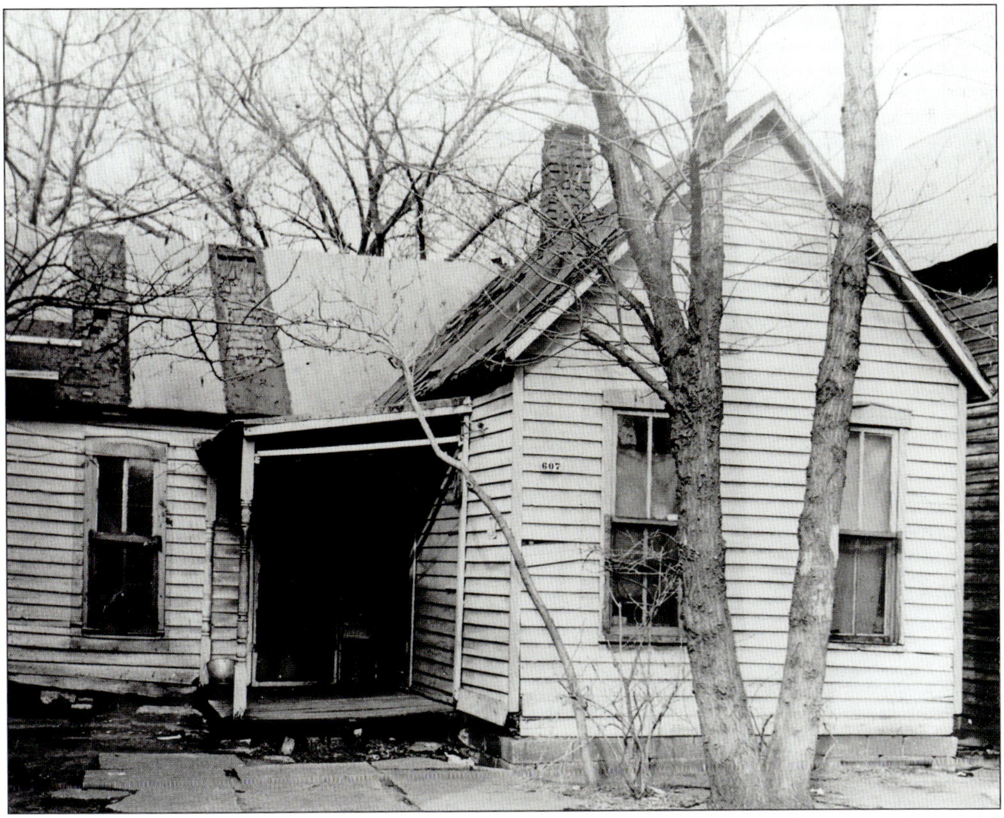

When the boardinghouse, formerly known as the First Presbyterian Church, was purchased for $400 by Dick Long in 1945, the building next to it was given to him as well. Until recently, it was thought that this was the church's parsonage. In fact, it was the home of Wesley and Millie Hodge, one of the earliest African American families in Wichita, who arrived in 1876. Millie, a member of Calvary Baptist Church, owned and operated the boardinghouse until her death in 1935. It was located at 607 North Main Street before it became one of the four founding buildings of Old Cowtown Museum, along with the First Presbyterian Church, jail, and the Munger House. (Above, courtesy *Wichita Eagle*; below, courtesy Keith Wondra.)

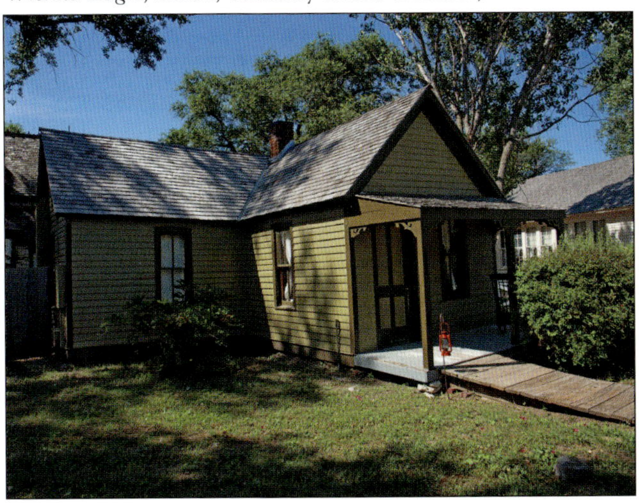

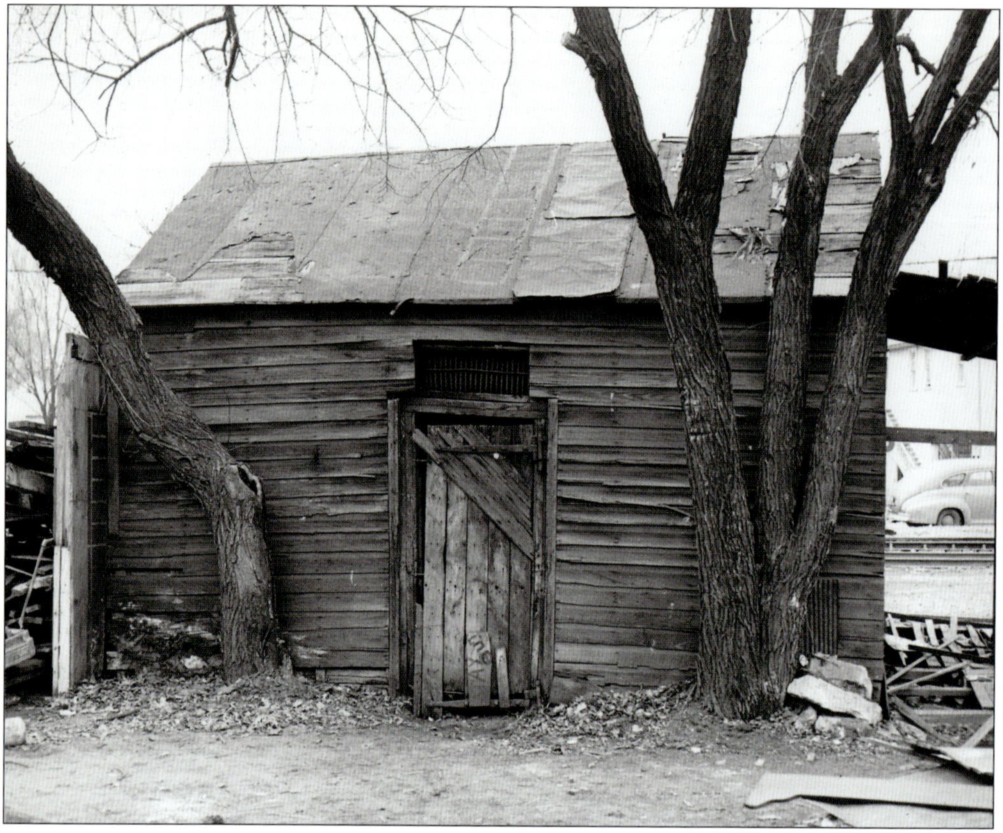

Wichita's first jail, or calaboose, was built at Second and Market Streets in 1871 and moved to Twelfth and Main Streets in 1874. The Wichita School District sold the building, which was being used for storage, to Historic Wichita, Inc. for $1, so that a new playground could be built at that location. The only renovations needed to the jail were new locks, which were donated by Fred J. Cooley, and keys, donated by Wichita Key, Lock and Safe Company. The jail was named the Wyatt Earp Memorial Jail in 1955 as part of the opening ceremony of Cow Town, with George Earp, first cousin of Wyatt Earp, in attendance. In reality, Wyatt Earp was hired by the city after the jail had already become a storage shed. (Above, courtesy *Wichita Eagle*; below, courtesy Keith Wondra.)

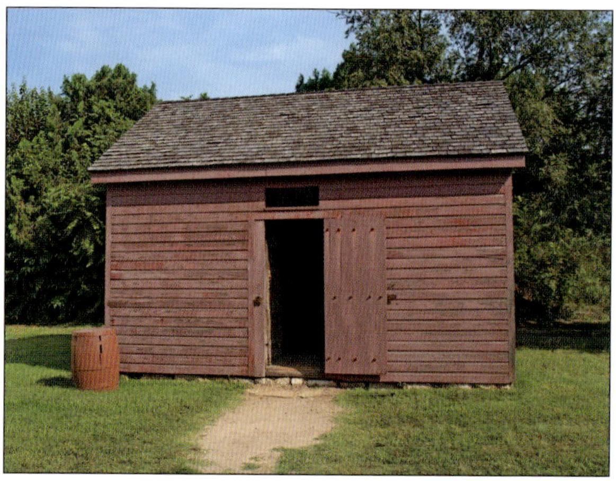

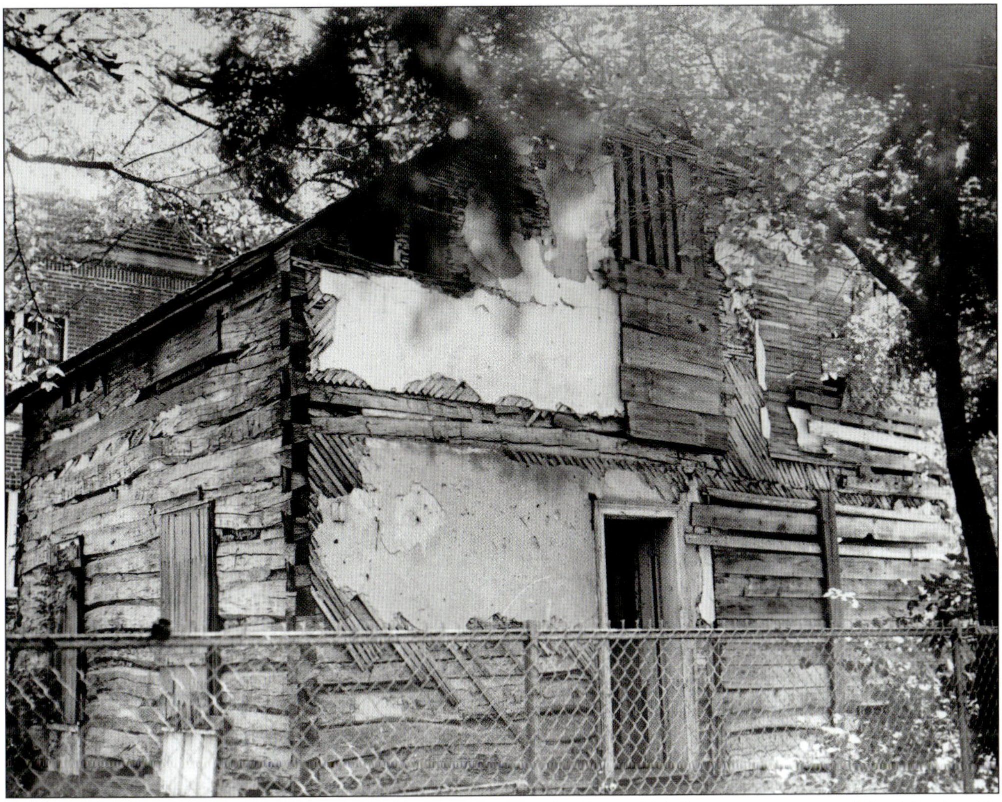

The Munger House, the first permanent structure built in Wichita, was erected by Darius S. Munger in 1869. Located at Ninth Street and Waco Avenue, it was used as the first post office, hotel and meeting place. W.C. Woodman bought the home from Munger in 1874 and renovated it into what he named Lakeside Manor. Dr. Dalton Fuller bought the renovated house in the 1920s and moved it to Back Bay Boulevard. The building was acquired by the Eunice Sterling Chapter of the Daughters of the American Revolution in 1944. The chapter donated it as shown above to Historic Wichita in 1952. It is the only building at Cowtown that is listed in the National Register of Historic Places. (Above, courtesy *Wichita Eagle*; below, courtesy Keith Wondra.)

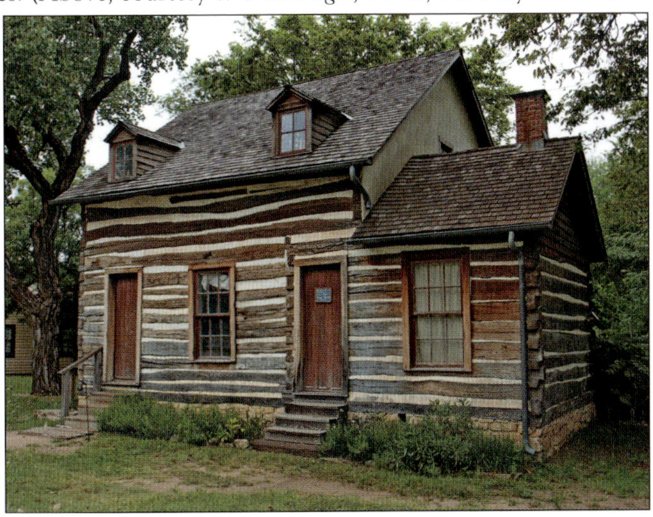

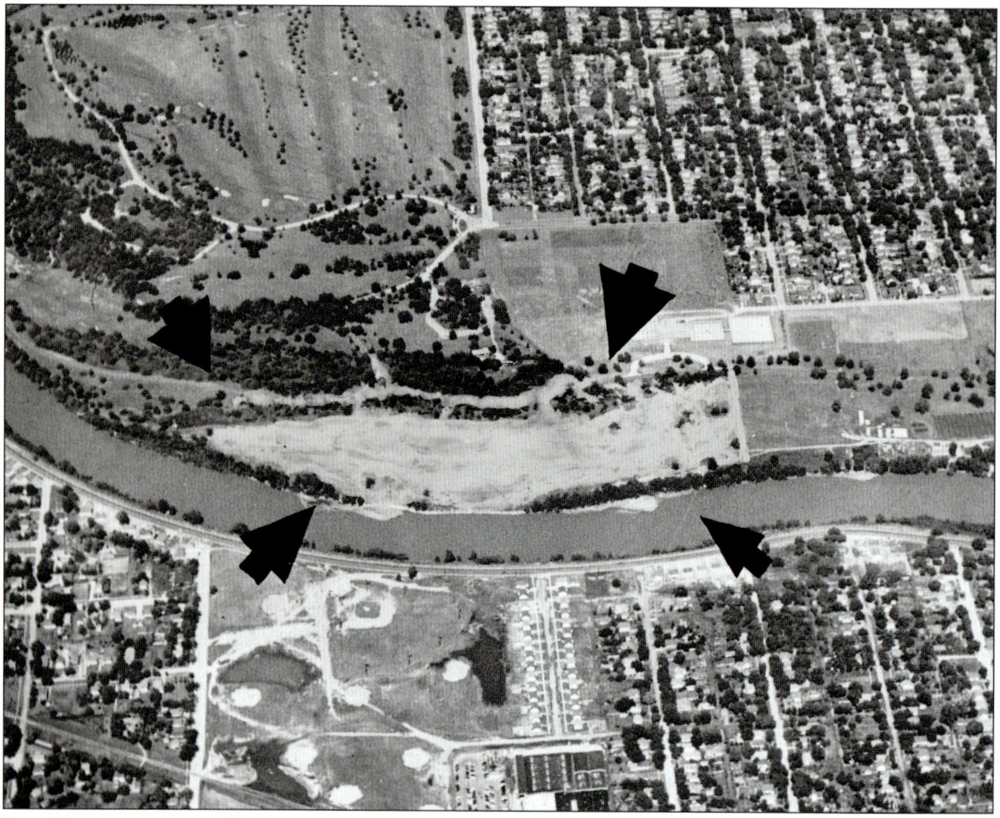

In 1951, Historic Wichita, Inc. leased 23 acres of land from the Wichita Water Company. As seen this c. 1951 aerial view, the land was north of the Big Arkansas River and south of the Wichita Water Company. Sim Park is in the upper left, with the land Old Cowtown Museum is on surrounded by the black arrows. (Courtesy *Wichita Eagle*.)

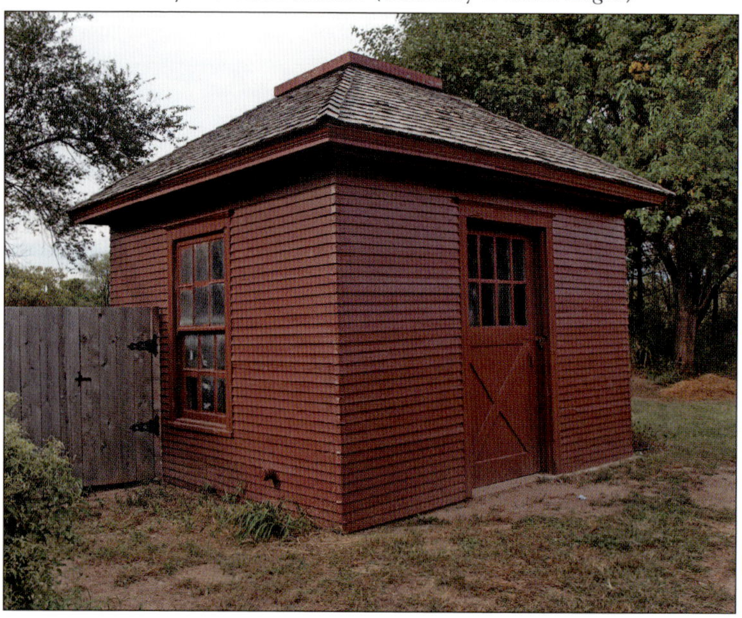

In the 1930s, the Wichita Water Company built six well houses north of the Arkansas River to be used as emergency wells. When Historic Wichita, Inc. leased the land, it inherited the well houses. Over the years, they were torn down, with only this one remaining. (Courtesy Keith Wondra.)

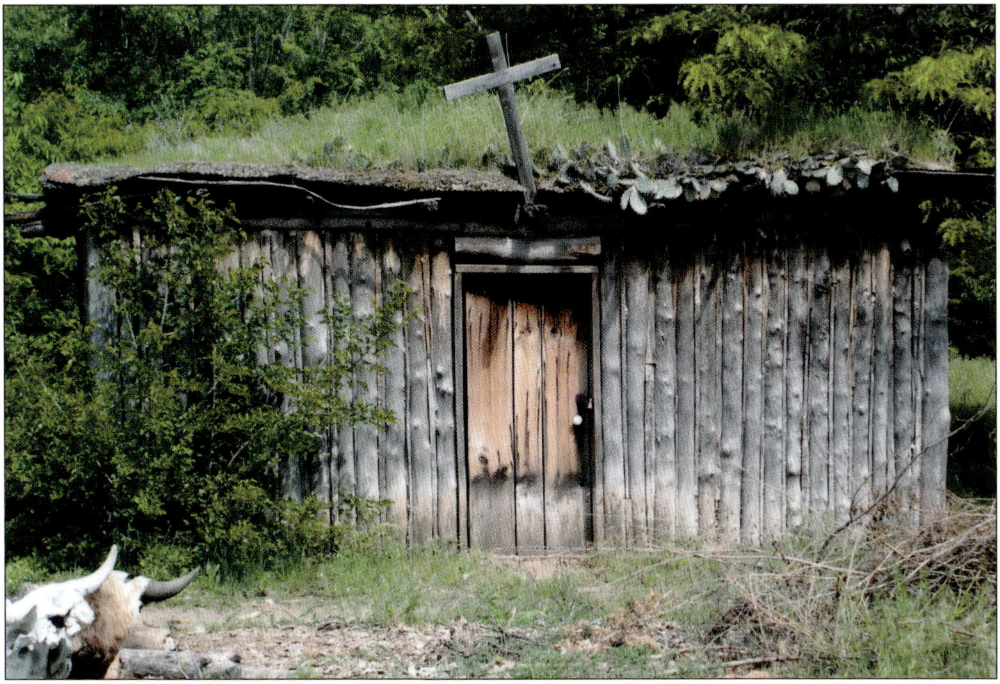

The replica of St. John's Episcopal Church (seen above), also known as Wichita's first school, was constructed in 1953 and sponsored by McCormick Armstrong. The church originally met in the Munger House with Rev. John Rice Hilton, until the original church was built from oak logs in 1870. The two-story building at 712 North Market, constructed in 1893, was also moved to Cowtown in 1953. The move was sponsored by Steffen's Dairy, with the intent to make the first floor a drugstore and the second floor a replica of a land office. However, a windstorm in 1953 knocked the building down (seen below), so it became the one-story Bon-Ton Drug Store.

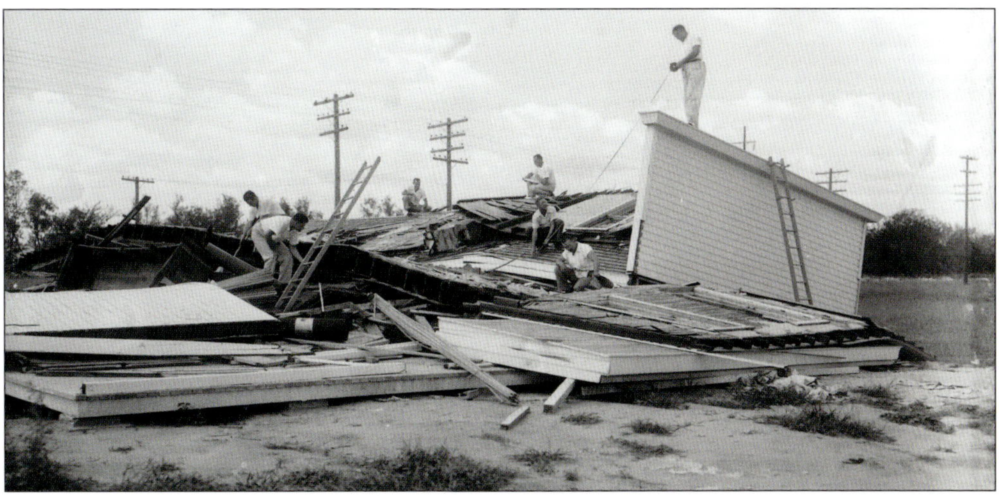

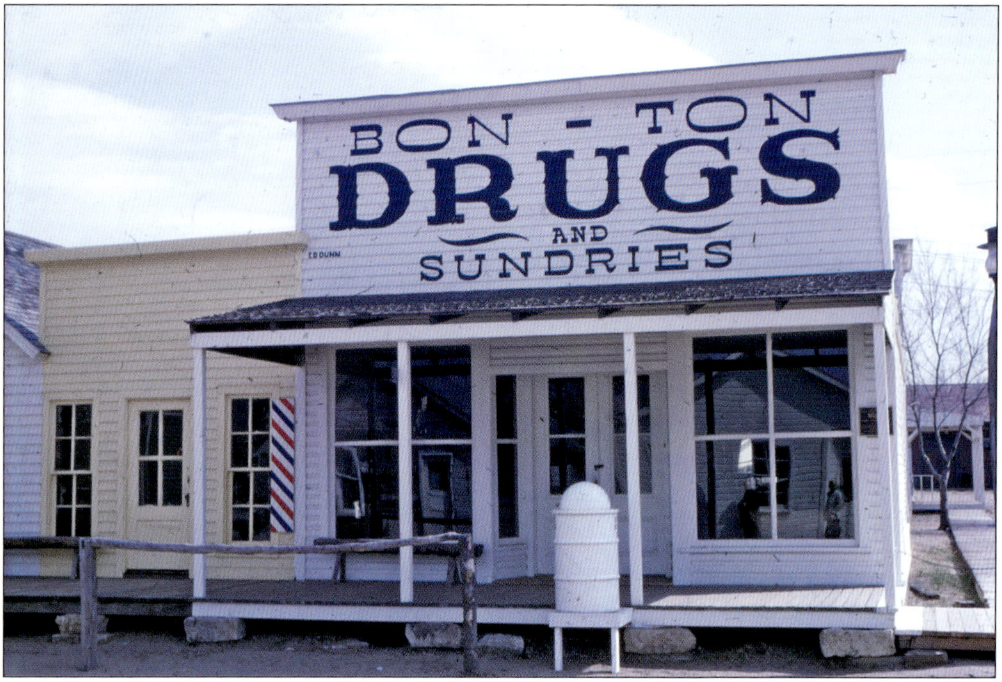

After the windstorm blew down the second story of the drugstore, plans were modified due to insurance only covering one story and not the damaged second story. The building included one of the first soda fountains in Kansas, which came from Junction City. The piece of the second story was used to erect the building that would become the Barber Shop (now the Land Office) on the left. In 1996, the structure was moved west of the general store, and it became the McGinn's Feed and Seed. (Above, courtesy Treva Mathur; below, courtesy Keith Wondra.)

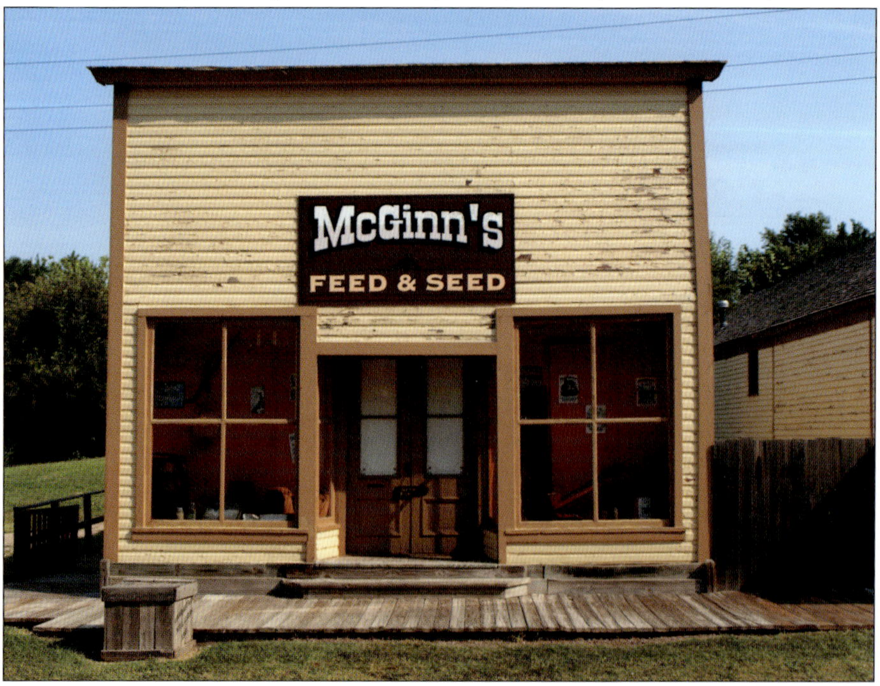

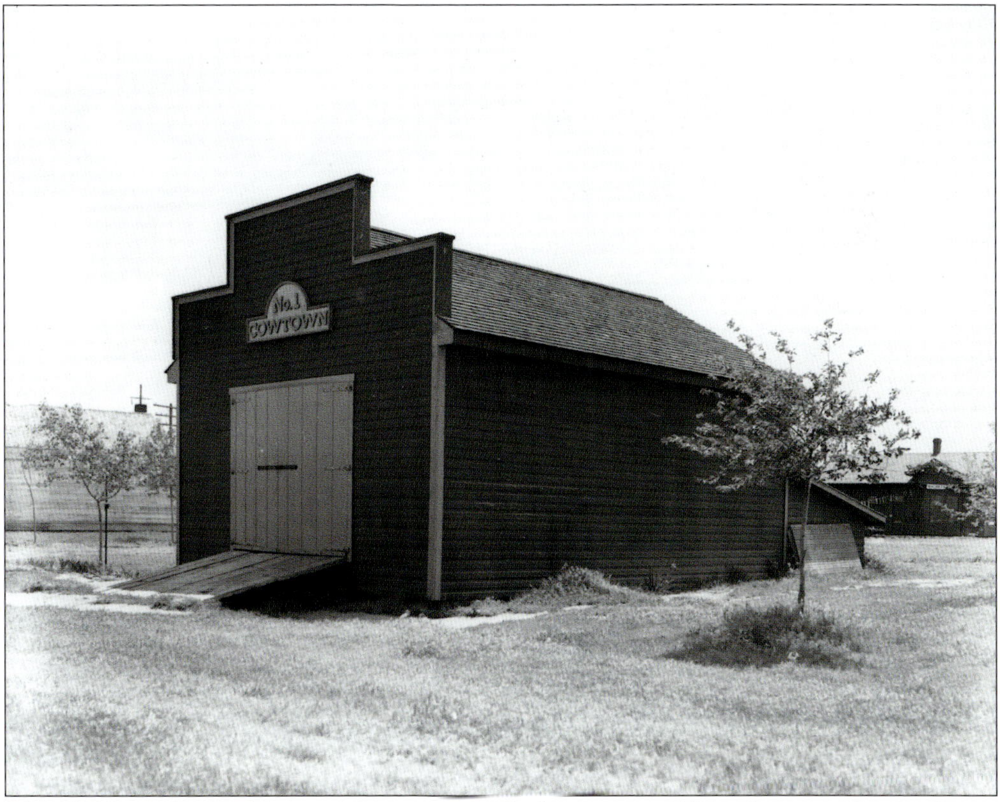

The Children's Corner Creative Emporium was built on-site in 1954 as home to the Cow Town Fire Station No. 1, which housed the museum's volunteer fire department. It was the second building erected on-site and the seventh located at the museum. After the fire barn was built on the east side of the museum around 1969, the structure became the Wells Fargo Building. It was later known as the Orientation Building and the doors on the north were eliminated. After the new Visitors Center opened in 2005, it became the Children's Corner Creative Emporium. (Below, courtesy Keith Wondra.)

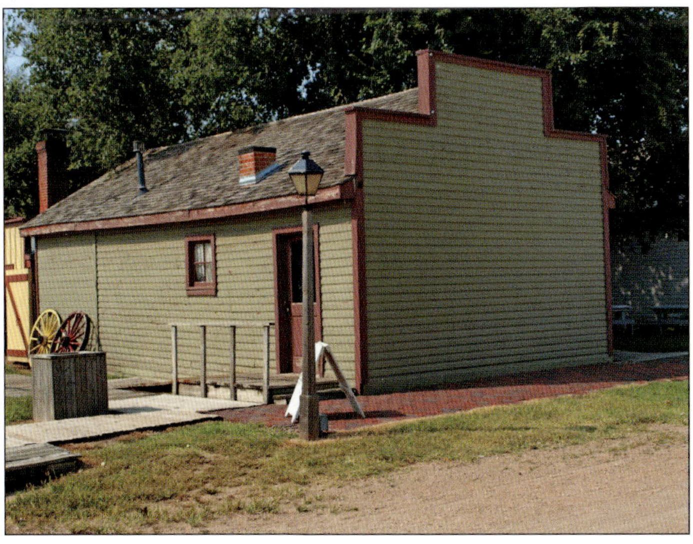

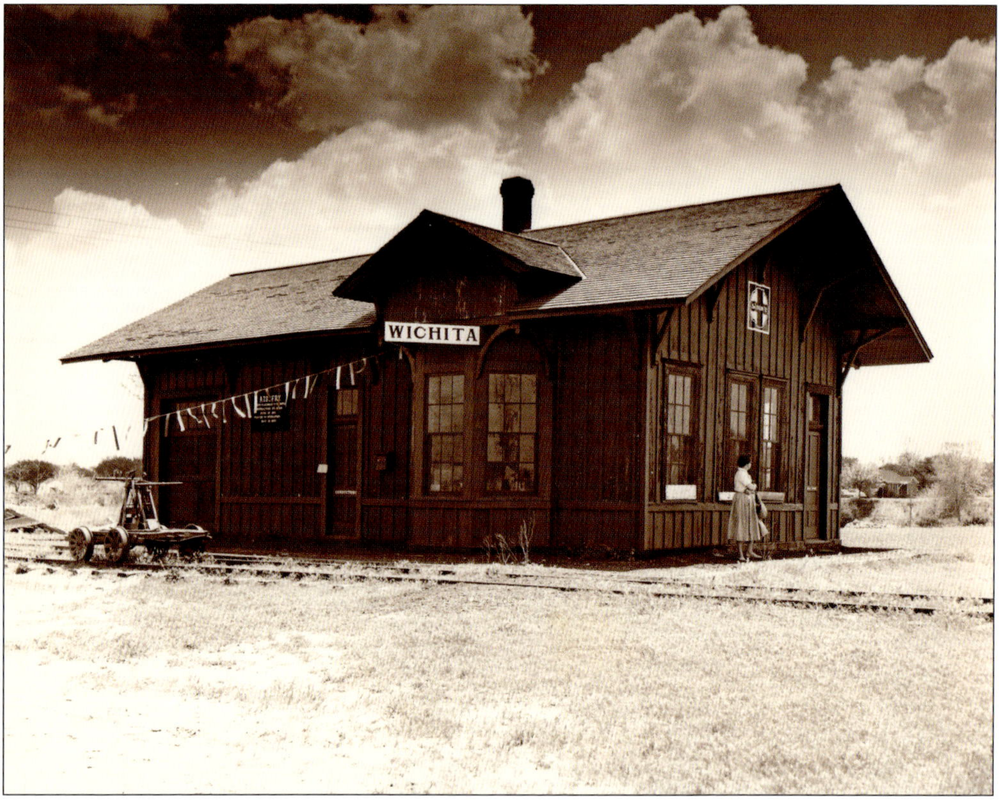

Railroads were a large part of Wichita's founding, and Wichita's re-created western village needed a depot. A delegation from the Santa Fe Railway and members of Historic Wichita, Inc. toured three possible candidates in the towns of Adams, Anness, and Eula, Kansas. Historic Wichita, Inc. decided on the Santa Fe Depot in Anness, Kansas, that was built in 1887. The building was given and moved to the museum Cowtown by the Santa Fe Railway in 1954. The depot is now known as the Wichita and Southwestern Depot, a re-created depot that represents the railroad that connected Wichita to Newton. (Below, courtesy Keith Wondra.)

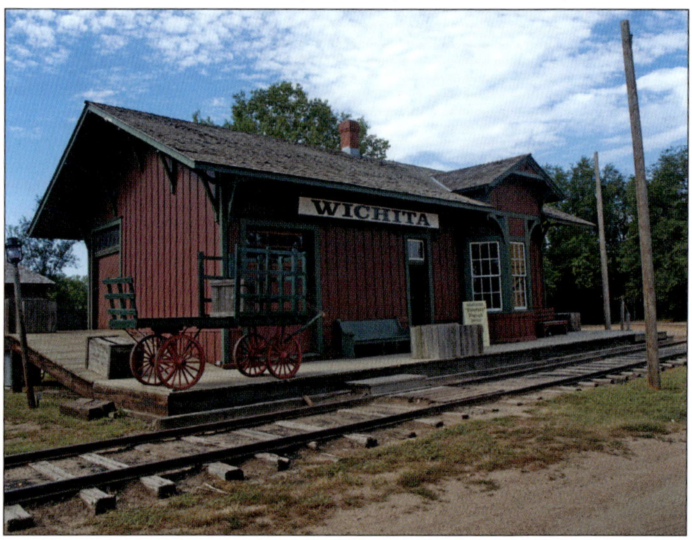

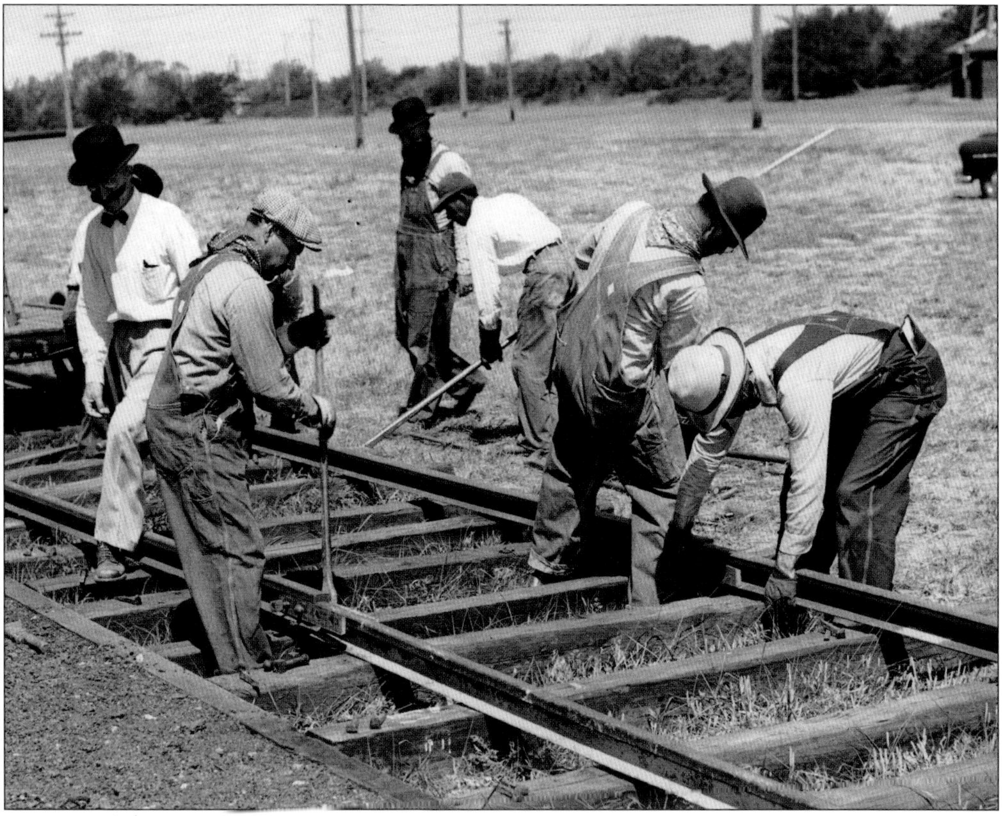

Not only did the Santa Fe Railway donate the depot from Anness, it also provided labor to lay track in front of the new depot in 1954. On June 24, 1954, a crew of seven men installed the tracks and also built re-created stockyards to the west of the depot. (Courtesy *Wichita Eagle*.)

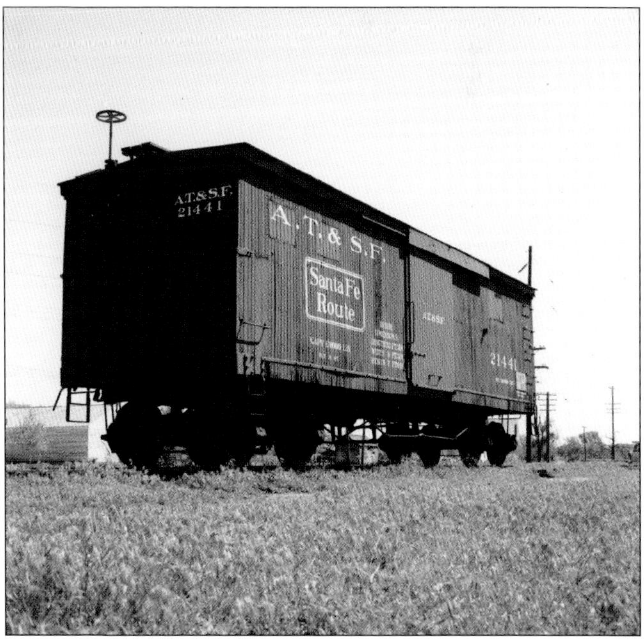

The Santa Fe Railway also donated and moved to the museum a Santa Fe boxcar of the cow town era. Santa Fe Railway assistant general manager C.S. Cravens rescued it from the junkyard. Due to its fragile state, the boxcar was shipped via a flatcar from Topeka to the West Wichita Shops for restoration. Once restoration was done, it was moved to the museum in 1955.

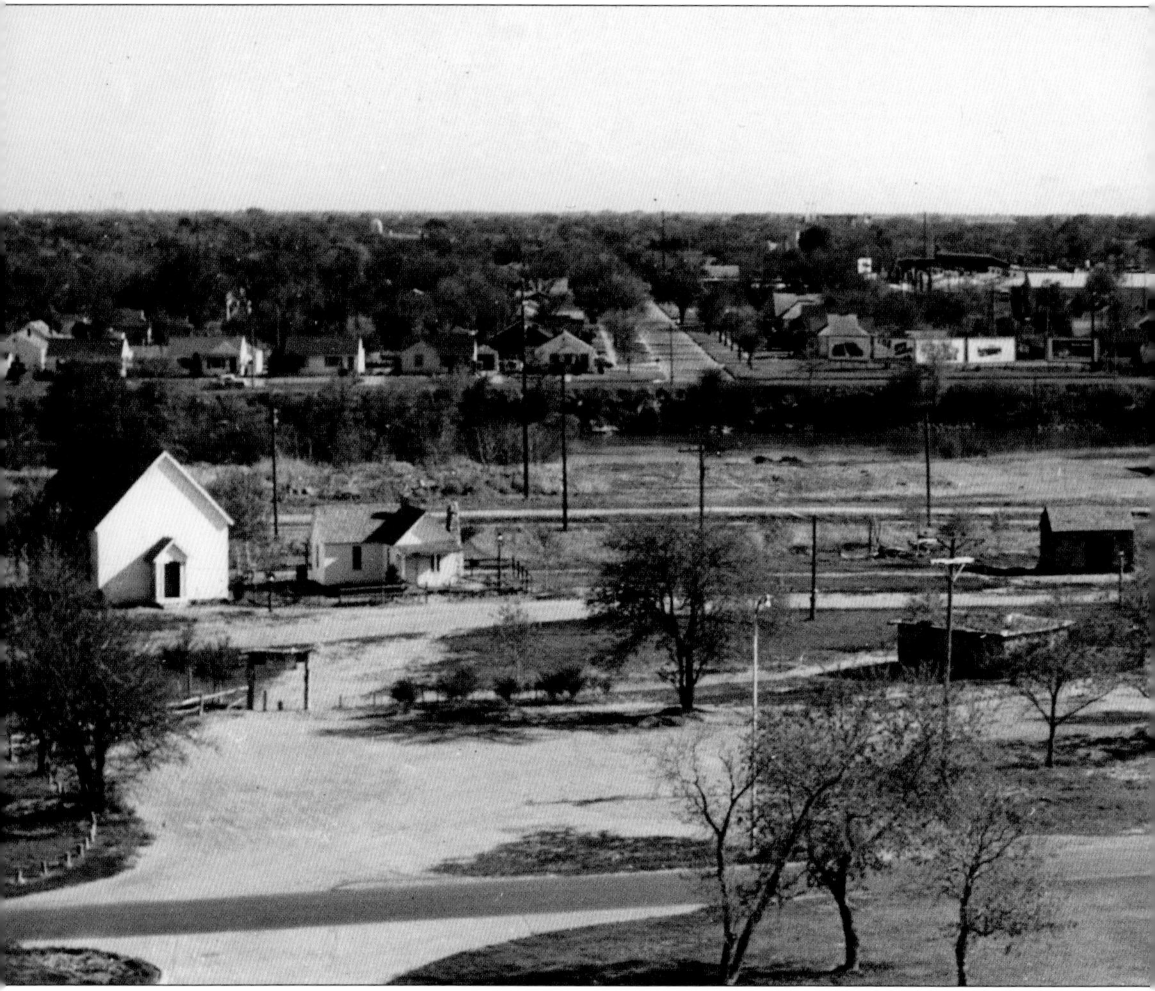

After the museum's opening in 1955, Old Cowtown Museum became an afterthought in Wichita. For much of the 1950s, the museum received little promotion, with even the Wichita Chamber of Commerce failing to mention it as one of Wichita's major attractions. Also, financial support from the city for Old Cowtown Museum varied from year to year. With scant support, the museum

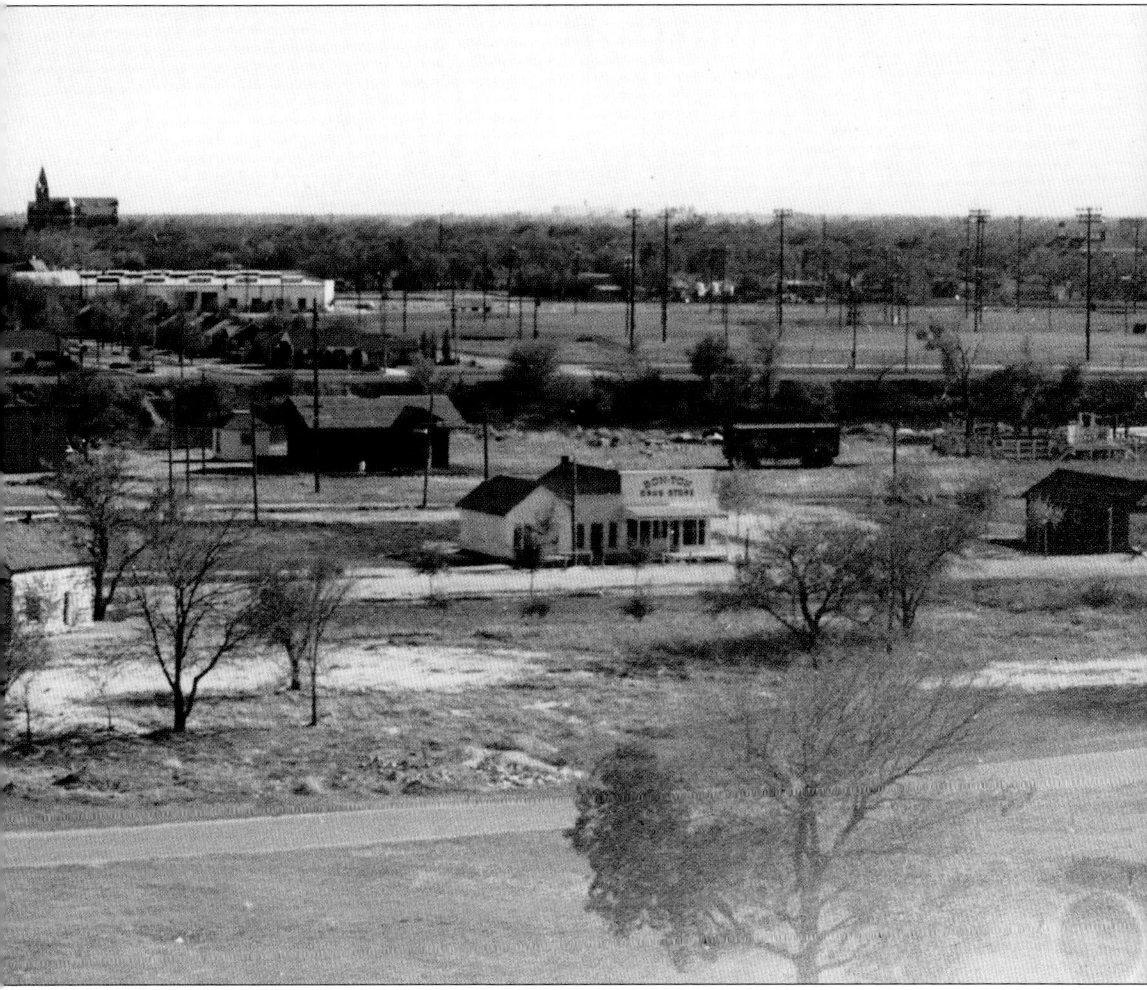

grew very little, as seen in this image showing the 11 buildings that would be at the museum for the next three years. It would not be until the celebration of the Kansas Centennial in 1961 that Old Cowtown Museum would be promoted as one of Wichita's major attractions.

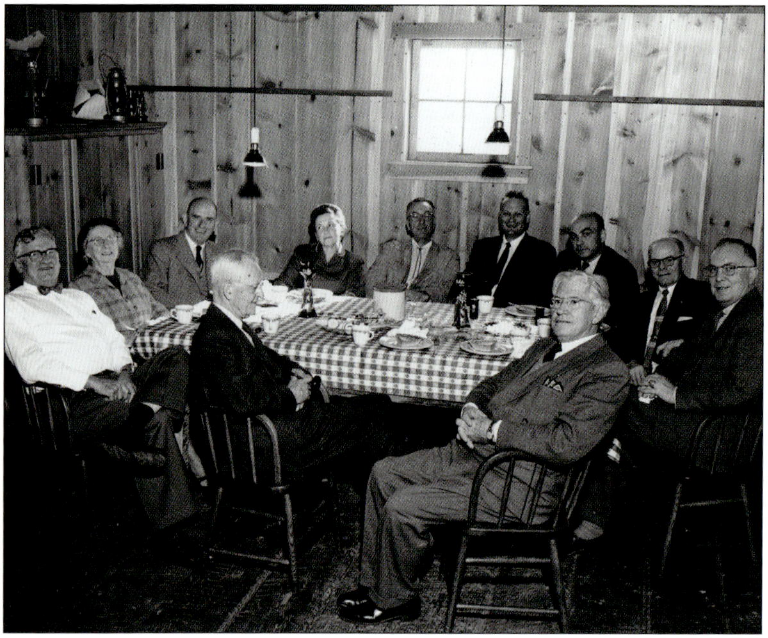

On December 9, 1953, Historic Wichita, Inc. held a board meeting inside the Cow Town Fire Station No. 1. In the photograph are, from left to right, (first row) O.A. Bell, R.T. Aitchison, Dr. Albert Kirk, and John D. McEwen; (second row) Lola Fisher, Dick Long, Mrs. Larry Roberts, Larry Roberts, Tom Fuller, Dr. Howard Clark, and Robert Israel Sr.

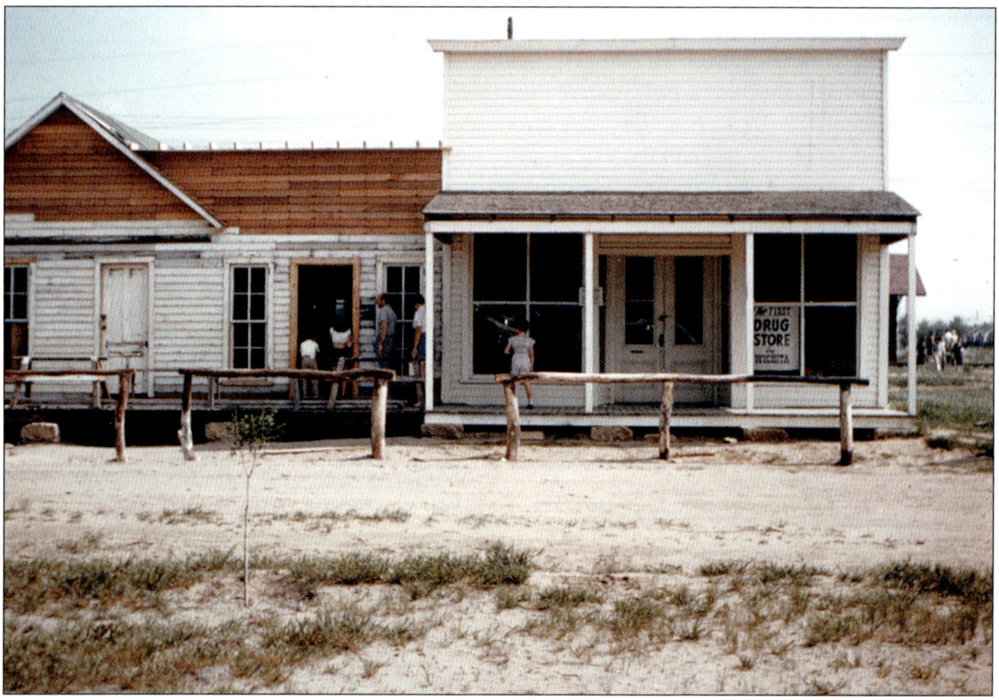

By 1955, Old Cowtown Museum had plans for 32 buildings, but only had 10 structures, which included, from left to right, the Post Office (originally the Wichita Township Hall), the Barber Shop (made out of the remains of the second story of the Drug Store), and the Drug Store (originally a two-story building). In the background is the depot, originally from Anness.

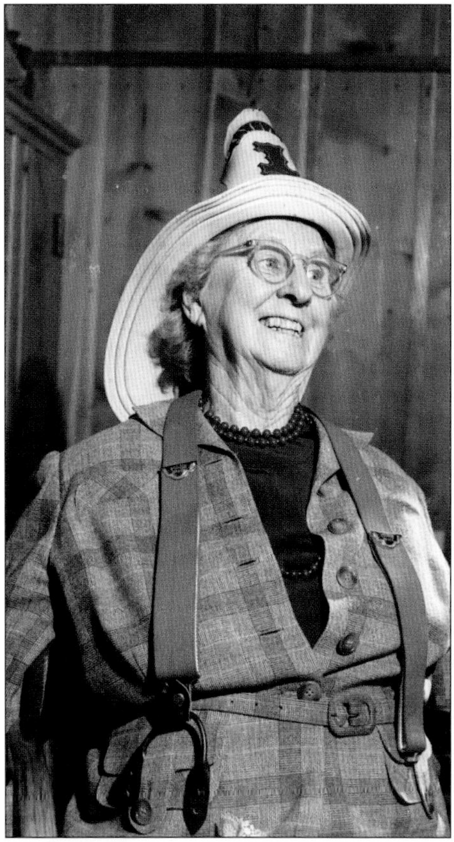

Pictured at right in 1953 is Lola Fisher, the first woman elected to Historic Wichita, Inc. board and the only woman in the volunteer fire department. Fisher was instrumental in the restoration of the First Presbyterian Church as a memorial to her husband, Jesse Clyde. Below, from left to right, Cowtown mayor Art Woodman, Cowtown historian Capt. John Coslett, and Cowtown vice mayor and membership chair John Bell are shown moving fire equipment outside the Cow Town Fire Department in the new fire station built around 1969. The fire equipment that was displayed in this building is now at the Kansas Firefighters Museum on South Broadway Street. (Below, courtesy *Wichita Eagle*.)

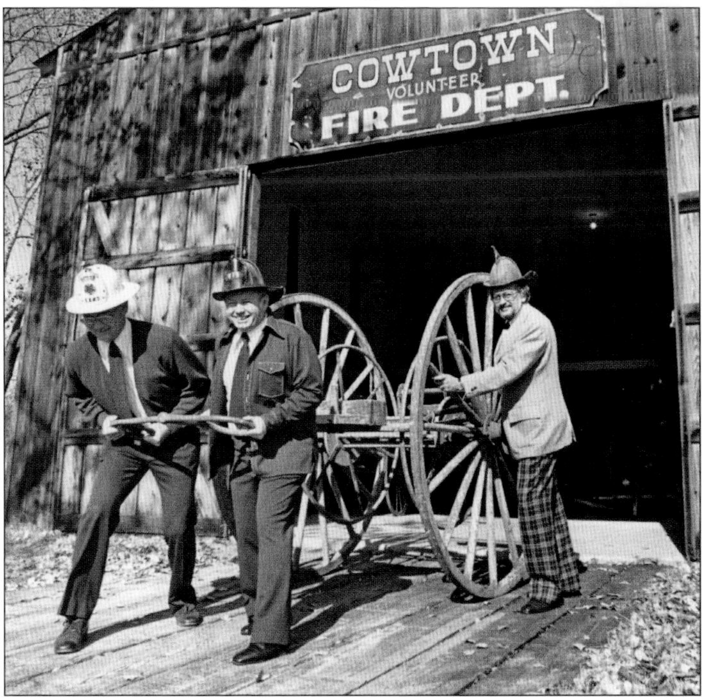

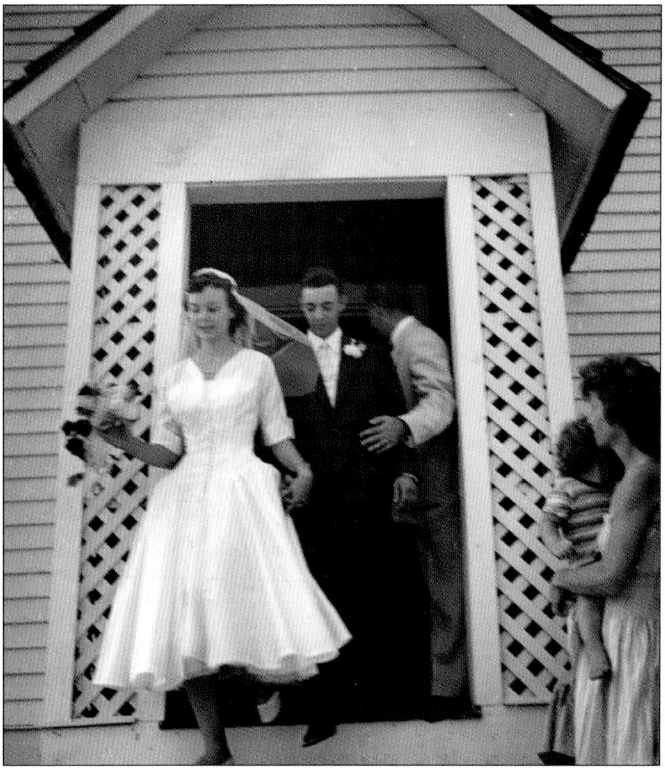

The wedding of Margaret Lofton and Kenneth Mantz of Udall was held at the First Presbyterian Church at Old Cowtown Museum, seen at left, as part of the museum's grand opening on July 13, 1955. Their original wedding venue had been destroyed by the Udall tornado of May 1955. The grand opening also included the premiere of the movie *Wichita,* starring Joel McCrea and Wichita's own Vera Miles, which was held at the Miller Theatre. Many other celebrities of the time visited the museum, such as Virginia Mayo, who was "sworn in" as mayor, in 1957. Mayo is shown below with Bob Israel. Her movie *The Big Land* premiered at the Miller Theatre in 1957. (Both, courtesy *Wichita Eagle.)*

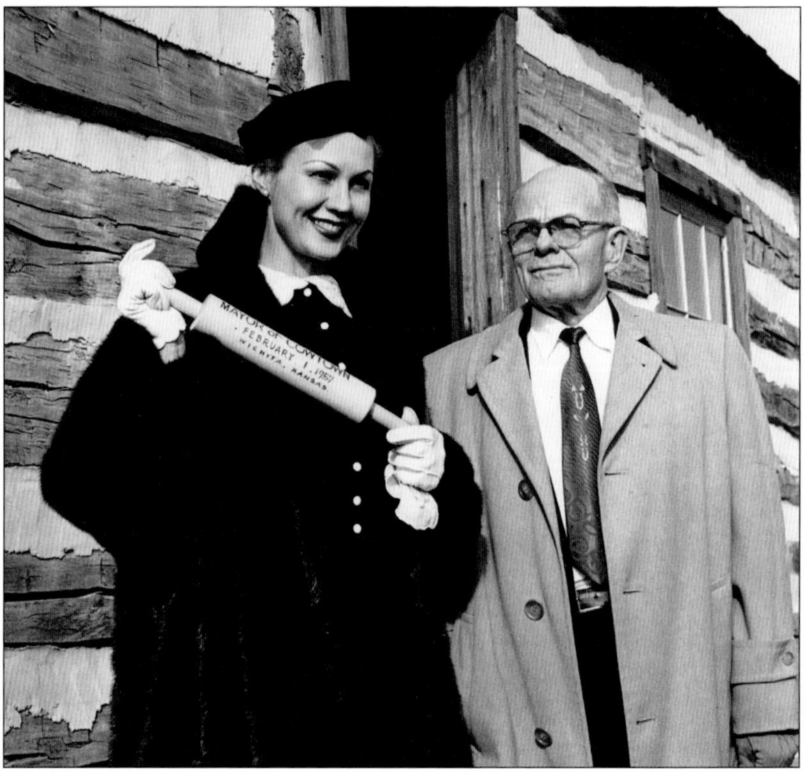

Two

LIVING HISTORY

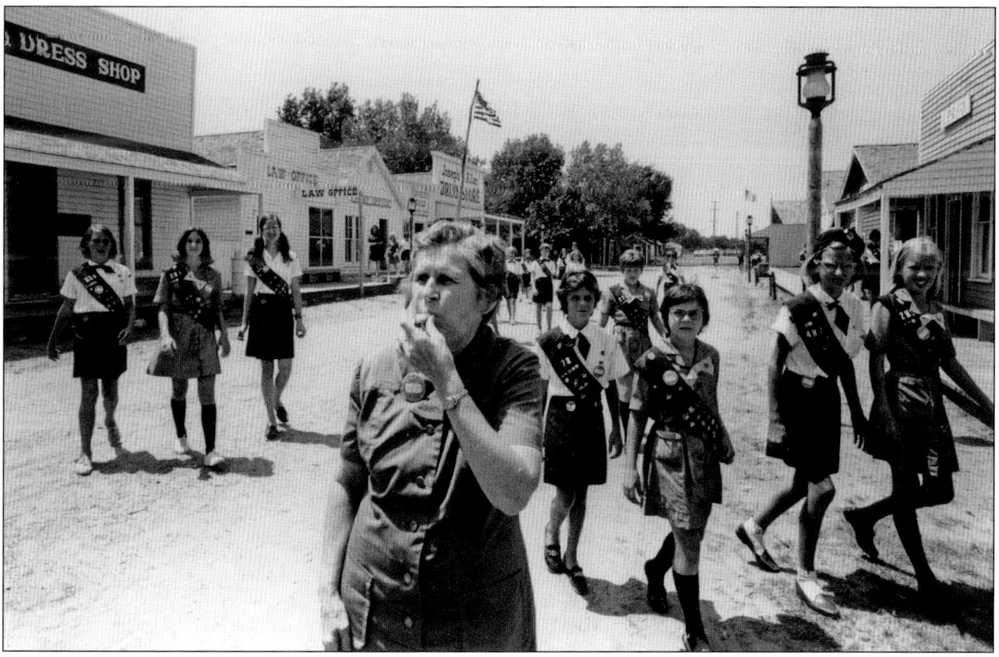

At the urging of Historic Wichita members Dick Long, Tom Fuller, and Bill Walker, the Wichita-area Girl Scouts agreed to serve as Cowtown guides during the busy summer months. Marge Kirby (center) became the founder and site director of the Girl Scouts at Old Cowtown. This started a bond that lasted generations with many fondly remembering their time at Old Cowtown Museum. (Courtesy Girl Scouts of Kansas Heartland.)

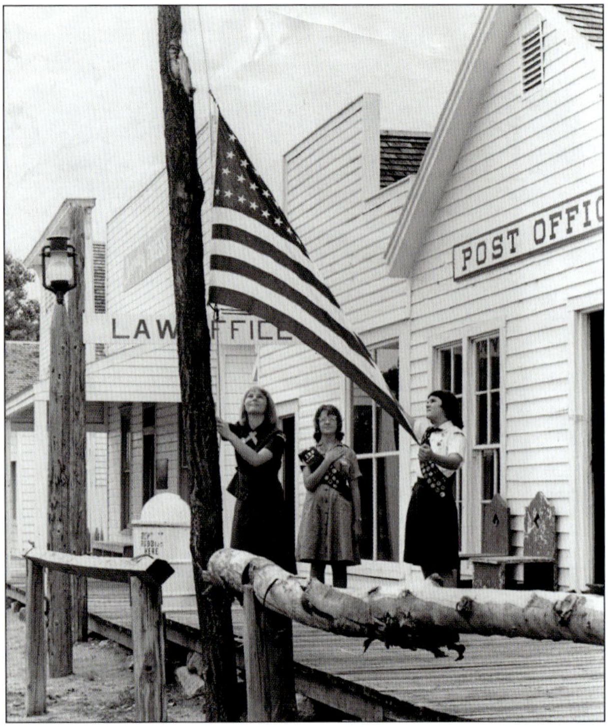

For the first 18 years of the project, Girl Scouts were assigned to each of the museum's buildings. Senior Girl Scouts were known as Cowtown museum aides, with Junior and Cadette Girl Scouts serving as Cowtown guides. They would be assigned a certain building and memorized a museum-approved script. At left, Sarah Cowles (left), Cathy Clark (center), and Sherry Horine raise a 37-star flag in front of the Post Office on June 8, 1965. By 1976, the Girl Scouts shifted from being guides to living history interpreters dressed in period clothing. Instead of being in each building, they were assigned an area such as the DeVore Farm, shown below. (Left, courtesy *Wichita Eagle*; below, courtesy Linda Thom.)

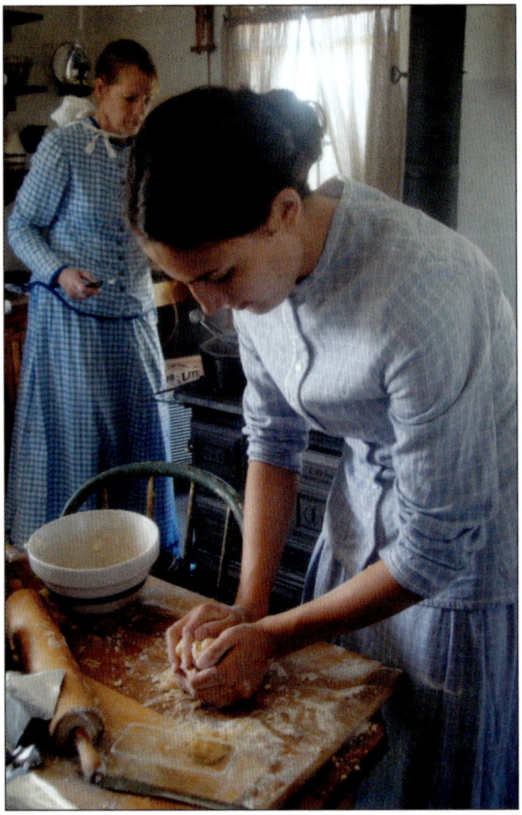

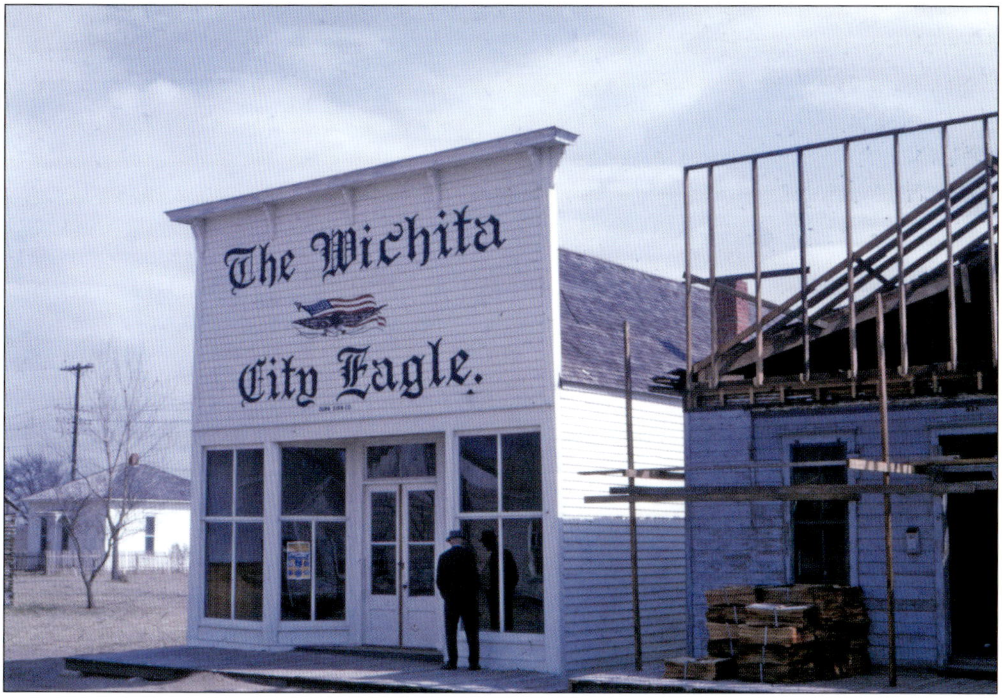

Since two of Old Cowtown Museum's founders, Dick Long and Dr. Albert Kirk, were also editors of the *Wichita Eagle*, it made sense that Old Cowtown Museum re-create the early home of the city's most famous newspaper. Larry Roberts, one of the museum's founders, acquired a vacant late-19th-century building located on the southwest corner of Ninth and Main Streets and donated it to the museum. It was moved to the re-created village in 1959 and opened to the public in 1960. The above image from 1962 also shows construction on the building that would become Fechheimer's Dry Goods and Clothing Store on the right. (Above, courtesy Treva Mathur; below, courtesy Keith Wondra.)

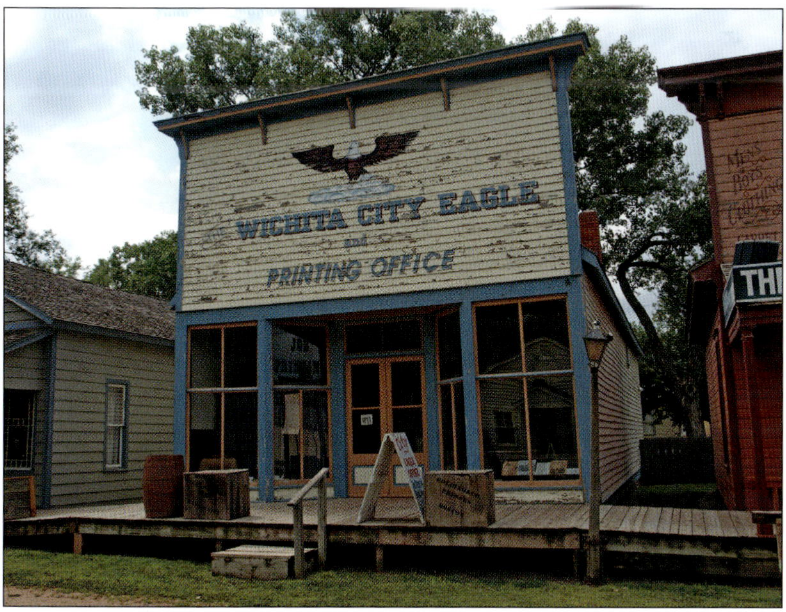

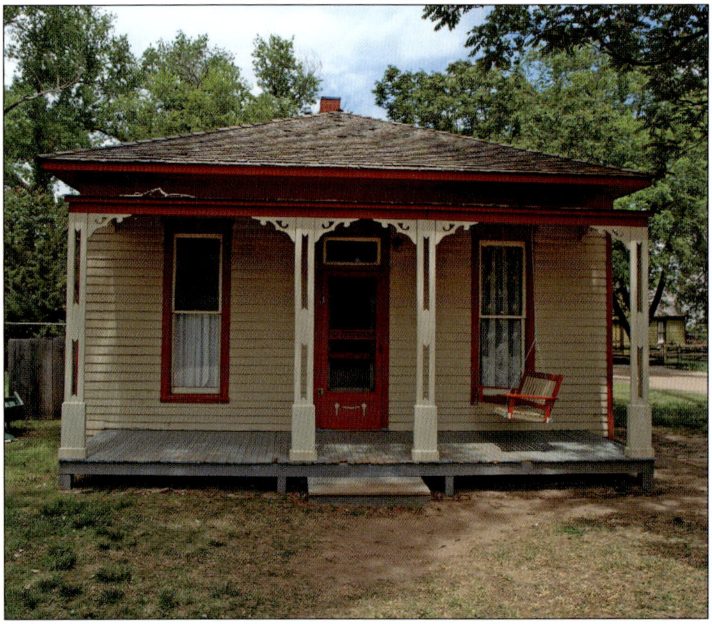

In 1961, Leo McKenzie, whose ancestors founded the Wichita Carriage Works in 1885, donated the McKenzie House to Old Cowtown Museum. The house was built by the donor's ancestors in the 1880s around Third and Water Streets in Wichita. Over the years, the house became a caretaker's residence, volunteer headquarters (with its most famous function being the Kirby House), and headquarters for the museum's Girl Scouts program. (Courtesy Keith Wondra.)

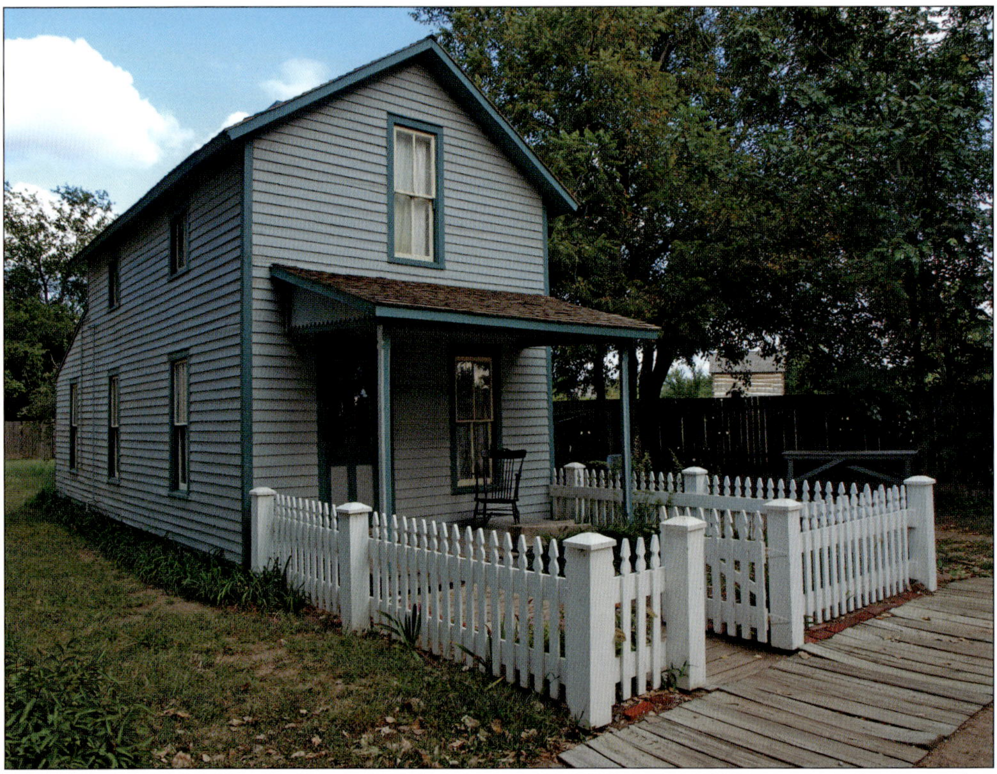

Also in 1961, Leo McKenzie donated the Story-and-a-Half House to Old Cowtown Museum. After its move to the museum, the house became part of the growing trend of promoting Wichita's early residents. Until the 1970s, it was promoted as "the restored childhood home of Billy the Kid" in museum brochures. As the museum transitioned in the 1980s, the house was renamed the Story-and-a-Half House. (Courtesy Keith Wondra.)

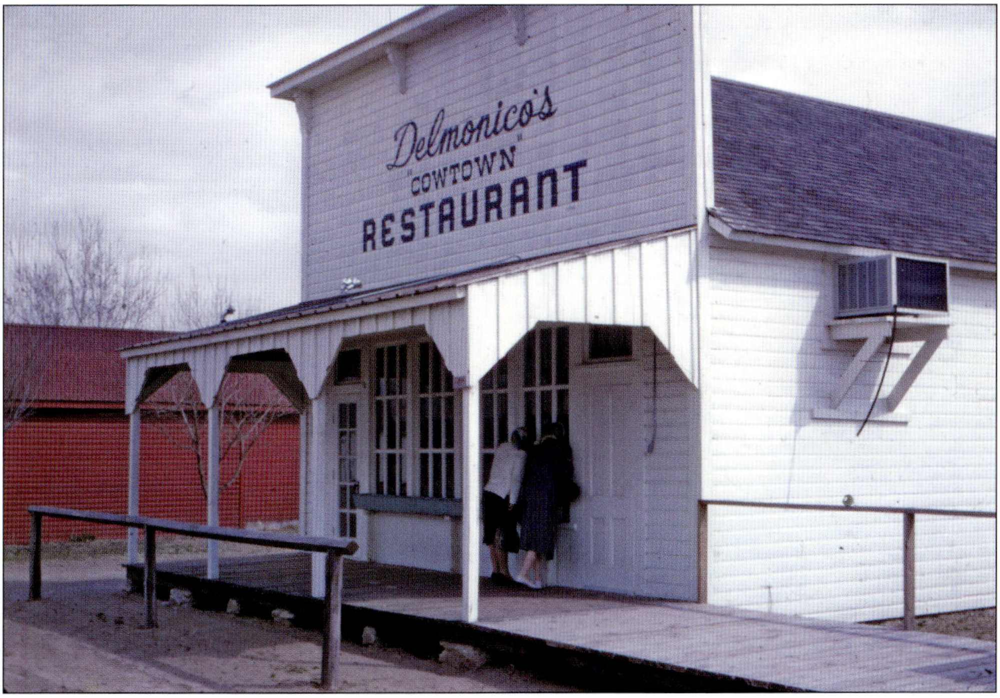

The feature of the Kansas Restaurant Association's 28th annual convention held in Wichita in 1961 was the dedication of the museum's restaurant, known as Delmonico's. Local grocer William Sutton built the structure at 816 East Market Street in 1904. John Jr. and Jim Jabara of Jabara's Market donated the building to Old Cowtown Museum in 1960, and it was home to Delmonico's Cowtown Restaurant until the early 1980s. It was renamed the Empire House Restaurant in the 1980s to more accurately portray Wichita's early history. With the opening of the DeVore Farm in the mid-1990s, the building became the museum's entrance and gift shop. It is now home to Empire Hall, a temporary exhibit space. (Above, courtesy Treva Mathur; below, courtesy Keith Wondra.)

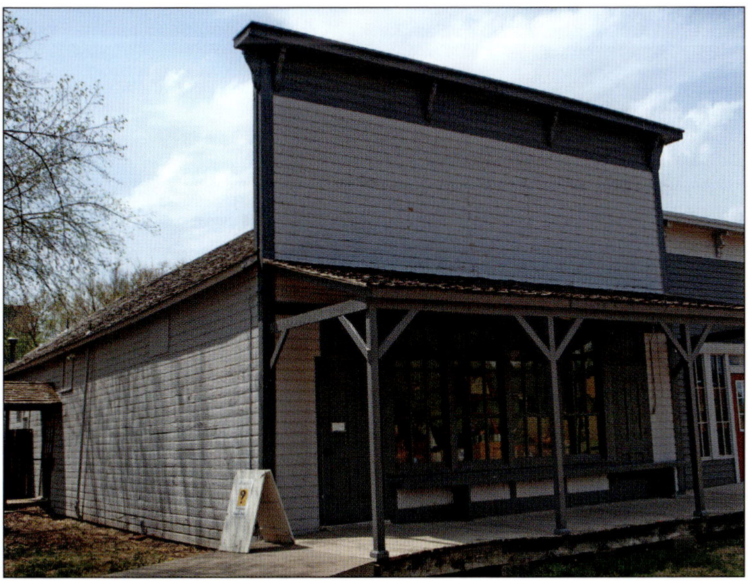

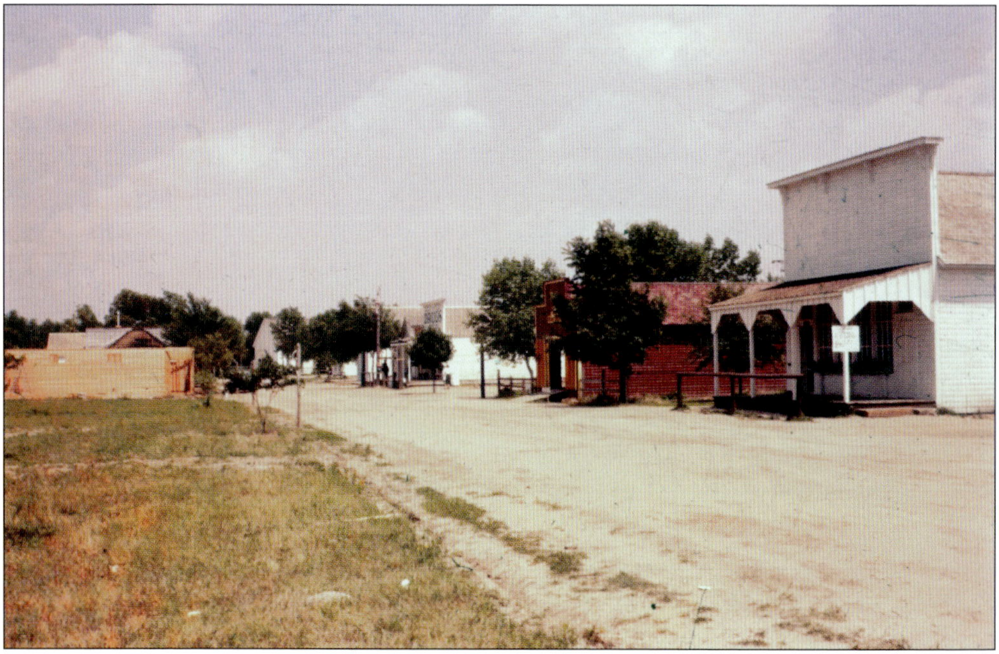

The celebration of the Kansas Centennial in 1961 gave Cowtown its biggest growth in the number of buildings, with 11 new buildings added by January 3, 1961, bringing the total to 18. According to Historic Wichita, Inc. directors, Old Cowtown Museum would have over 70 buildings by the end of 1961. In the above picture, the bank is being built in 1961 on the left, with the structure that would become Delmonico's Cowtown Restaurant on the right. By the end of 1961, the museum had 26 buildings—a far cry from the over 70 buildings planned. (Below, courtesy Treva Mathur.)

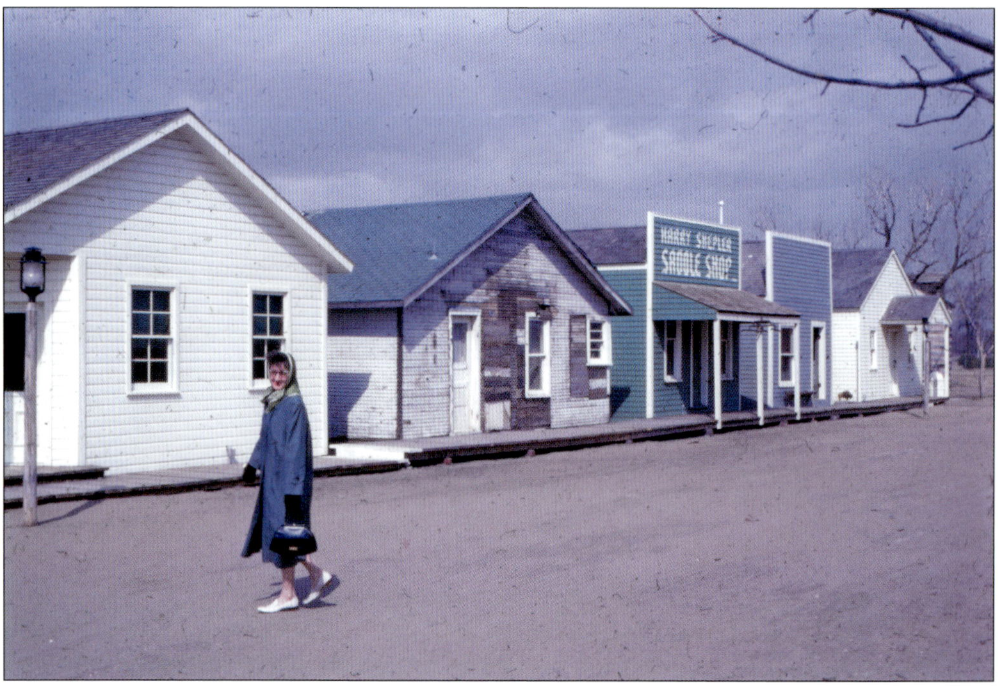

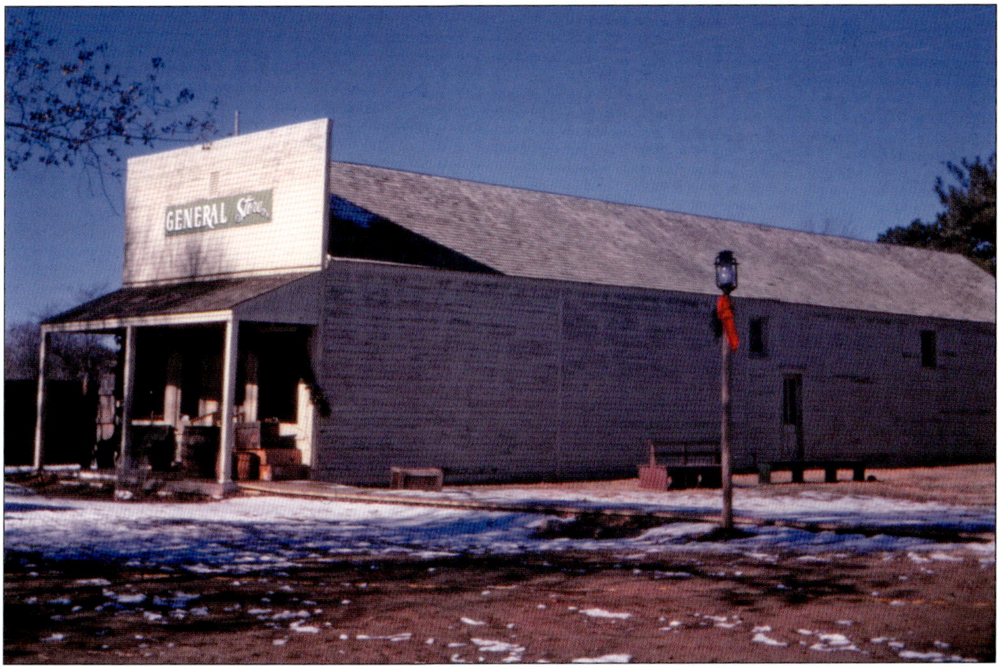

The acquisition of Old Cowtown Museum's General Store continues the museum's role in preserving not just buildings from Wichita's past but also ones from communities outside of the city. The General Store was built in 1884 in Garden Plain, Kansas. Originally home to the A.K. Masters General Store, the structure had many owners, ending with Alois Stepanek and his son Gerald. When they were planning to expand their business with a new grocery and meat market in 1964, the Stepaneks donated the historic structure to Old Cowtown Museum. Due to its length, the building was moved to the museum in three sections. (Below, courtesy Keith Wondra.)

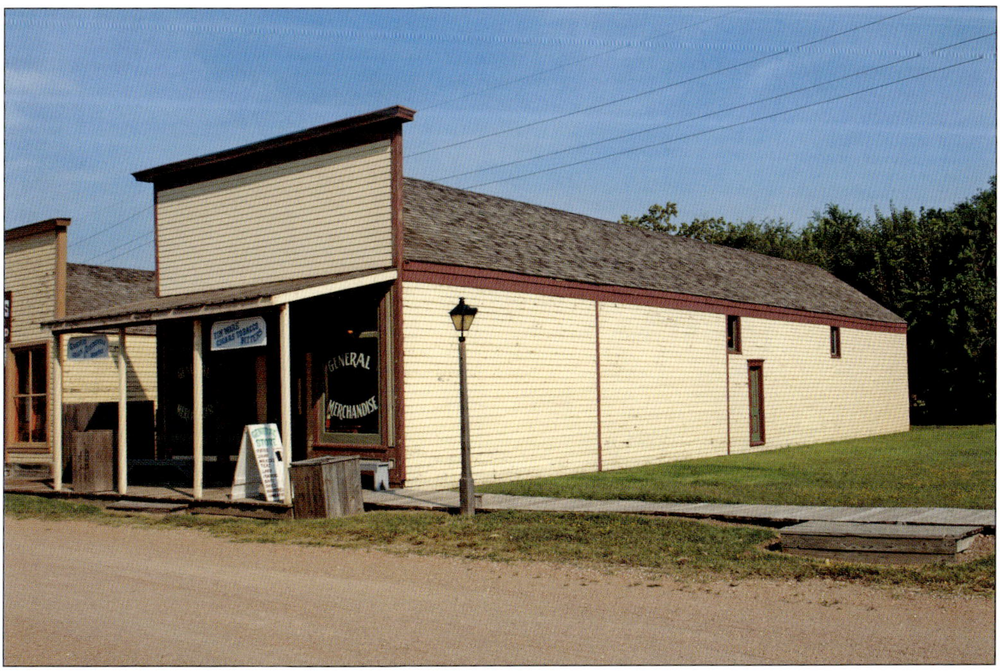

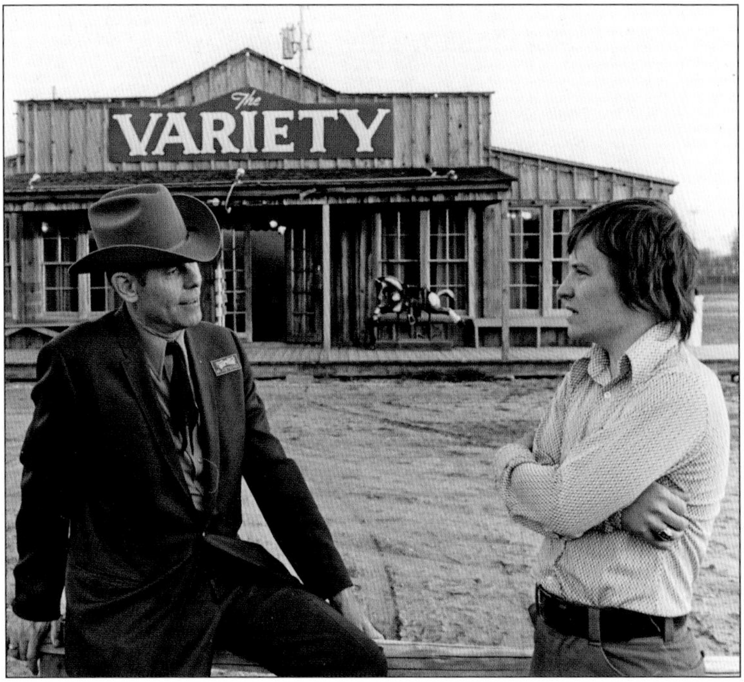

Even though the building was erected in 1961 as a venue where Wichitans could dance and party, the Variety Theater became home to melodramas and dinner theater. These ended in the mid-1990s. Here, Tom Frye (right), one of the Crown Players, talks during the 1973 season with Robert Goetschius, Old Cowtown Museum business manager. (Courtesy *Wichita Eagle*.)

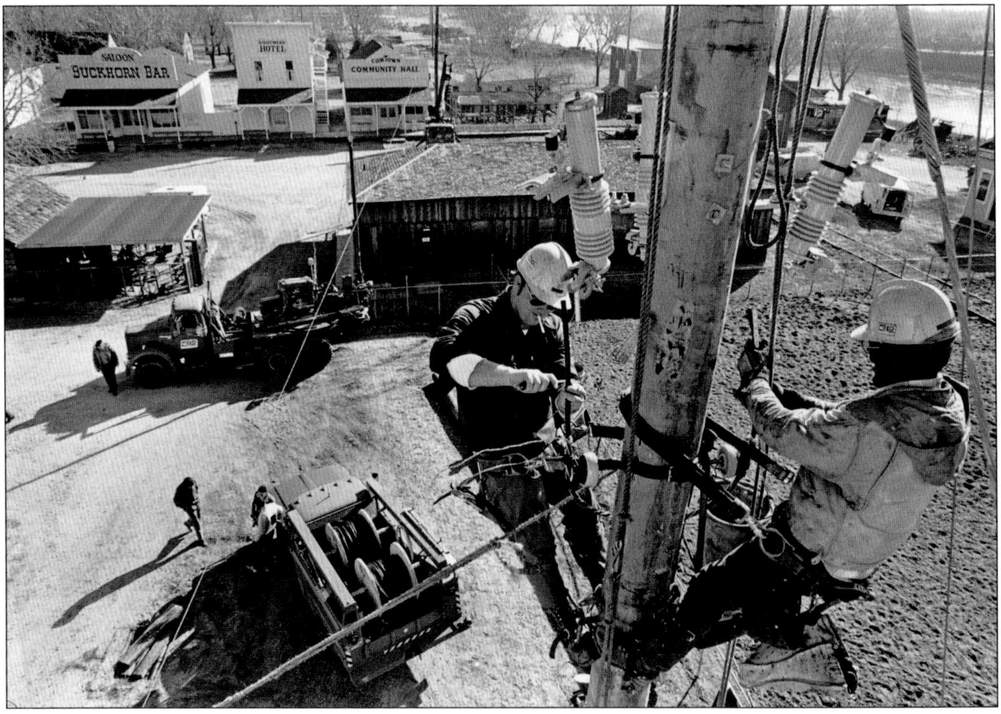

Over the years, volunteers and Old Cowtown Museum have gone hand in hand. Even businesses got involved, such as these Kansas Gas & Electric (now Westar) workers observing National Electric Week by volunteering at the museum in 1974. They relocated overhead electrical distribution lines underground, installed additional receptacles, and corrected electrical problems. (Courtesy *Wichita Eagle*.)

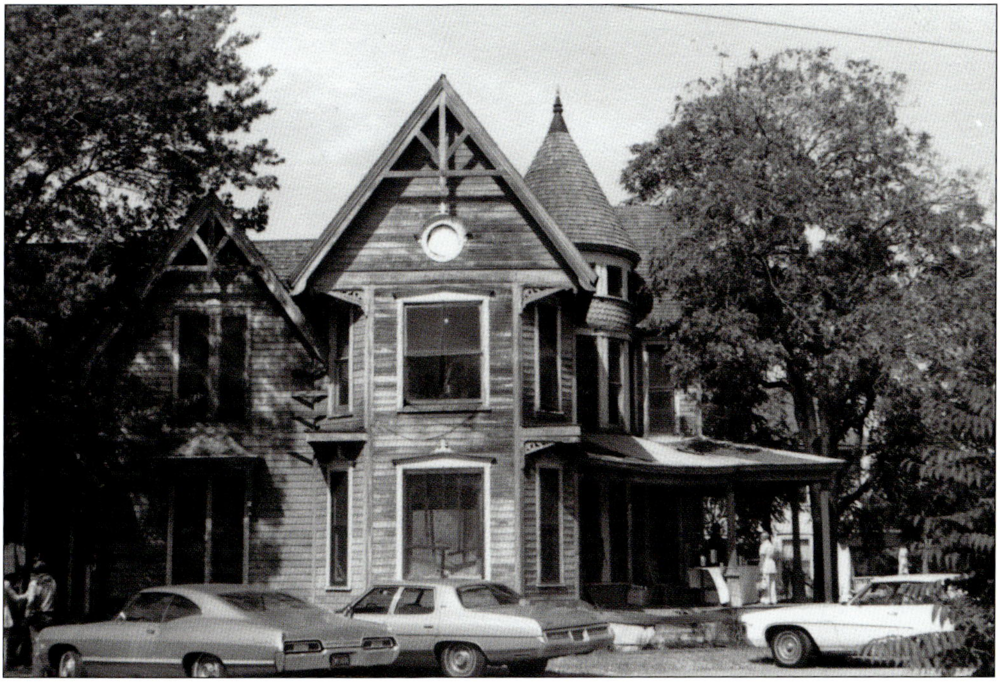

In 1874, Marshall Murdock built the Murdock House on the northwest corner of Murdock and St. Francis Streets. A hundred years later, the Midtown Citizens Association saved the Murdock House from demolition and opened the home for tours. This started the Midtown Citizens Association's annual historic home tours, now held yearly in October. Later, in 1974, the house (without the additions from the early 1900s) was moved to Old Cowtown Museum. After its restoration, the house opened to the public in 1983 with a yellow paint scheme. For years, the home was painted brown, and in 2009, the current color scheme was applied to the structure. (Below, courtesy Keith Wondra.)

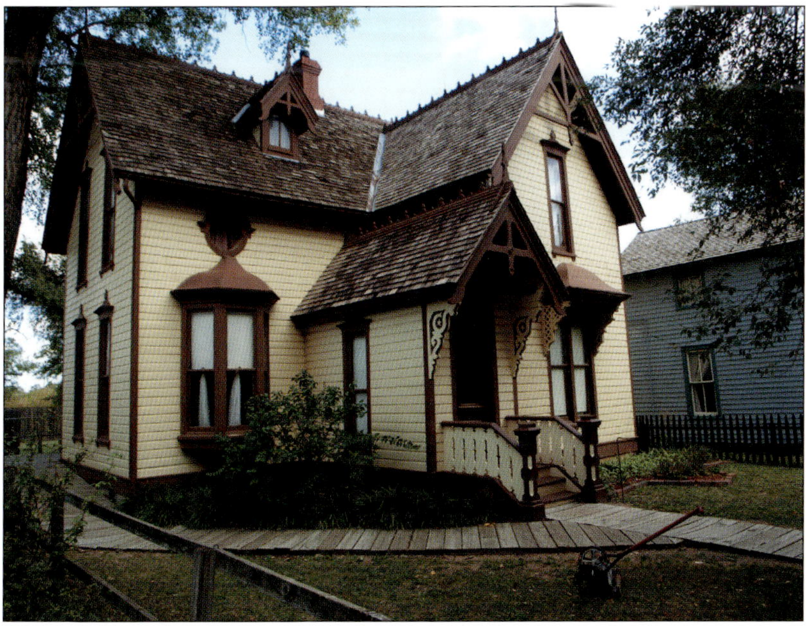

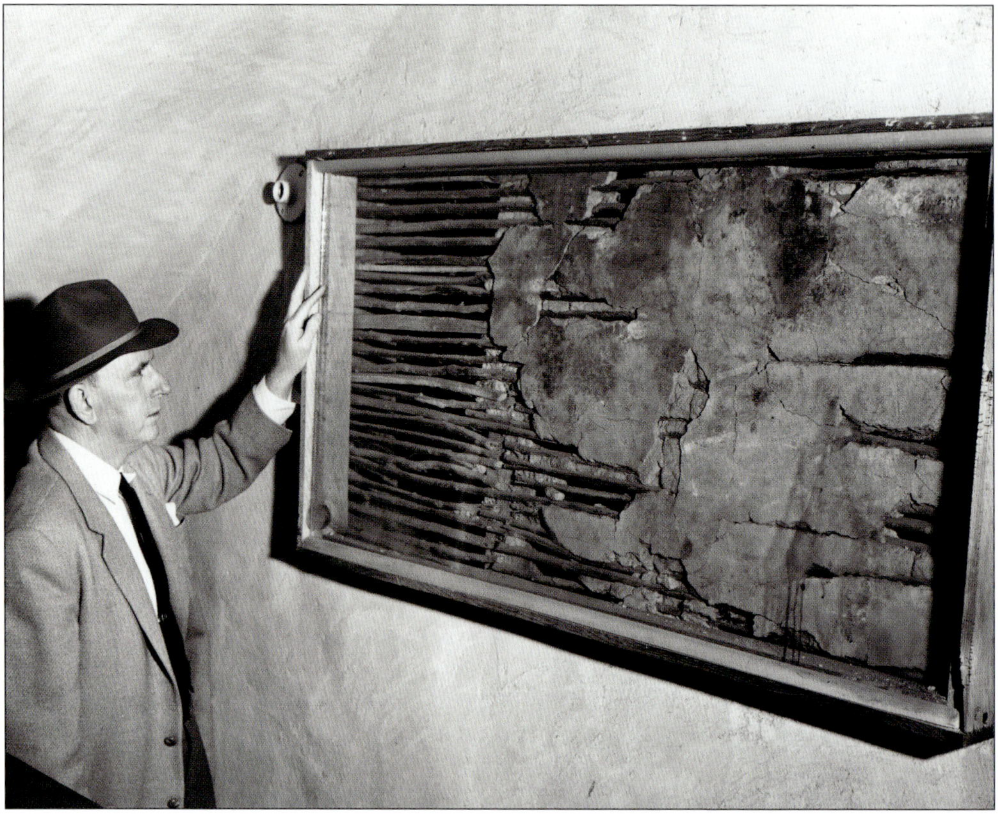

When the Munger House was restored in the 1950s, Old Cowtown Museum framed two sections of the original 1868–1869 wall. They show how Darius Munger constructed the walls from old plaster made with sand from the Arkansas River, lime from clamshells burned with wood from the riverbank, and willow withes bound with buffalo hair. Above, Dick Long, president of Historic Wichita, Inc., inspects one of the two framed sections of the Munger House. Below is one of the framed sections on the second story of the Munger House in 2015. (Below, courtesy Keith Wondra.)

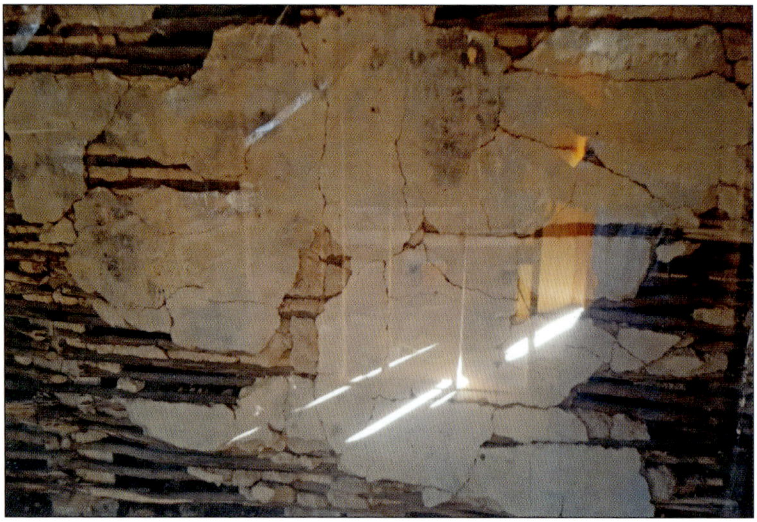

For years, there was a staircase in the middle of the Munger House that led to the second story, and the public was allowed up the stairs. The stairs were added to the house when it was owned by W.C. Woodman. The restoration of the house in the 1990s led to the removal of these interior stairs.

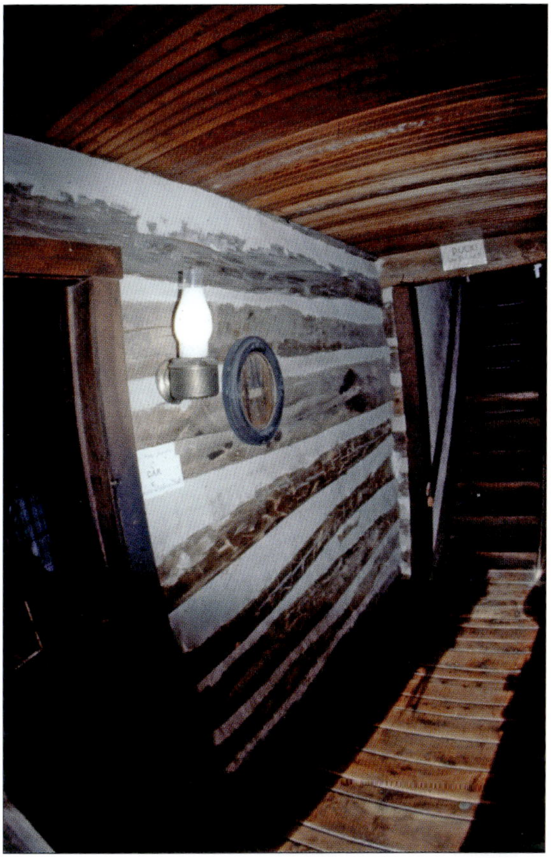

When the Munger House had hotel rooms upstairs, there were exterior stairs for guests to have uninterrupted access to their rooms. After the structure's move to Old Cowtown Museum in 1952, stairs were added. Due to the Americans with Disabilities Act (ADA) and fire code, the stairs were removed in the late 1990s.

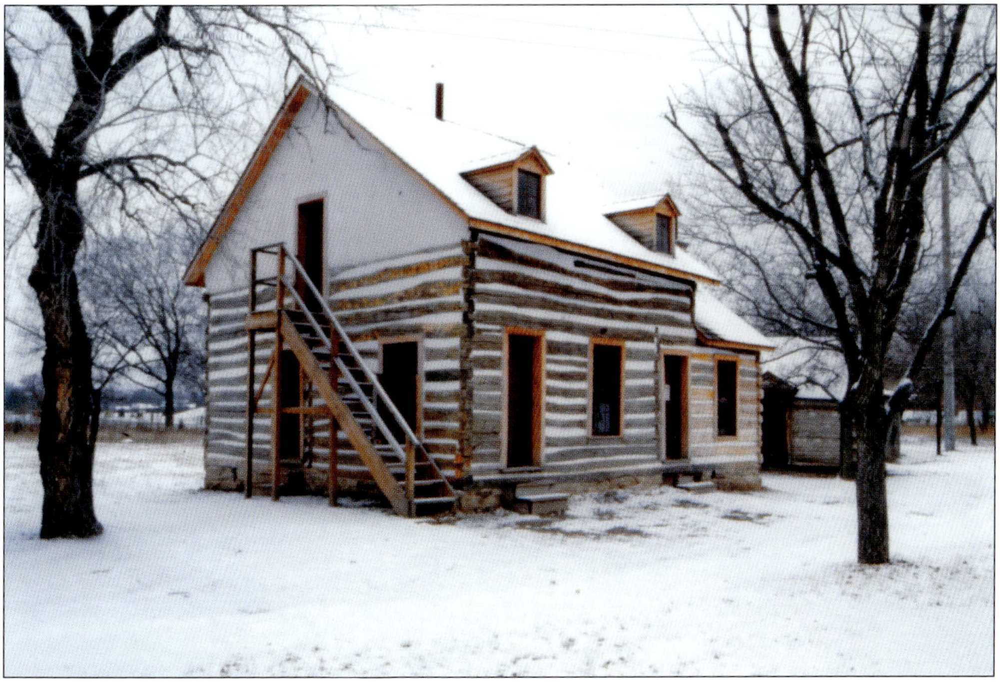

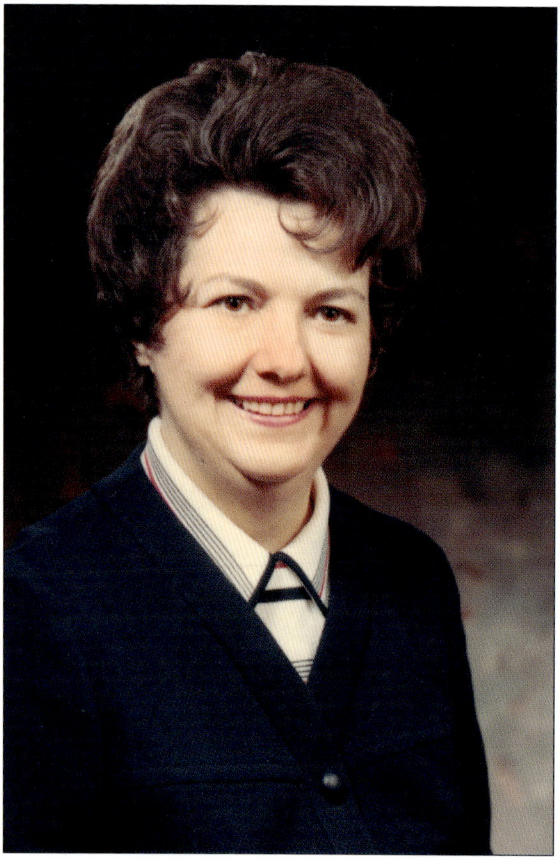

By the middle of the 1970s, Old Cowtown Museum began to professionalize with the hiring of Marjorie "Pat" Brooks as business manager. She became the first woman to run the museum. One of her first hires was Stan Harder as curator. Under his watch, the museum started the process of becoming more historically authentic. It renamed buildings to more accurate early Wichita names. Harder also removed mannequins put in the buildings during the 1950s. Also removed were the old wire and wood barriers that protected exhibits as visitors walked through the area.

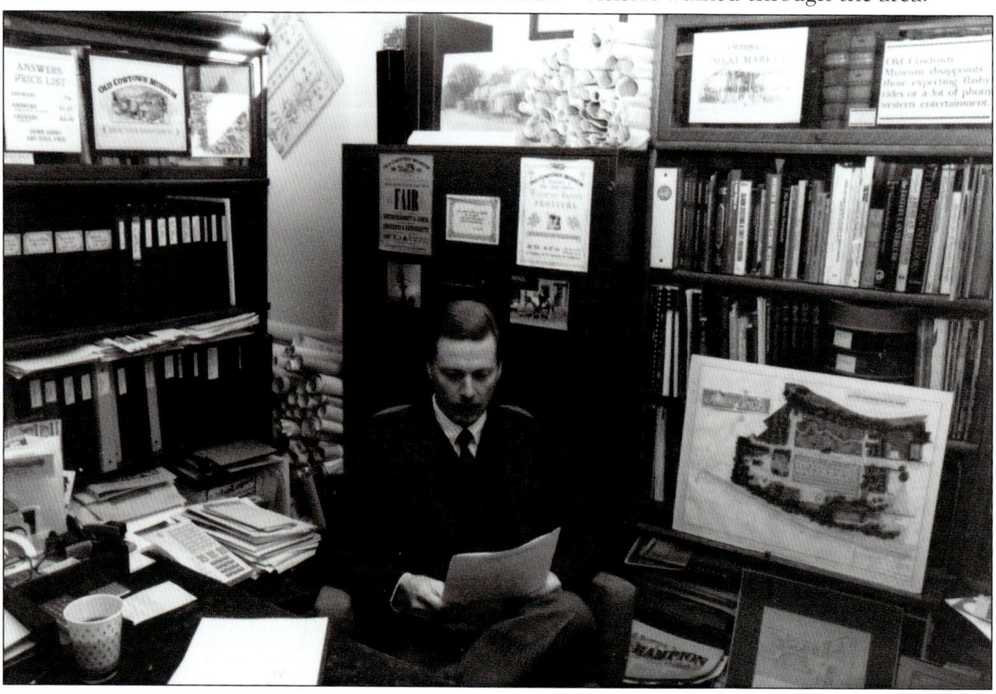

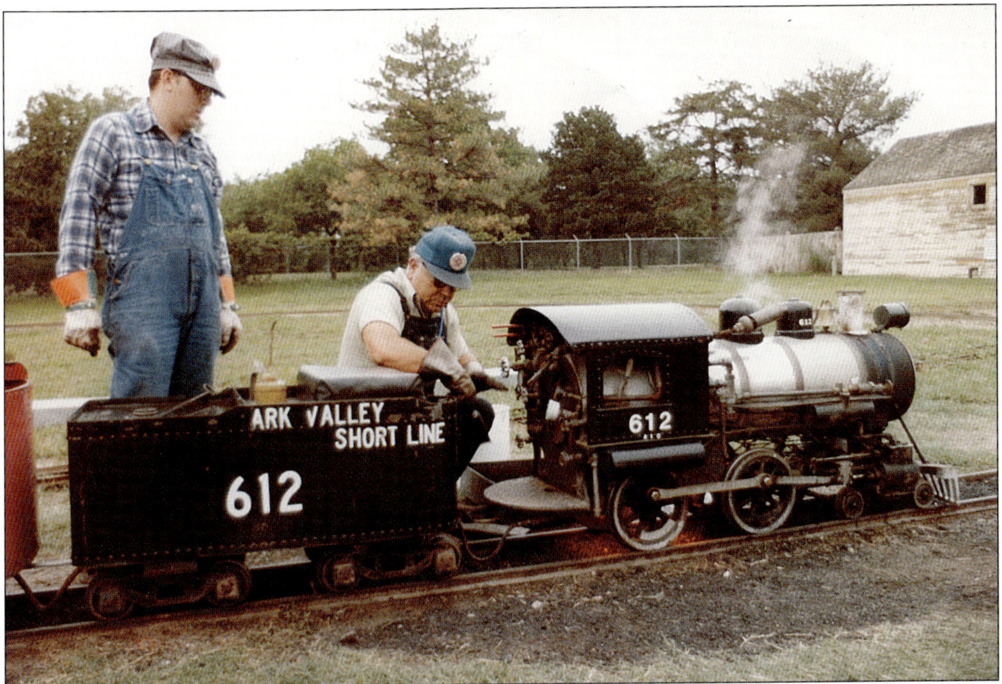

During the 1980s, Old Cowtown Museum started a move to become more historically accurate. This move drove out some of the longtime veteran Cowtown volunteers, including Charley George (above right, with Randy Spillman), who ran a small train ride beside the Variety Theater (above), and C.I. Blair (below), who worked in the Carpentry Shop demonstrating woodcraft and selling wooden tops. Cowtown staff asked George to remove his train due to it being inaccurate to the museum's time period. They also asked Blair to move from the museum grounds to the commercial area west of the Variety Theater and the Empire House. Instead of complying with the museum's demands, Blair and George quit volunteering at the museum.

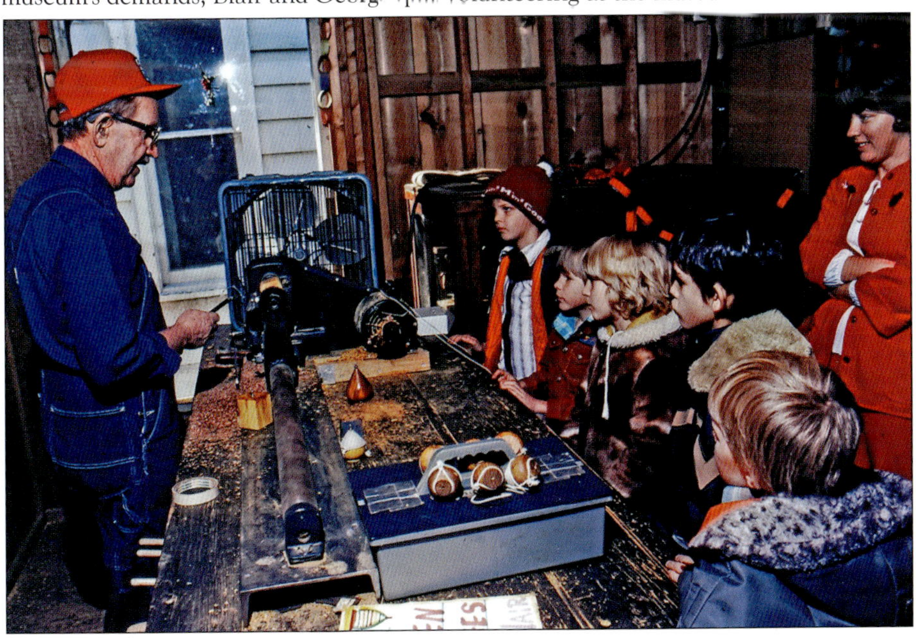

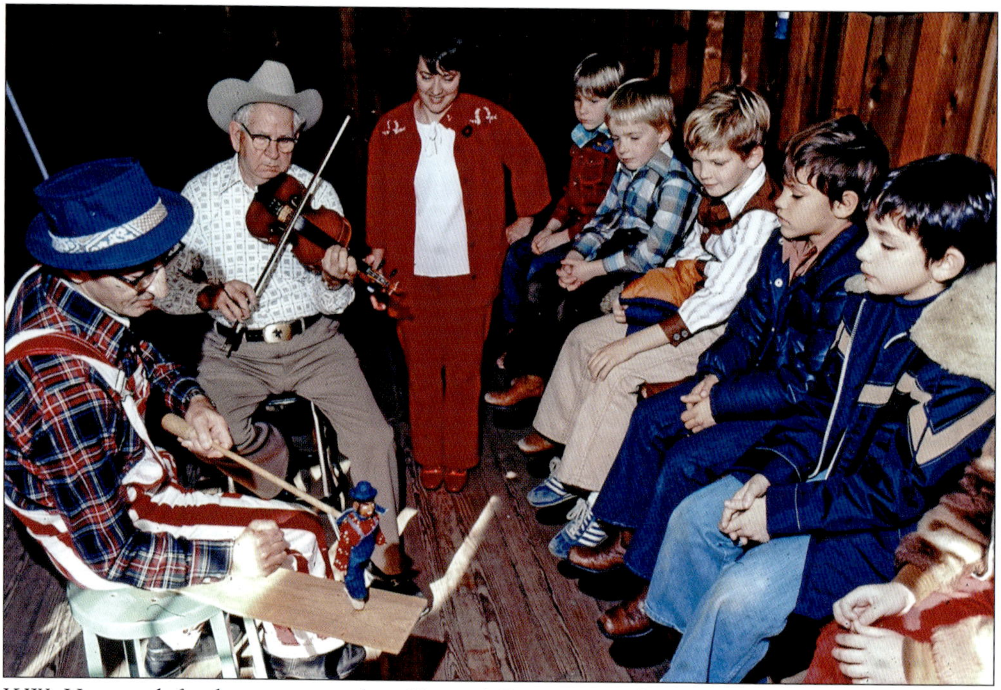

K.W. Hunter, left, demonstrates his *Cloggin' Dancer* wood carving to Andale Elementary schoolchildren, with Everett Fielder on the fiddle. Agnes George, room mother, is in the middle with students looking on the right. The impression of Hunter's *Cloggin' Dancer* is one that remains to many of the museum's now grown-up visitors.

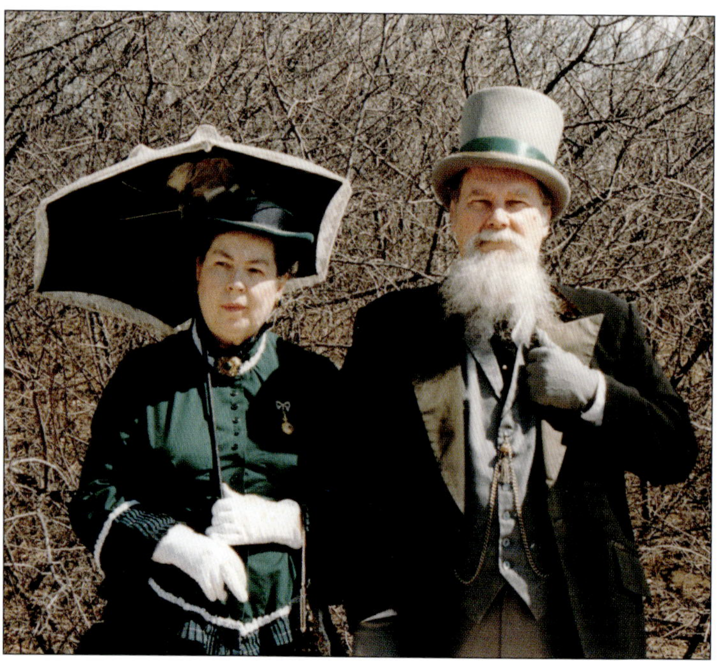

In what started out as a means of transportation for their daughter Karyl, Ron and Karlina Dodd became involved with Old Cowtown Museum. While on the grounds one day, curator Stan Harder noted that Ron bore a striking resemblance to pioneer doctor Andrew Fabrique. After doing research, the family became the Fabrique family, with Karlina playing Sarah, Ron as Dr. Fabrique, and Karyl as Mattie Lee Fabrique—roles they all played until the late 1990s.

One of Old Cowtown Museum's many volunteers was Marie MacDonald, a broadcaster for local radio and television stations KFDI, KARD-TV (now KSNW), and KFH. She also was an editor and writer for the *Wichita Beacon*, the *Wichita Eagle*, and the *Wichita Eagle-Beacon.* After retirement, MacDonald became an ambassador for Old Cowtown Museum, portraying Julia Munger and Victoria Murdock. MacDonald died on December 24, 1992, at the age of 82.

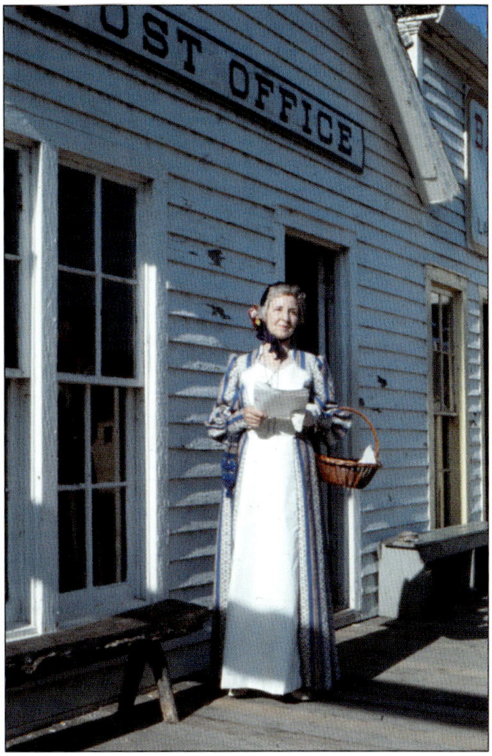

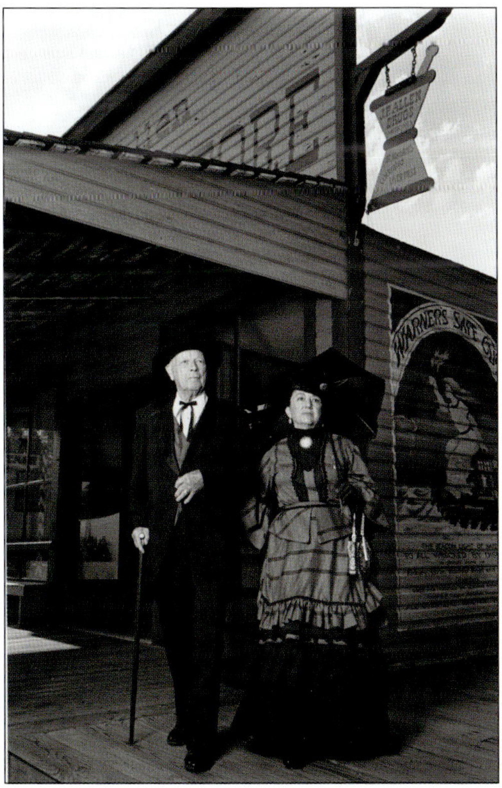

Two more of Old Cowtown Museum's many volunteers were Roy and Wilma Sehnert. Roy worked for the *Wichita Eagle*, where his first job was as the personal driver of Victor Murdock. Wilma was the founder of the Dixie Lee Saloon Girls and president of the Cowtown Social Club. Roy died on August 6, 1996, at the age of 99, and Wilma died on February 9, 2006, at the age of 82.

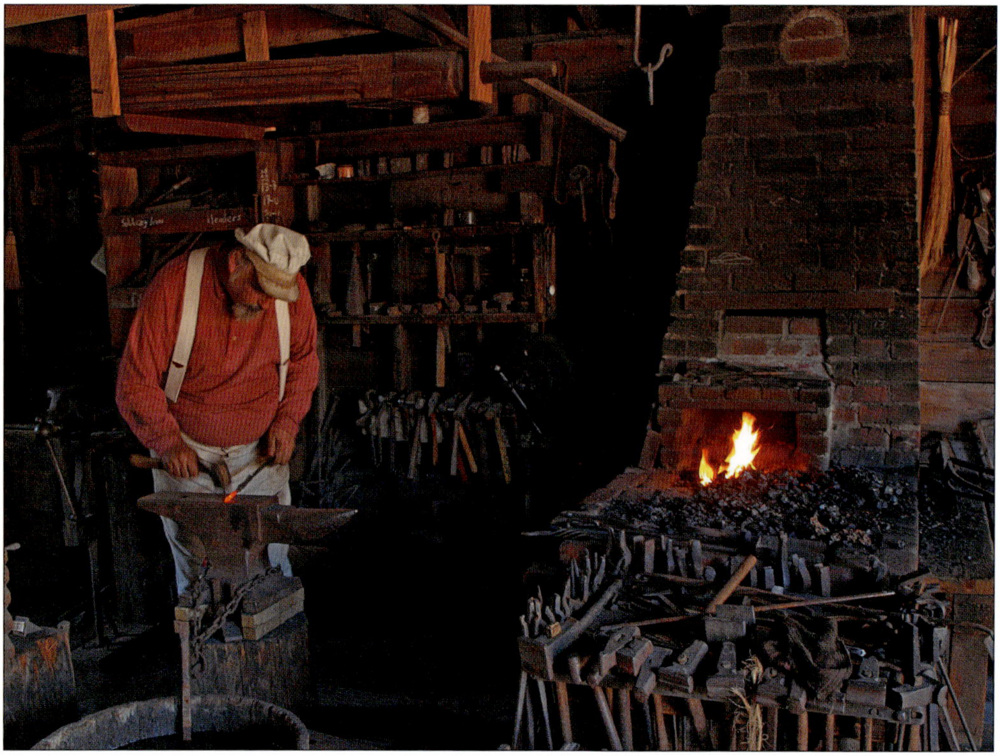

In the 1980s, Old Cowtown Museum started concentrating on living history, a trend that was occurring nationally at institutions such as Bent's Old Fort and Fort Larned. One of the holdovers from the Old West theme, the Blacksmith Shop, seen above, along with the Print Shop, below, became the main focus of the museum's living history program. (Above, courtesy Keith Wondra.)

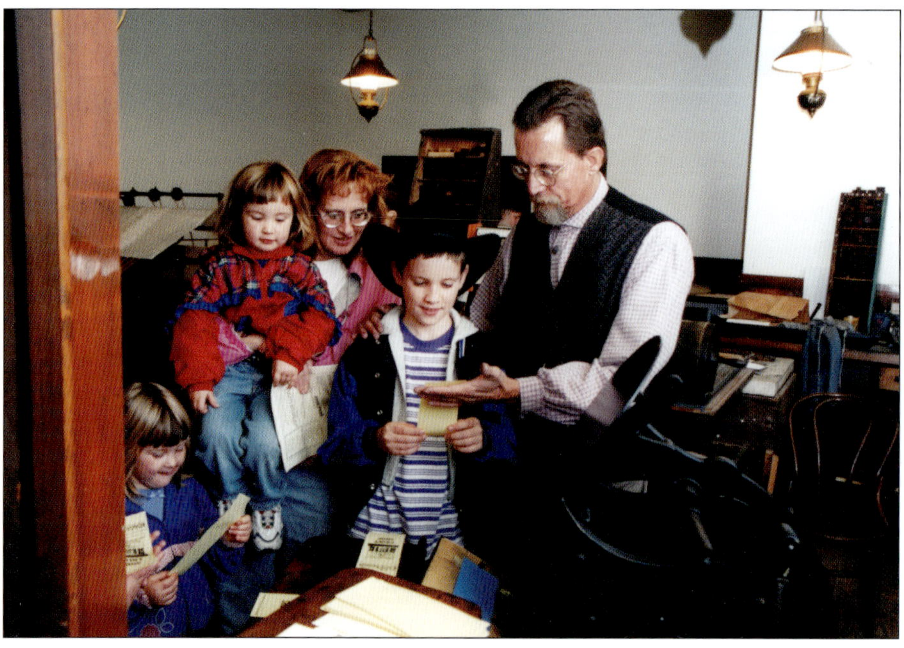

Three

Events and Groups

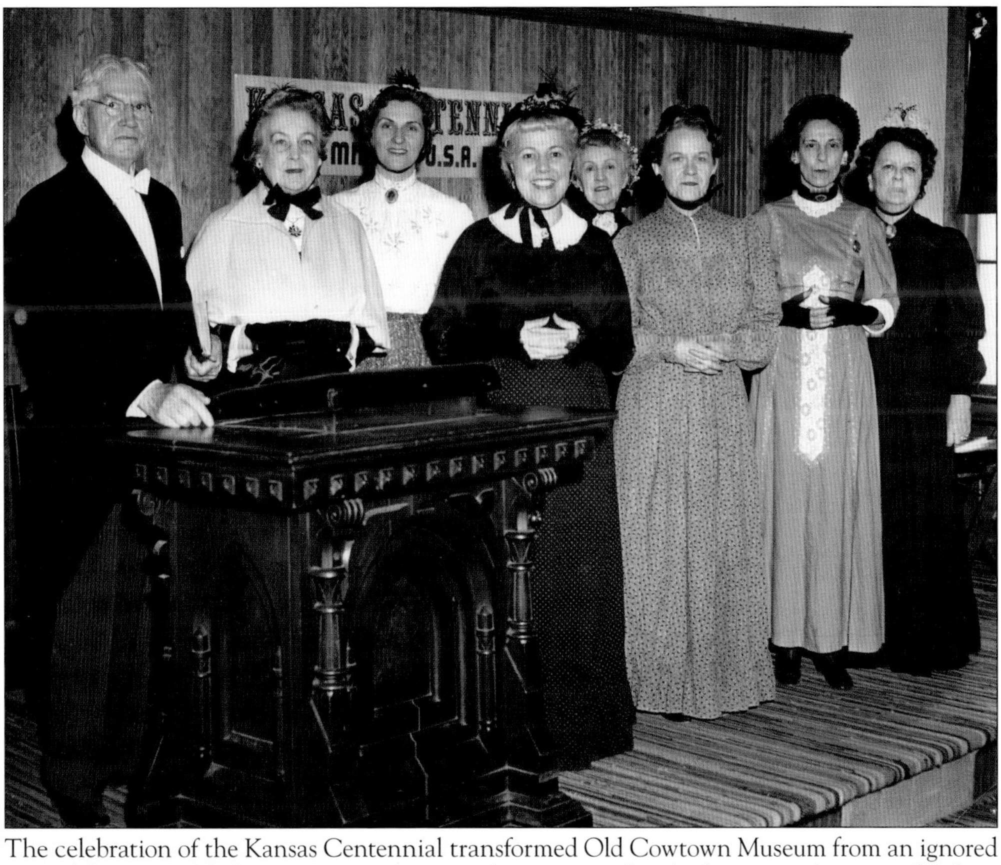

The celebration of the Kansas Centennial transformed Old Cowtown Museum from an ignored part of the city to Wichita's signature location for centennial and other citywide events. Wichita officially celebrated the centennial July 4–16, with the museum having gunfights along with reenactments inside the First Presbyterian Church, as shown here. (Courtesy *Wichita Eagle*.)

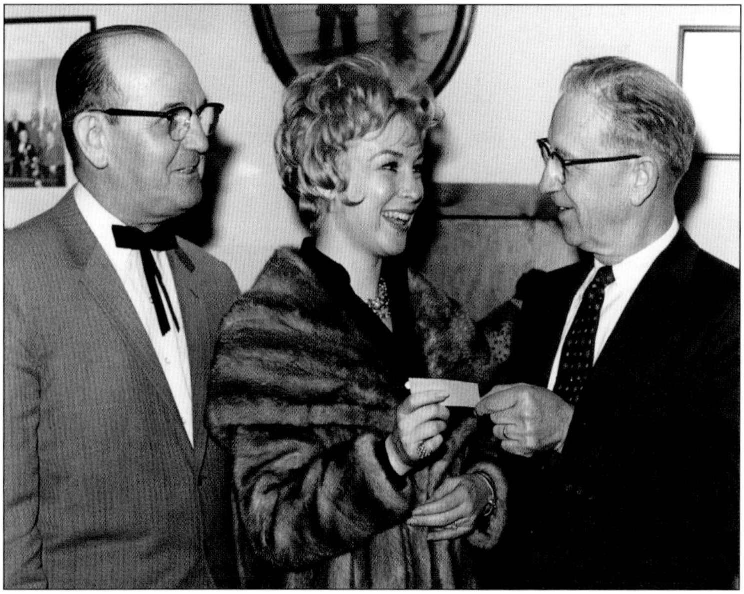

Over the years, several celebrities visited Old Cowtown Museum, including Barbara Eden (who went on to *I Dream of Jeannie* fame). During her 1961 visit, J.O. Wilson (right), president of Historic Wichita, Inc., presents a new Cowtown citizen card to Eden while Phil Manning (left), Old Cowtown Museum business manager, looks on. (Courtesy *Wichita Eagle.)*

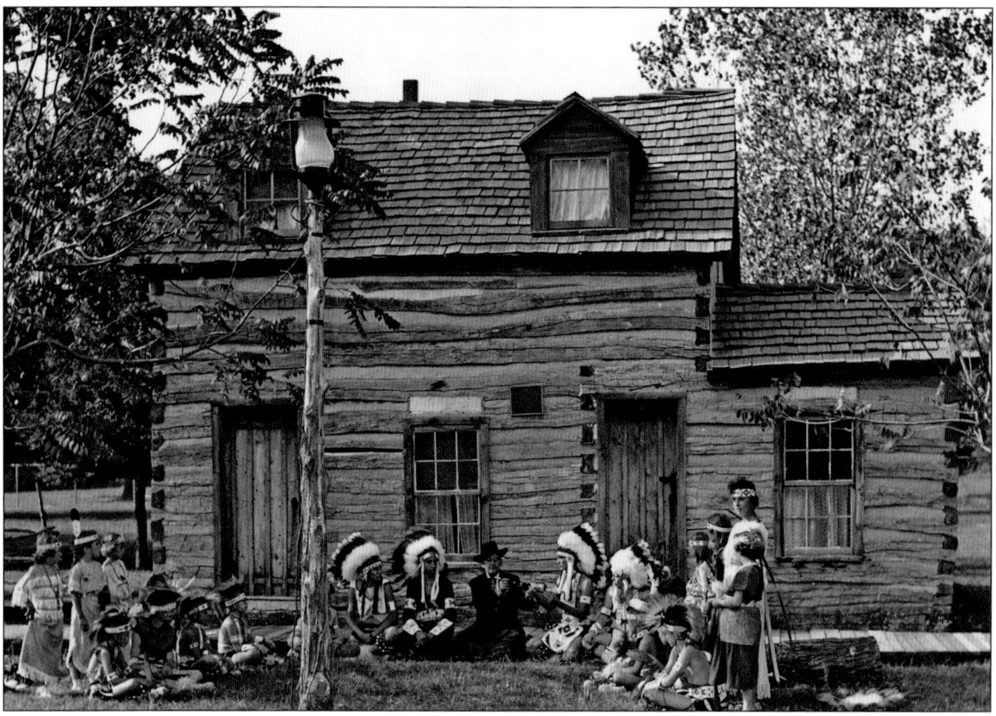

In 1963, the local Hon-Pe-Aika Indian dancers performed at the museum and posed for a photograph in front of the Munger House, the museum's most famous building. Larry Roberts, one of Old Cowtown Museum's founders and board members, is in the middle "smoking a peace pipe." This is one of the ways Old Cowtown Museum portrayed Native Americans in the 1960s.

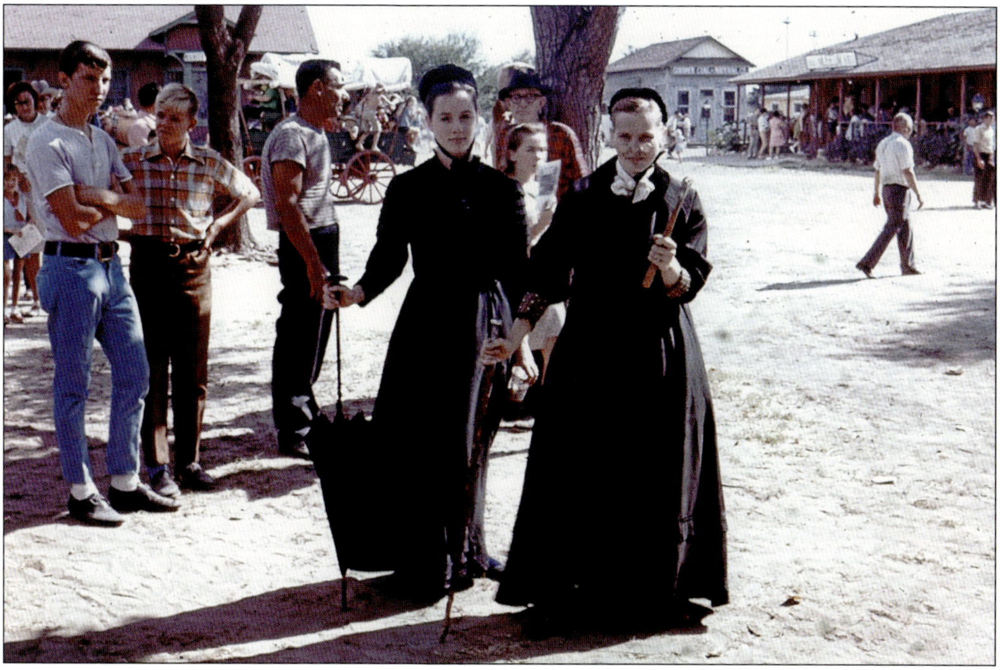

Started in 1966, the Chisholm Trail Jubilee Celebration began as a daylong event that paid tribute to Jesse Chisholm, whose trail went through what would become Wichita. Intermixed between gunfights and can-can girls was a "reenactment" of Carrie Nation's raid on the Buckhorn Bar. Here, Nattily Dowd (left) and Kathleen Garrett pose during a 1960s Chisholm Trail Jubilee Celebration.

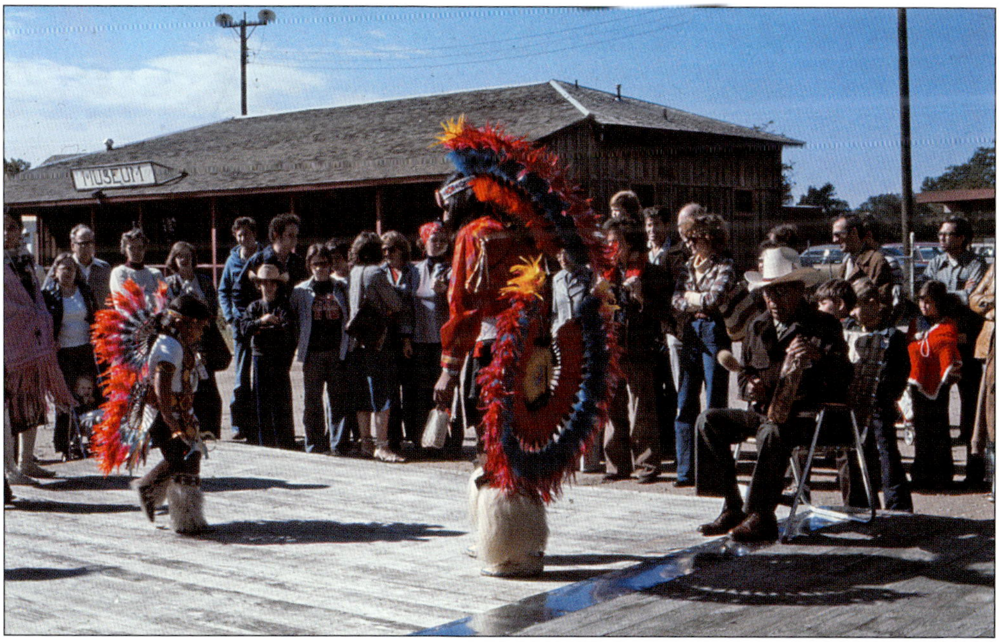

To counter the negative image that Hon-Pe-Aika dancers portrayed, powwows started at Old Cowtown Museum in 1969. They continued until the Mid-America All-Indian Center opened east of the museum in 1976 at the confluence of the Big and Little Arkansas Rivers. In the distance is the museum building that was constructed in 1963 and housed exhibits until 1986.

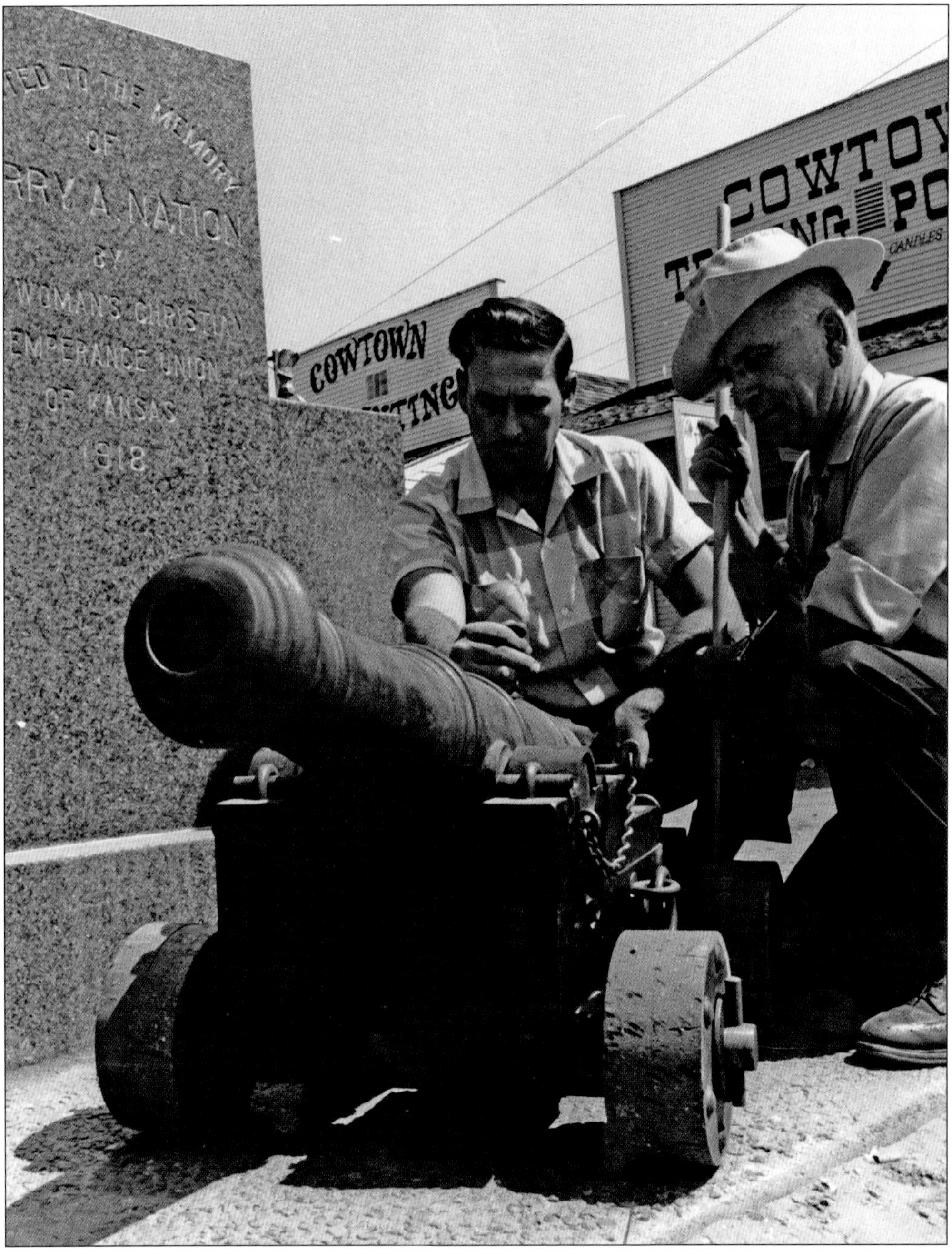

On April 28, 1957, approximately 27 men who shared a common passion for old guns formed the Chisholm Trail Antique Gun Association. Seven years later, they started having their meetings in Fritz Snitzler's Saloon and began running the Gunsmith Shop. During the Chisholm Trail Centennial celebration on August 22, 1967, a cannon was fired at 2:00 p.m. to signal the beginning of the celebration. Here, Dean Harrington (left) and Clyde Williams, both members of the Chisholm Trail Antique Gun Association, prepare the cannon for firing. After years of a love-hate relationship, the museum and the Chisholm Trail Antique Gun Association parted ways in 1979.

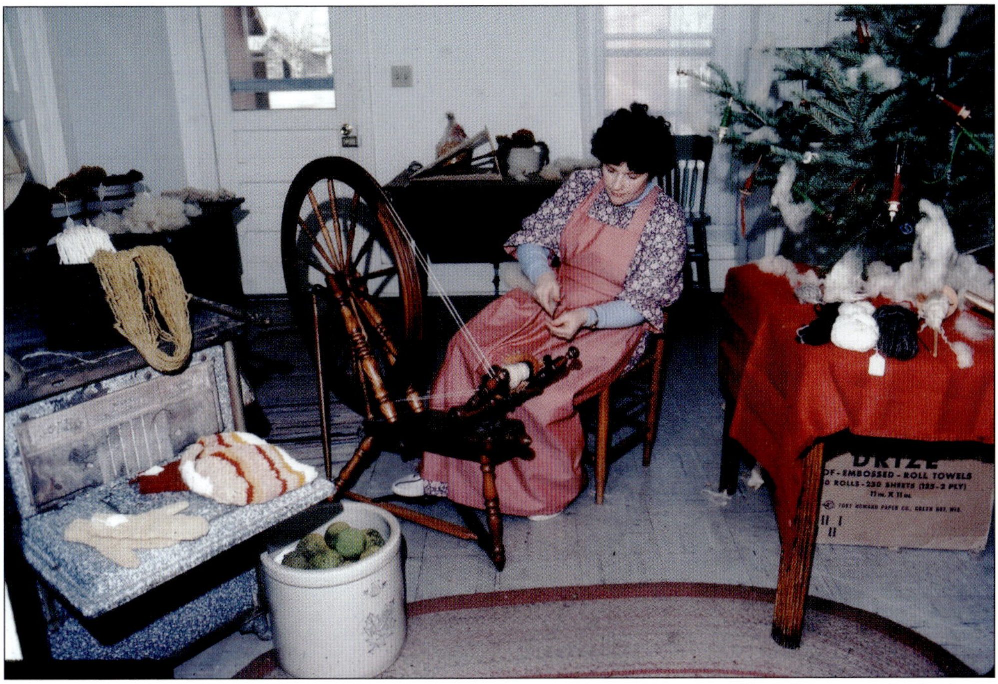

When "Christmas Through the Windows" started in 1975, visitors strolled the grounds, looking at reenactments through the windows of the historic structures, as seen above. Seven years later, the event started to have other activities that included Girl Scouts singing Christmas carols and Father Christmas roaming the dusty streets. Due to the museum's expanding collection, Old Cowtown Museum renamed the event Old Fashioned Christmas, and the building interiors were decorated and opened to visitors, such as the Murdock House front parlor, seen below. The event became the museum's signature event and, for many Wichitans, the start of the Christmas season. (Below, courtesy Keith Wondra.)

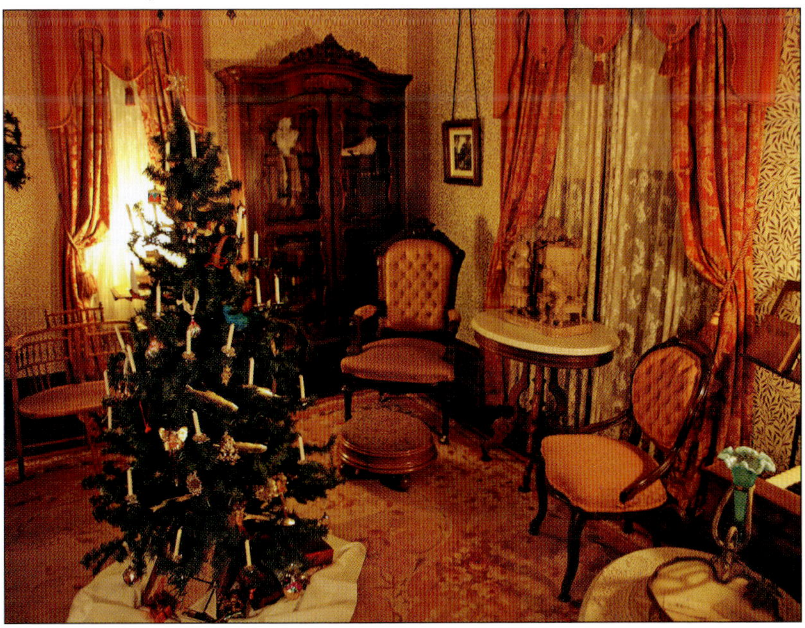

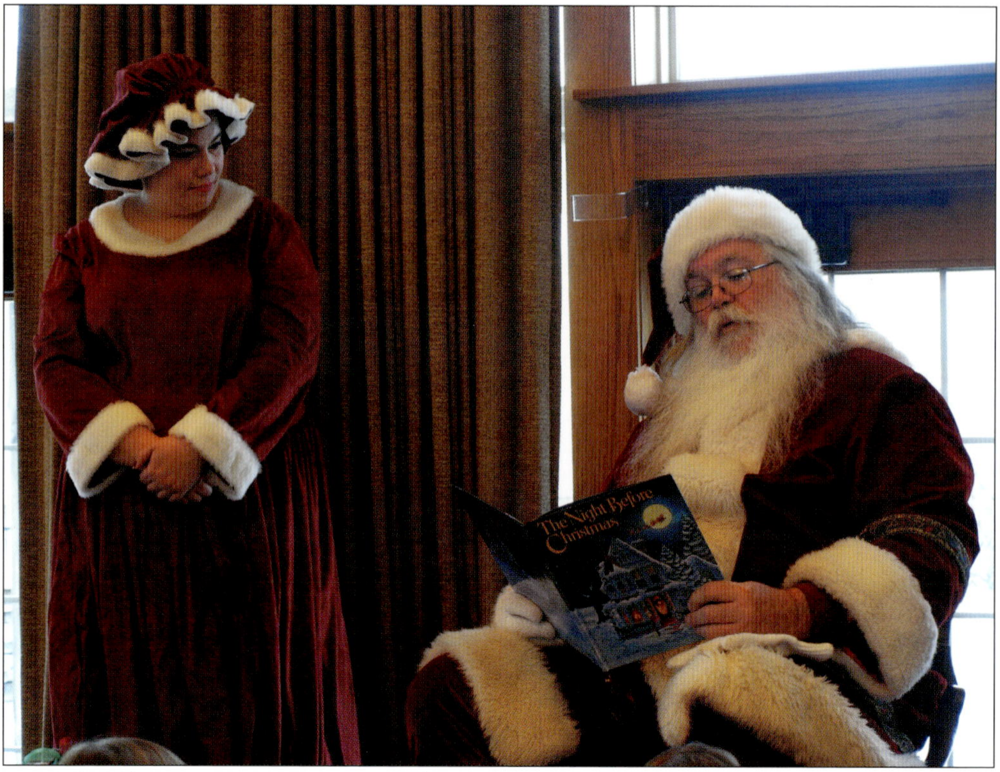

In 2005, Old Cowtown Museum created "Breakfast With Santa" as an addition to its popular Christmas event. The event's festivities include arts and crafts and a catered breakfast. The highlight of the event is the arrival of Santa Claus via the stagecoach, where he then concludes the event by reading Clement C. Moore's "A Visit from St. Nicholas." (Courtesy Keith Wondra.)

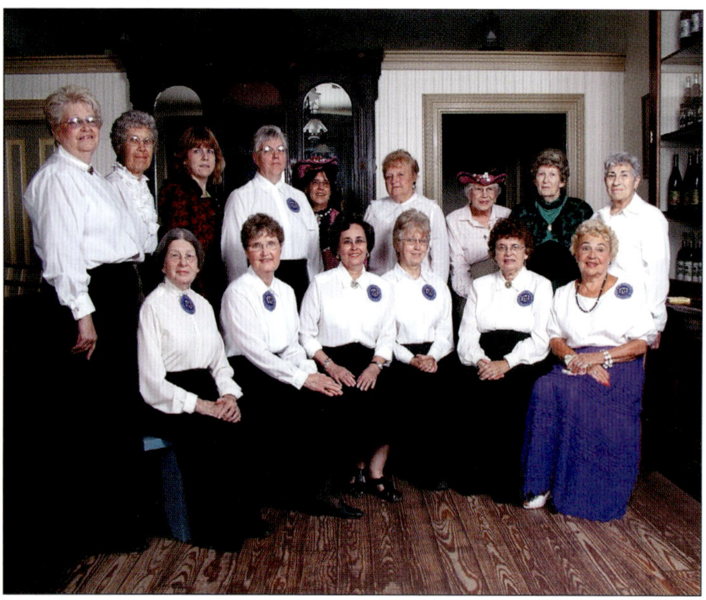

One of the oldest groups at Old Cowtown Museum is the Cowtown Social Club, founded in 1975 as a group to support and fund the museum through donations of time and money. Over the years, the club has funded construction of a bandstand and creation of the dress shop, and made fresh evergreen wreaths for the Christmas events, while funding these projects by selling homemade crafts and goodies. (Courtesy Greg Hunt.)

In 1977, to reinterpret the folkways of 1865 to 1880, the Harvest Home Festival was added. The event was the museum's answer to the Folk-Life Festival that was successful but discontinued in 1976. The Harvest Home Festival featured crafts, judging operation of an apple press (below), and display of antiques. Along with the crafts and judging came musical acts, such as the museum's Snitzies Fritzies (now the Dixie Lee Saloon Girls), musicians on banjos and fiddles, choral groups, and folk dancers. All of the performers were clad in period attire. Meticulously researched by curator Stan Harder and assistant director Patricia Christgau, it became one of the museum's signature events.

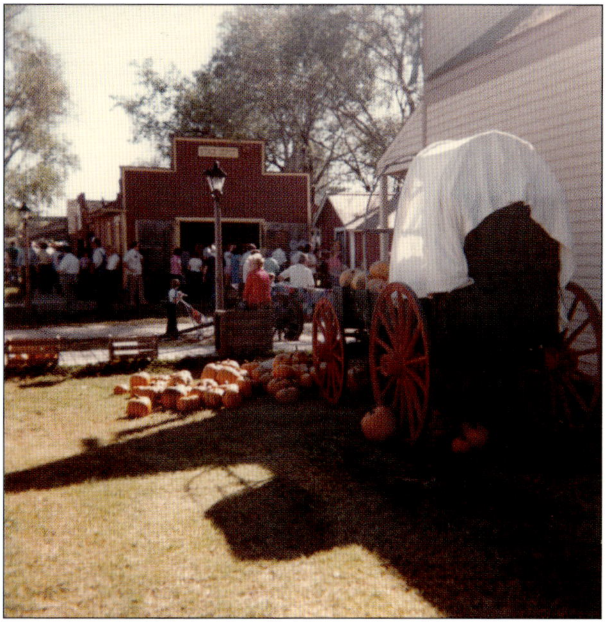

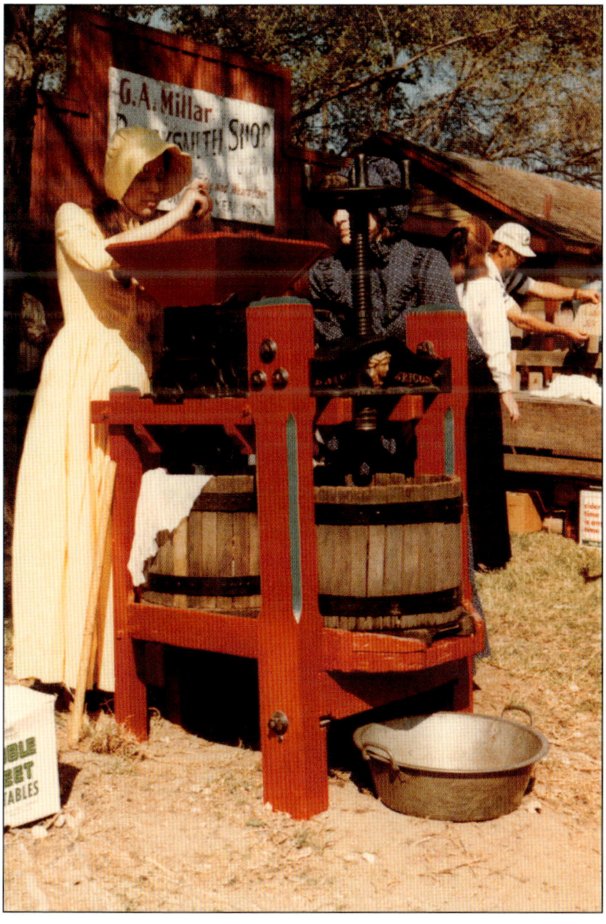

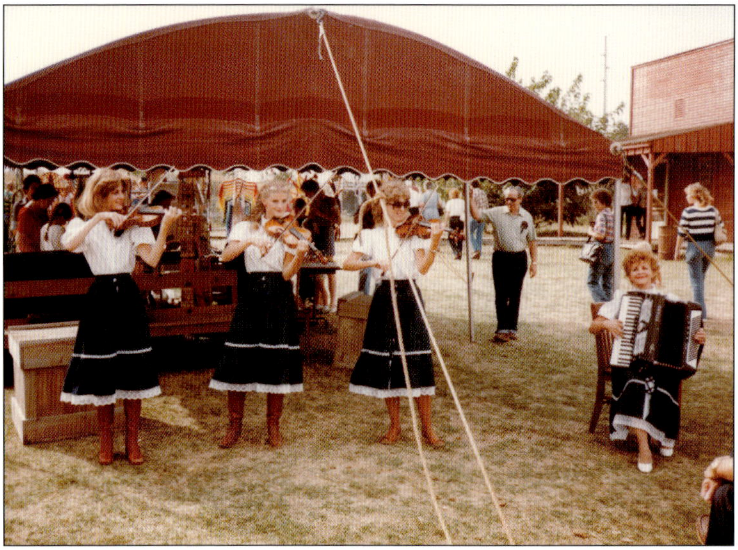

Four years later, the Harvest Home Festival was renamed the Old Sedgwick County Fair as a thank-you to Sedgwick County for providing the funding of the museum's growing number of staff. From left to right, Dana Scheer, Allison Peterson, Valerie Sullivan, and Ruth Scheer perform during the 1983 Old Sedgwick County Fair.

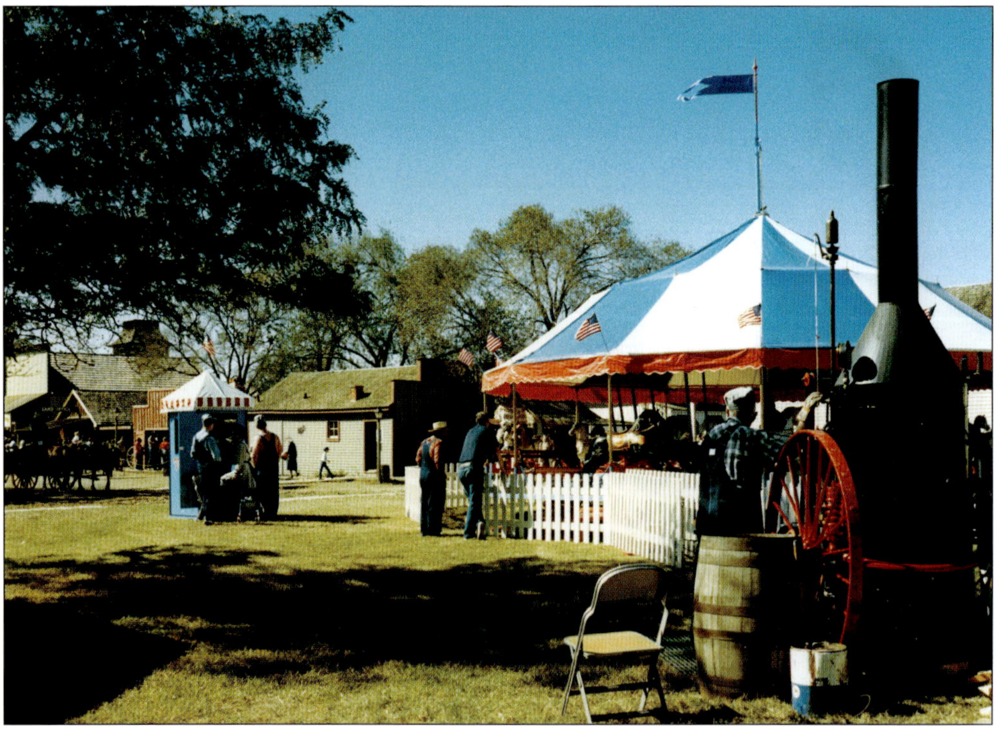

Starting with the 1988 Old Sedgwick County Fair, Jerry Ottaway, co-owner of Carousel Skate Center and son of the founder of Joyland Amusement Park, displayed an 1895 steam-operated carousel restored with the help of his son Gary and father, Herb. The carousel remained a popular attraction at the Cowtown event until 1993, when Ottaway sold the popular ride. (Courtesy Jim Powell.)

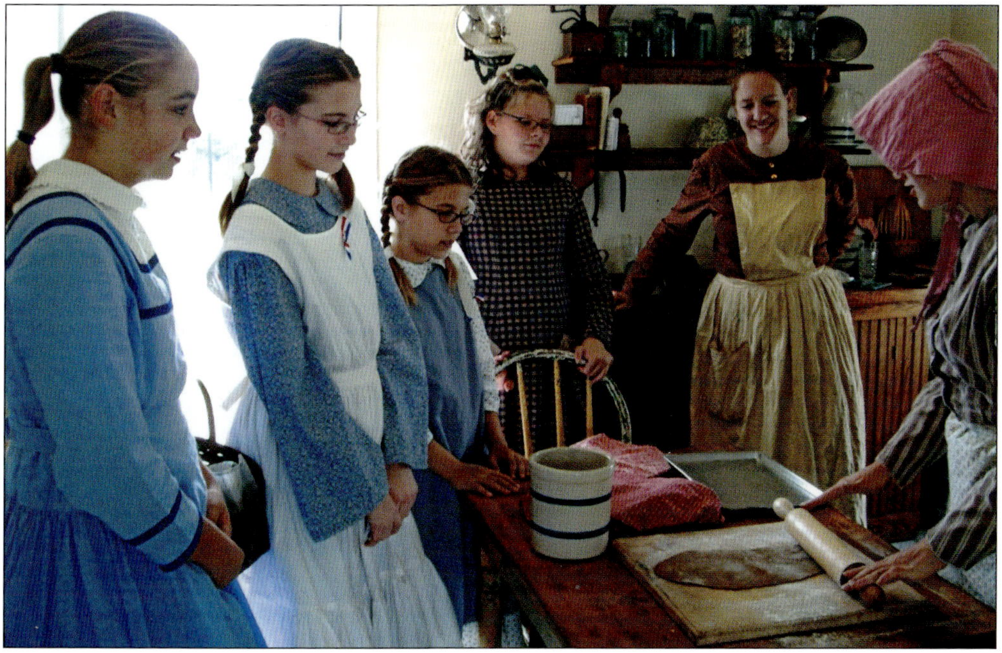

Quoted in the October 4, 1995, *Wichita Eagle,* Stan Harder claims the museum's county fair event "replicated the look and feel of an 1870s county fair in [that] . . . almost everyone and everything that represented agriculture and commerce in society was present at the fair. Everyone wanted to be seen or to show off their accomplishments as well as see what their friends had brought to the fair."

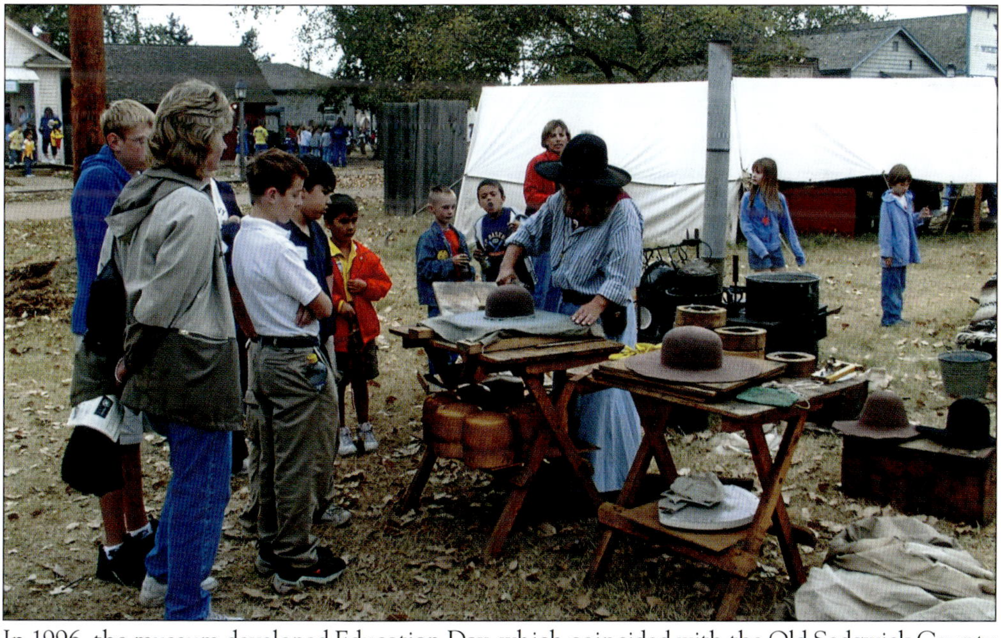

In 1996, the museum developed Education Day, which coincided with the Old Sedgwick County Fair. The education day taught schoolchildren the function of county fairs, from competitive judging to the process of showing animals. Even though the Old Sedgwick County Fair ended in 2011, Education Day is still one of the museum's important educational tools.

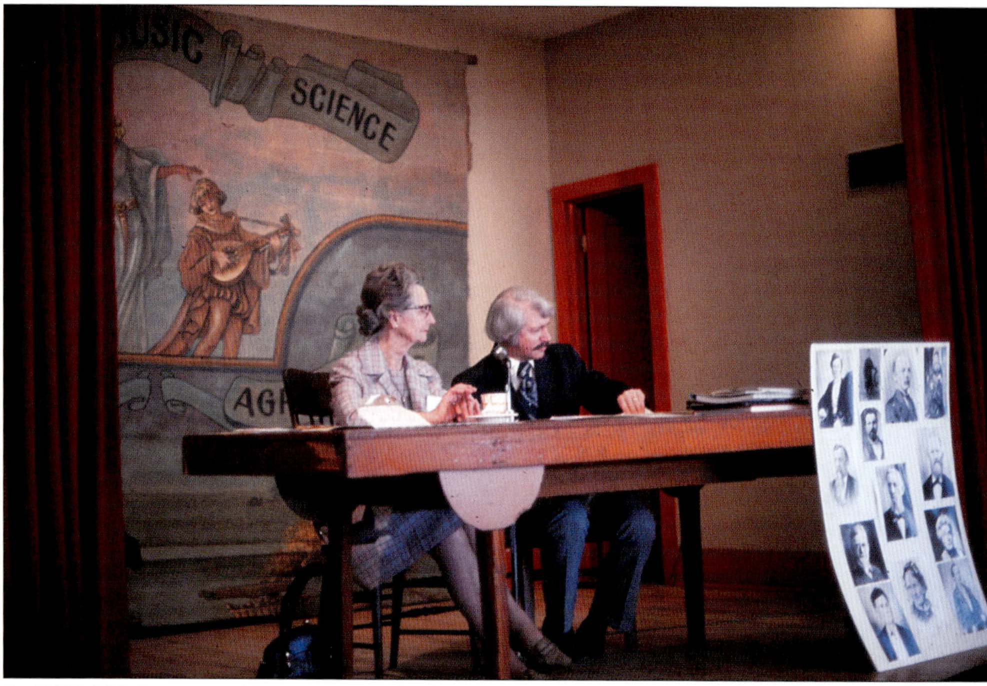

In 1977, Old Cowtown Museum started a docent training course to help provide vibrant learning experiences to groups that toured the museum. Above, Ignace Mead Jones, granddaughter of James R. Mead, and Wichita city historian Bill Ellington present a talk on early families of Wichita as part of the 1977 Cowtown docent training course. Also presented was a talk on the museum's origin and history given by Don Fitch, Kenneth Breese, Tom Fuller, and Phil Manning while moderated by John M. Bell. Below, from left to right, are Phil Manning, Don Fitch, John Bell, Kenneth Davis, and Tom Fuller as part of the 1977 Cowtown docent training course.

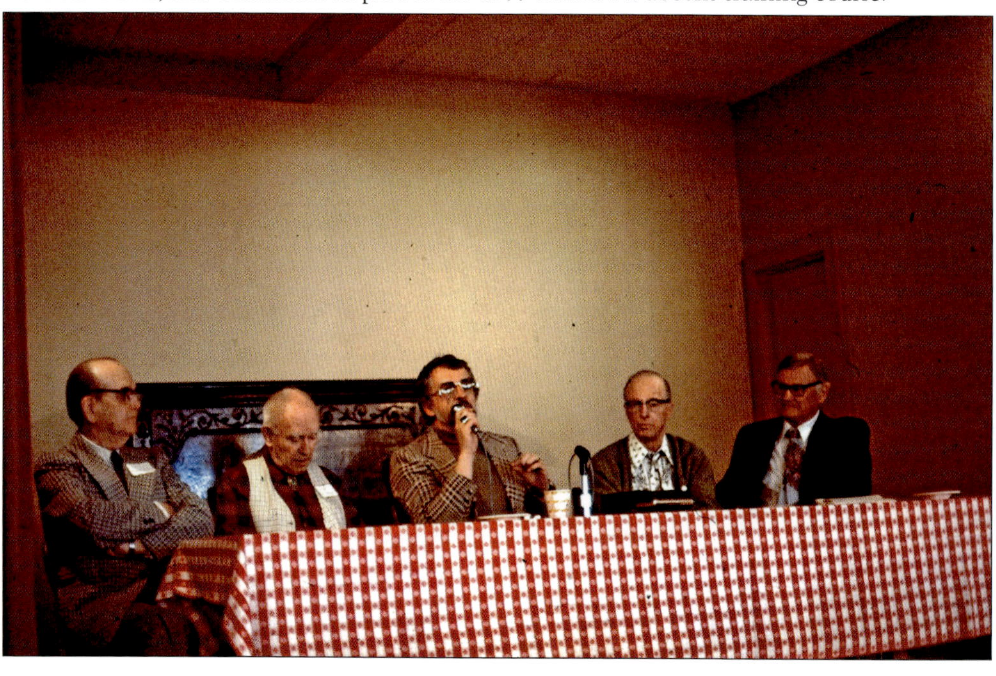

In late 1978, Wilma Sehnert (leaning on the table) started the Dixie Lee Saloon Girls as a new focus for the Buckhorn Bar, since nothing took place in the building. In the beginning, Sehnert did research on dances, costumes, and music from the 1870s. Originally, the group was called the Snitzies Fritzies after Fritz Snitzler, a longtime Wichita saloon owner. Older members of his family objected to the name, and it became the Dixie Lee Saloon Girls. What was going to be a onetime show became a staple group at Cowtown that performs to this day. (Right, courtesy Howard Eastwood.)

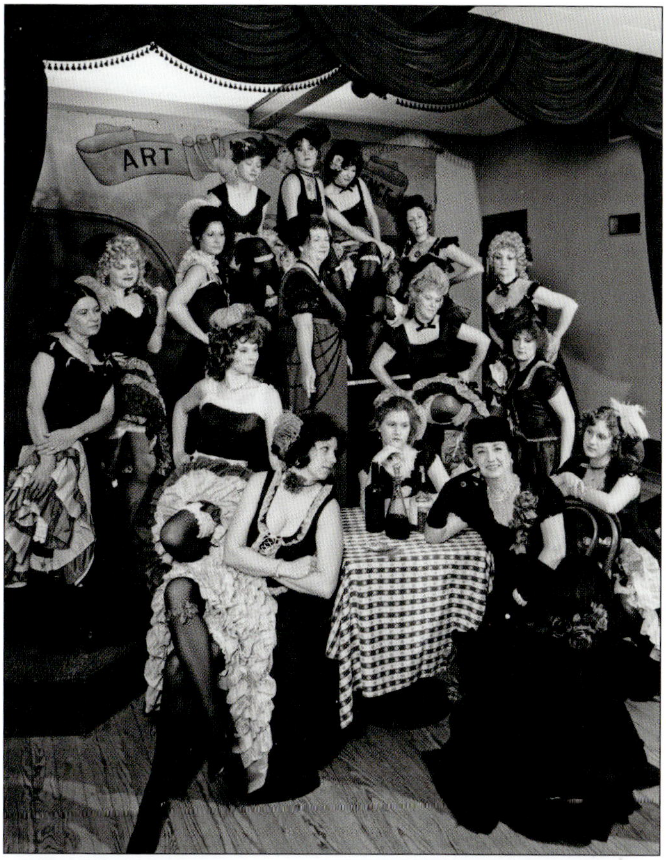

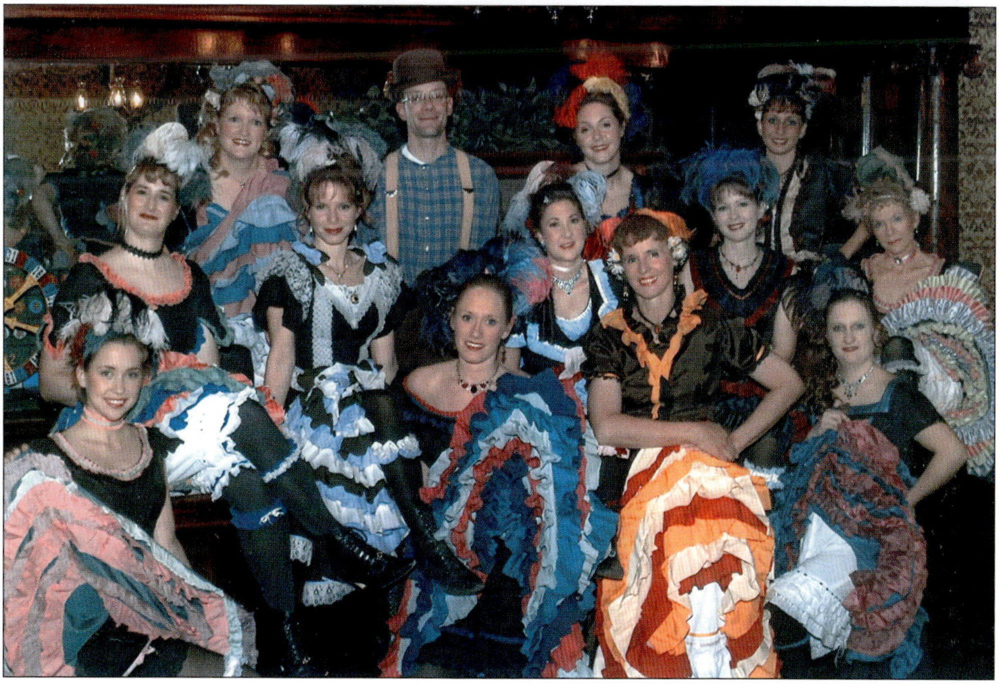

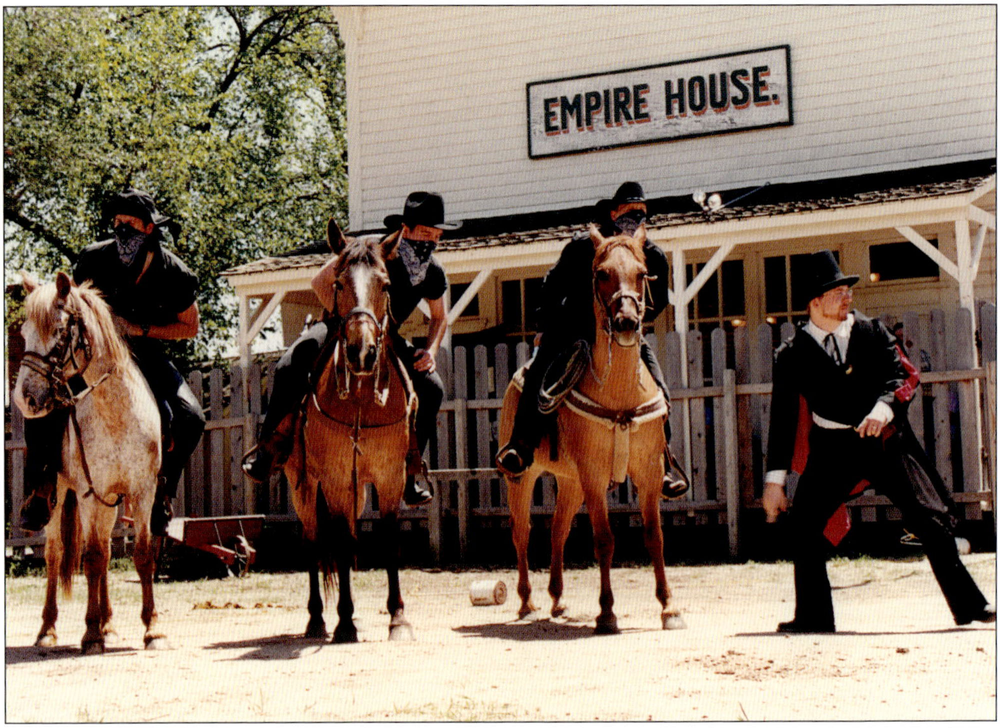

Above, starting in 1974, Old Cowtown Museum became home to the first performance of *The Wonderful Story of Windwagon Smith* during the Wichitennial River Festival, now the Wichita Riverfest. Mary Jane Teall, founder and director of the Wichita Community Theater, directed the first performance based on Walt Disney's animated film *The Saga of Windwagon Smith*. After some reworking, the play became *The Legend of Windwagon Smith* in 1976. It was a part of every Wichitennial River Festival and was performed at the museum until 1998. Below, as part of the House of Schwan's 50th anniversary during the 2010 Wichita Riverfest, the world-famous Budweiser Clydesdales are led through the streets of the museum. (Below, courtesy Keith Wondra.)

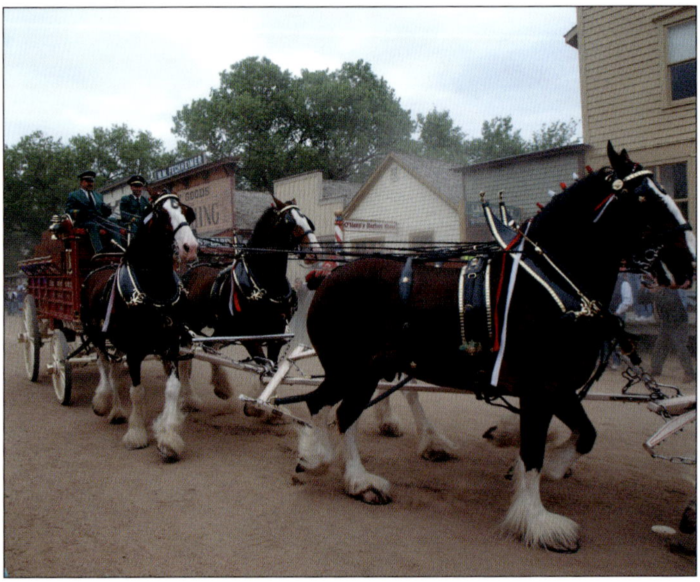

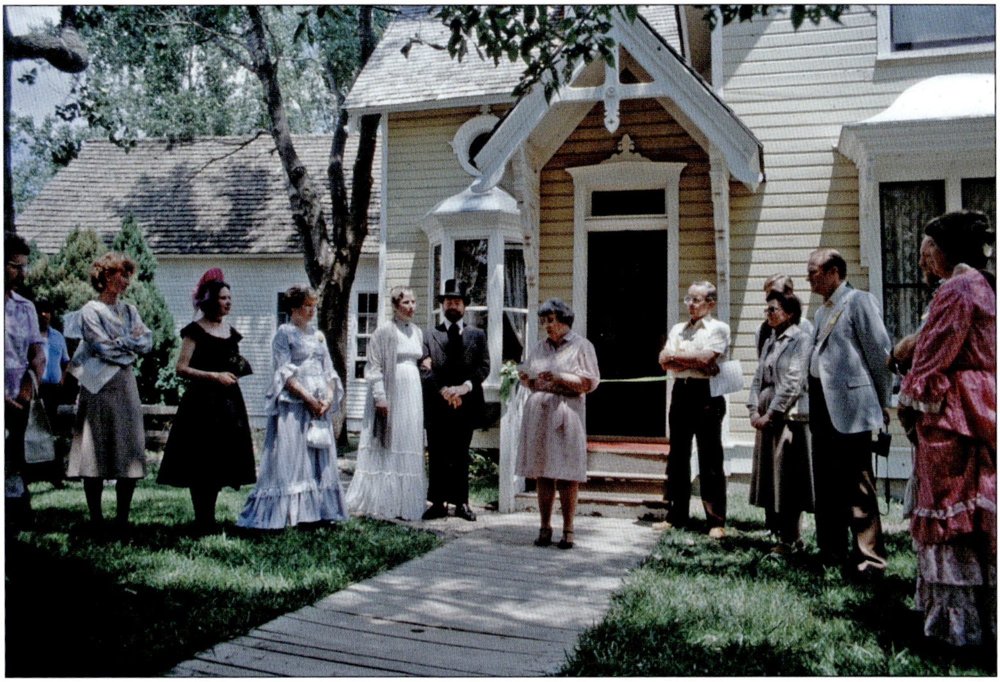

On June 1982, eight years after its move to Old Cowtown Museum and its restoration, the Murdock House ribbon cutting occurred. Mary Manlove, one of the volunteers, is speaking in the center with Mid-Town Citizens Association members looking on. The ribbon cutting was part of the second annual Victorian Garden Festival in 1982.

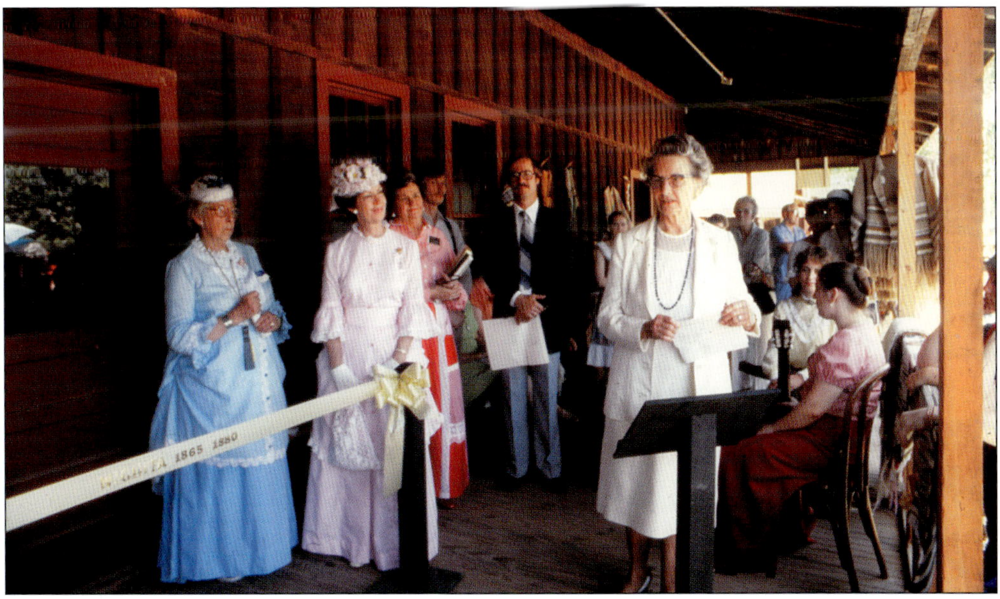

One of the last exhibits in the Museum Building was the "Wichita 1865–1880" exhibit. The ribbon cutting brought dignitaries to the museum, including Ignace Mead Jones, granddaughter of James R. Mead, who spoke at the event. The museum building and exhibit were torn down in 1986. Museum business manager Pat Brooks and curator Stan Harder are third and fourth from the left.

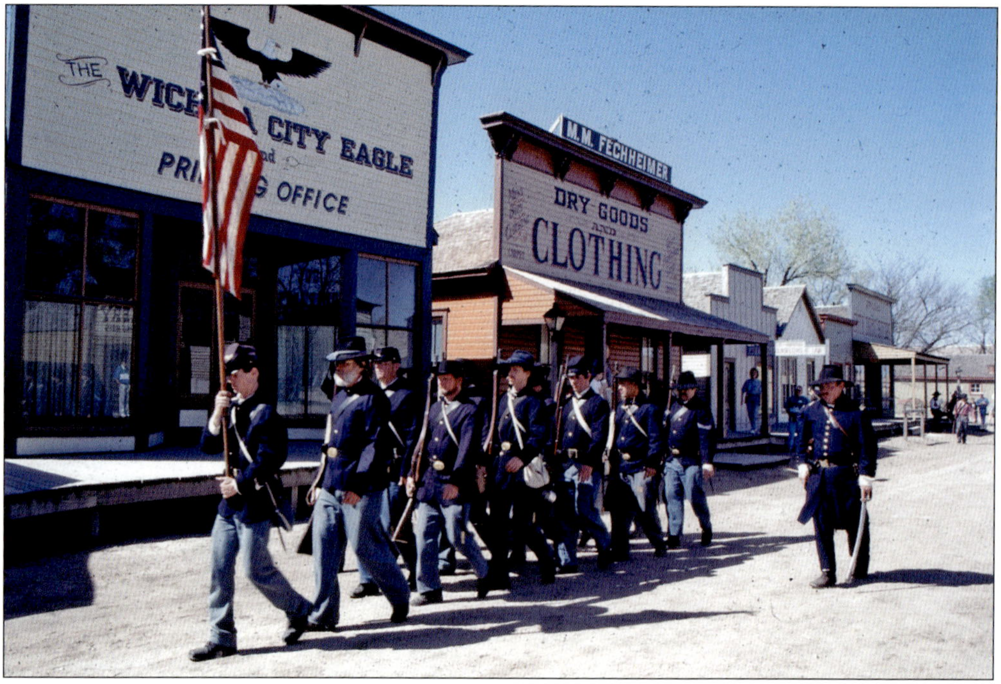

In the 1990s, Old Cowtown Museum started to tap into the growing fascination with the Civil War—even though no battles occurred near Wichita. The festivities became one of the largest-attended of all of the museum's major events. In recent years, the Civil War events have become more historically accurate in terms of clothing and battle formations. As early as 1985, Old Cowtown Museum put together the reenactment of 1870s Independence Day celebration, including anvil shootings, gunfights, and patriotic speeches. Below, standing are, from left to right, Keith Thompson, Helen Brown, Nancy Cammerer Oberg, and Crystal Meek. In the wagon in the background are Wilma and Roy Sehnert. (Below, courtesy Dennis Kennedy.)

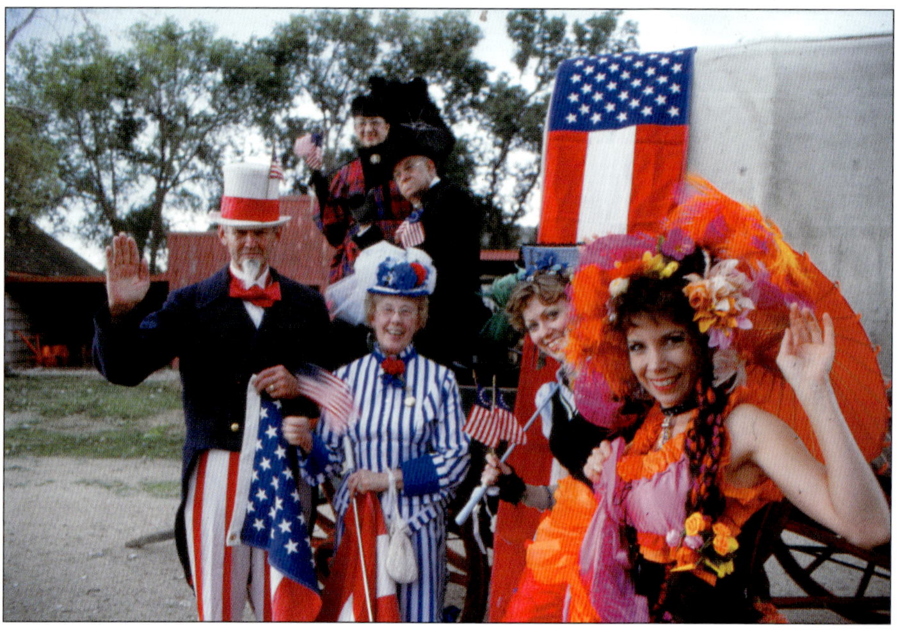

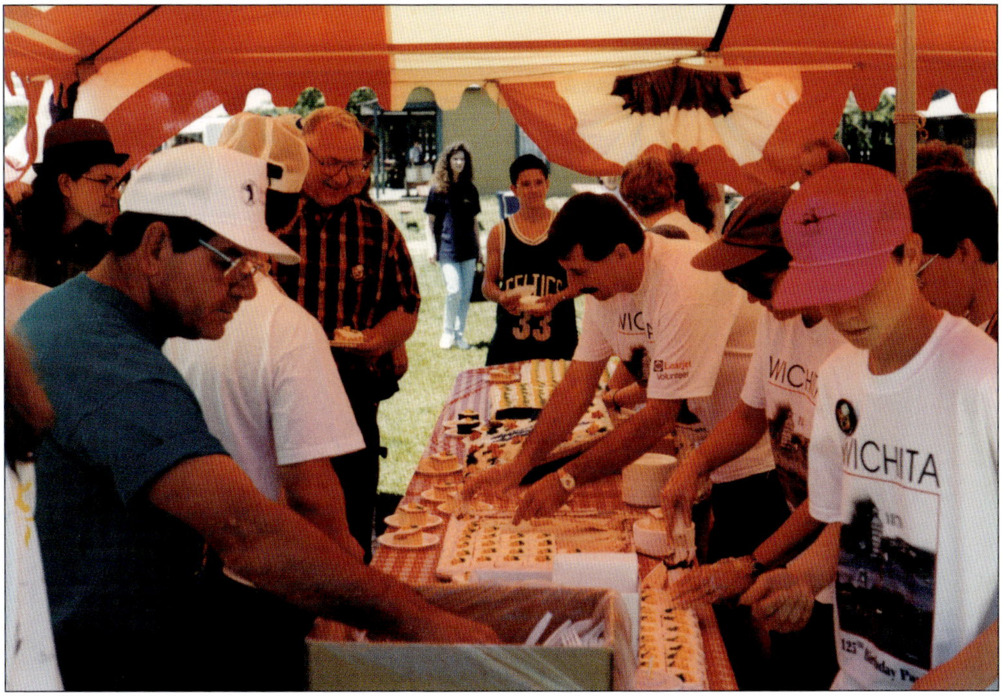

In 1995, Old Cowtown Museum continued its role as the place for historical anniversaries in Wichita's history. During the 19th annual Old Sedgwick County Fair held October 7–8, 1995, the museum celebrated Wichita's 125th birthday. Even though the celebration was a low-key event, other institutions like the Wichita-Sedgwick County Historical Museum did not even plan a celebration for the 125th birthday, and the city's convention and visitors bureau completely forgot.

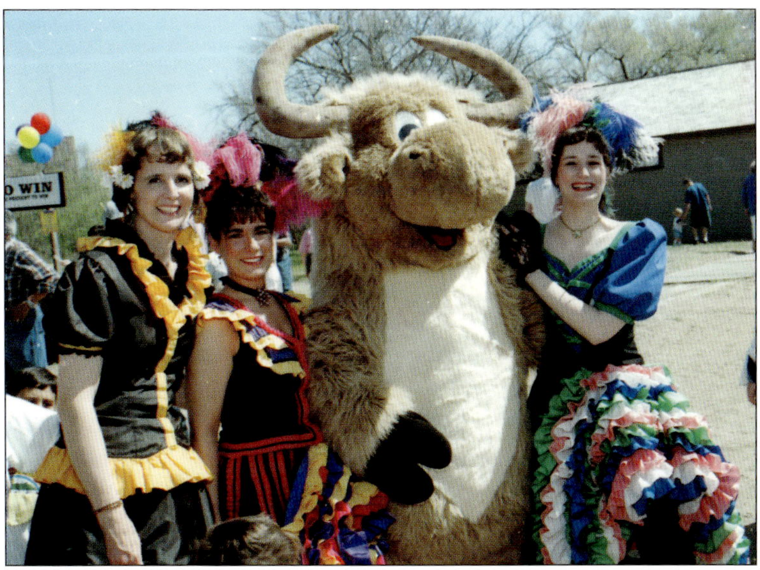

On April 19, 1997, warm weather brought 3,400 people out to celebrate the 125th birthday of the *Wichita Eagle* at Old Cowtown Museum. Festivities included wagon rides, 6,000 slices of birthday cake, and free root beer. Here, Yak, the mascot of the paper's kids section, poses with some of the Dixie Lee Dancers.

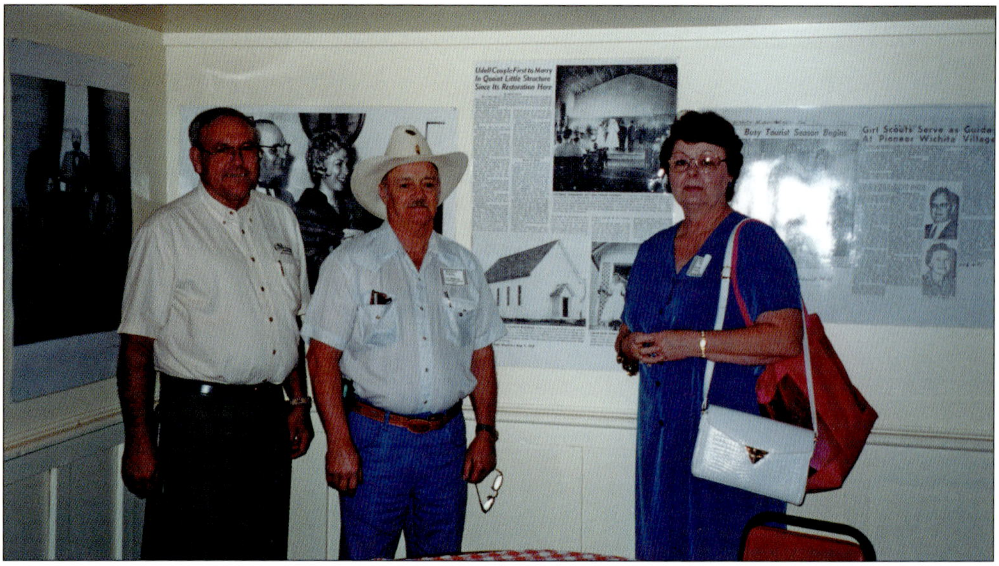

In 2000, Old Cowtown Museum celebrated its 50th anniversary with a reunion of the first couple married at the museum in 1955, Ken and Margaret Mantz. Also included was an oral history project documenting visitors' memories. Here, museum board member Les Drum (left) poses with Ken and Margaret Mantz during Old Cowtown Museum's 50th anniversary.

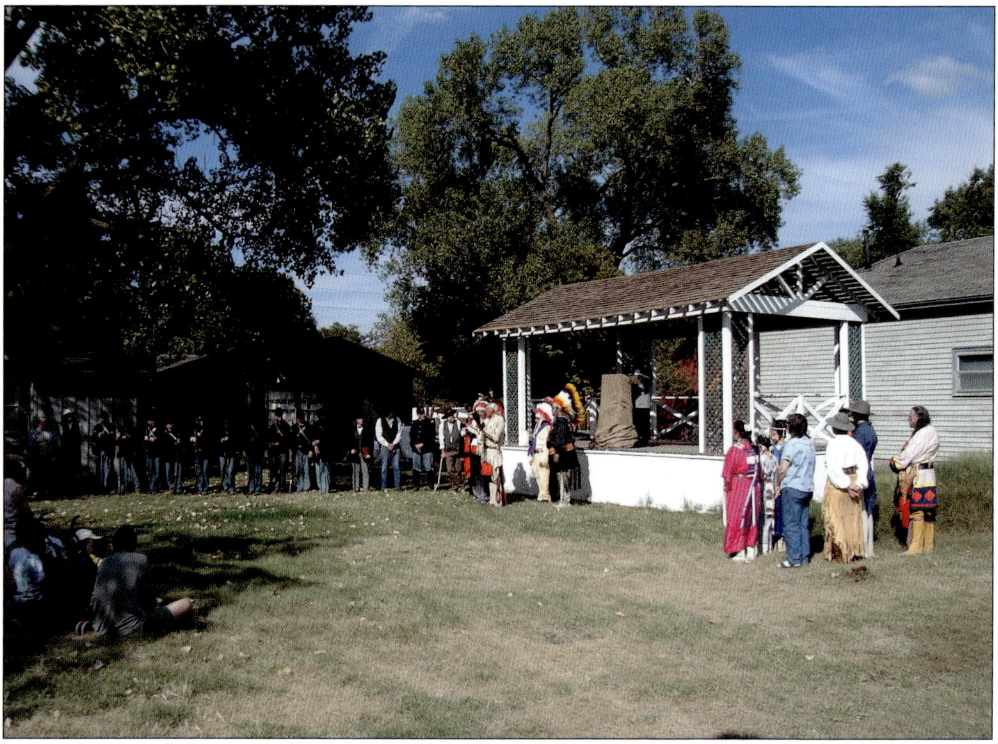

On September 24, 2005, Old Cowtown Museum celebrated the 140th anniversary of the Little Arkansas River Peace Treaty. The treaty opened the state up to settlement and brought the arrival of the railroads. For the celebration, several descendants of the treaty's key players were in attendance. (Courtesy Doug McGovern.)

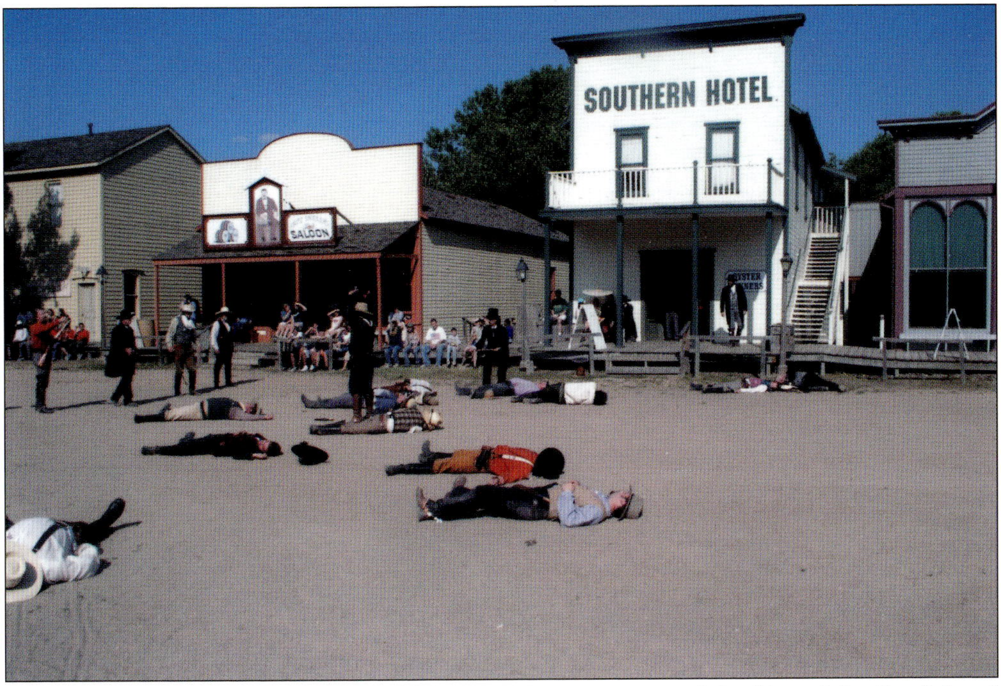

As a response to the visiting public, Old Cowtown Museum created the "Age of the Gunfighter" event in 2002. From 2003 to 2006, the museum hosted the American Federation of Old West Reenactors' Midwest Regional Gunfight and Living History Championships, which drew reenactors and living history interpreters from across the nation to the event. In 2008, it became more of a regional event, with groups from Kansas and the surrounding states participating in skits and quick-draw competitions, below. Included in recent years was the "Amazon Run," a re-creation of the time when "women of ill repute" ran to the Arkansas River to bathe and ran back to town while the cowboys bet on who would win. (Below, courtesy Keith Wondra.)

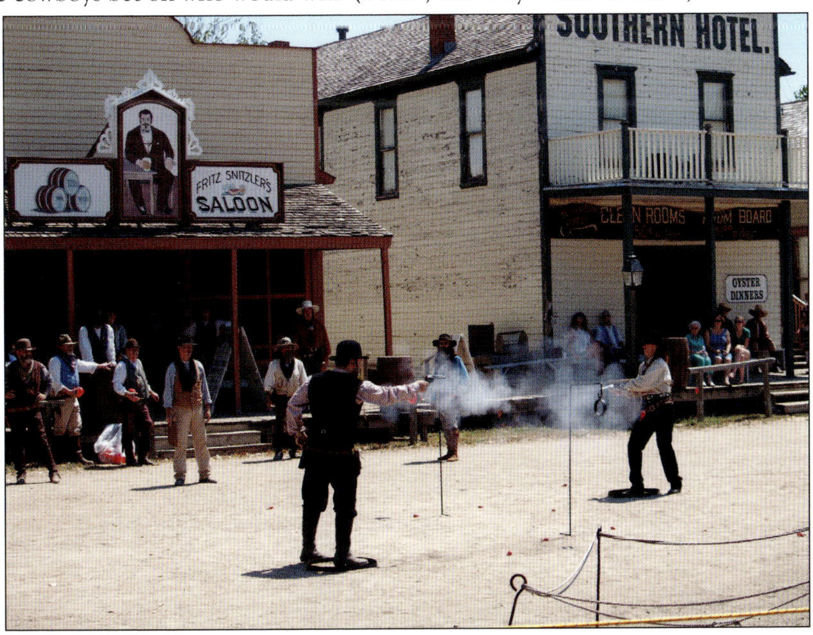

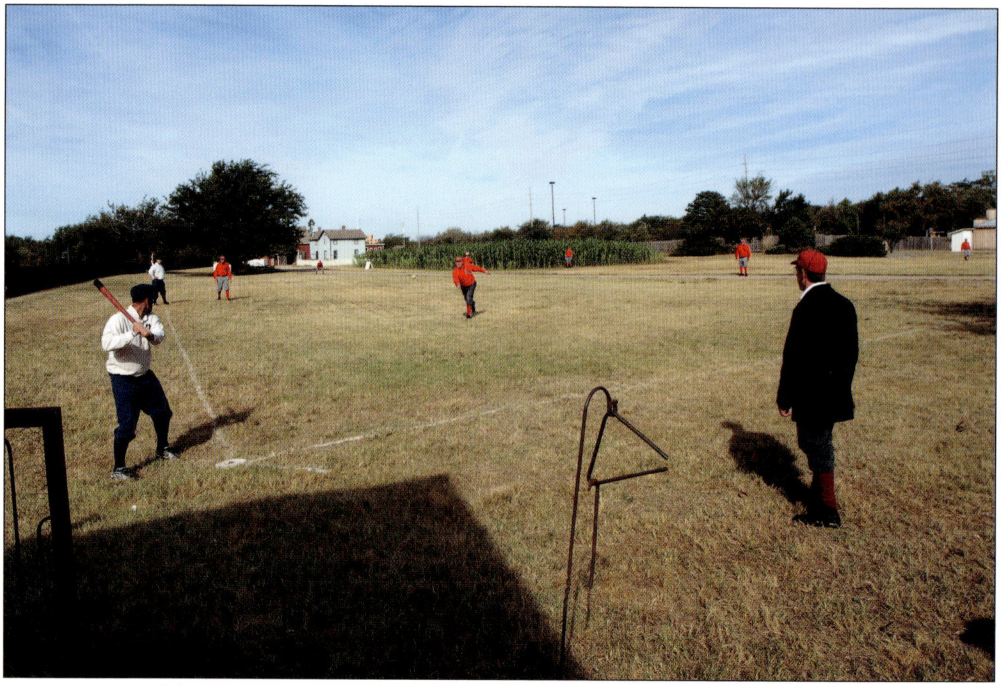

As a way for Old Cowtown Museum to reach out to new groups and interests beyond just the Old West or agricultural history, the Cowtown Vintage Base Ball Club was created in 2004 by Gary Lee and Vance Davis. They based the teams and uniforms on two 1870s baseball clubs in Wichita, the Red Stockings and the Bulldozers. The organization, composed of players in the 14-to-65 age group and with several father-son combinations, was started as an avenue to portray another aspect of Wichita history instead of only dancers, such as Entre Nous and the Dixie Lee Saloon Girls. The group plays about 20 games a year at Cowtown, across Kansas, and in other states, including a game before the championship game of the National Baseball Congress at Lawrence-Dumont Stadium. (Both, courtesy Keith Wondra.)

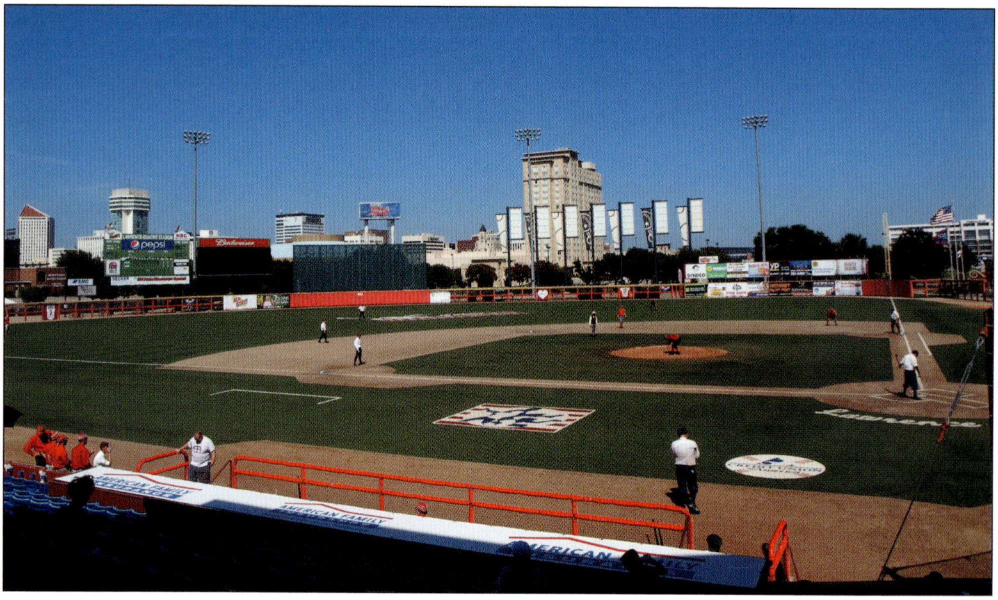

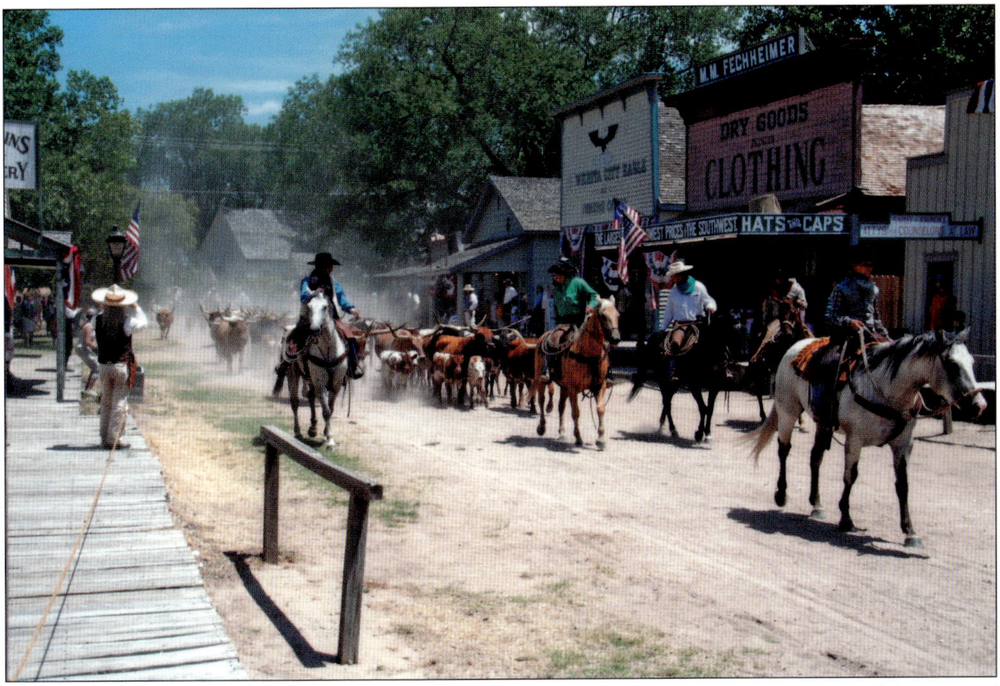

Beginning in 2003, Old Cowtown Museum started the Rails & Trails event as a celebration of the cattle trails and the railroad's impact on Wichita's history. The highlight of the event was herding of 15 to 25 longhorn cattle through the streets of the museum. Along with cattle drives, the event brought in descendants of famous people in Wichita and Kansas history, such as Beverly J. Murphy, great-great-granddaughter of Jesse Chisholm, the man who started the famous trail that went through what would become Wichita. The popular event ended in 2008. (Above, courtesy Charlayne Talley and Old Cowtown Museum.)

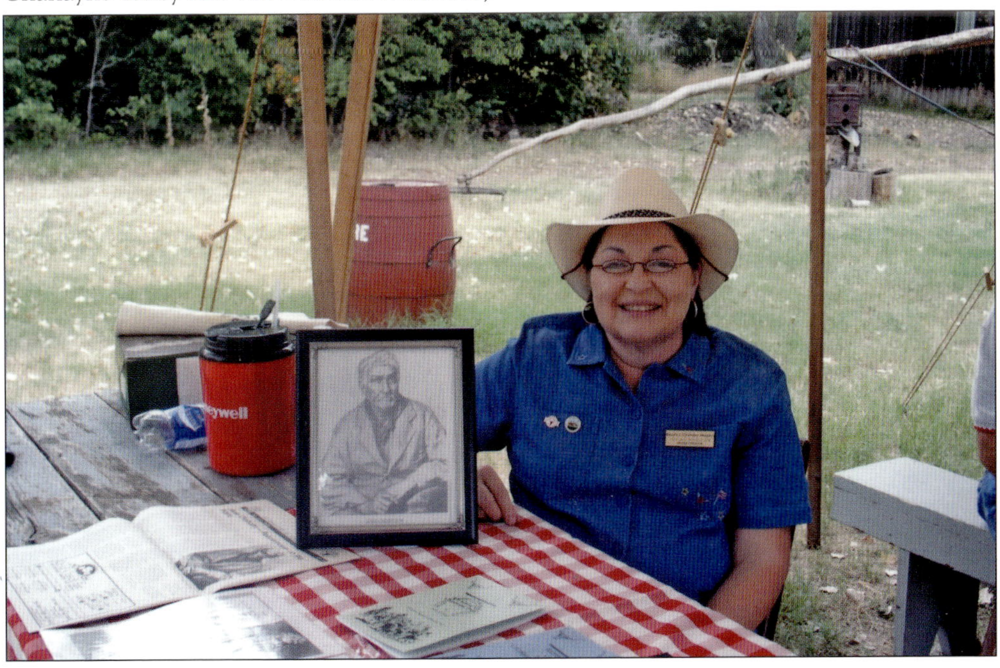

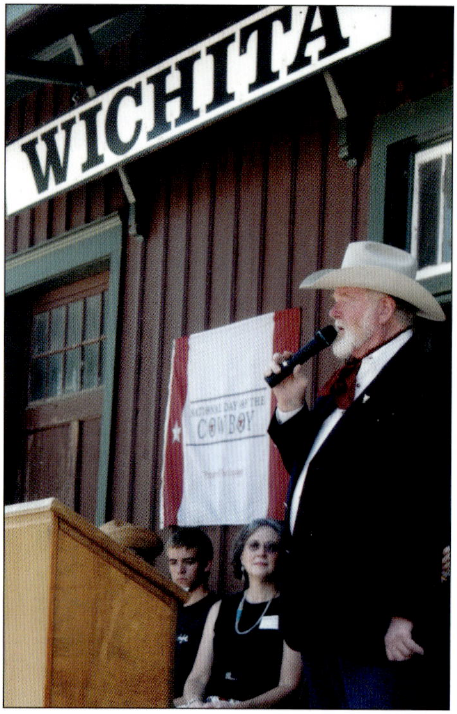

During the 2006 Rails & Trails event, Old Cowtown Museum celebrated the National Day of the Cowboy, which featured Red Steagall, an award-winning western musician and poet. Along with Steagall, Kansas governor Kathy Sebelius attended the festivities. The event was one of the largest in Kansas to honor the American cowboy. (Courtesy Paul Soutar.)

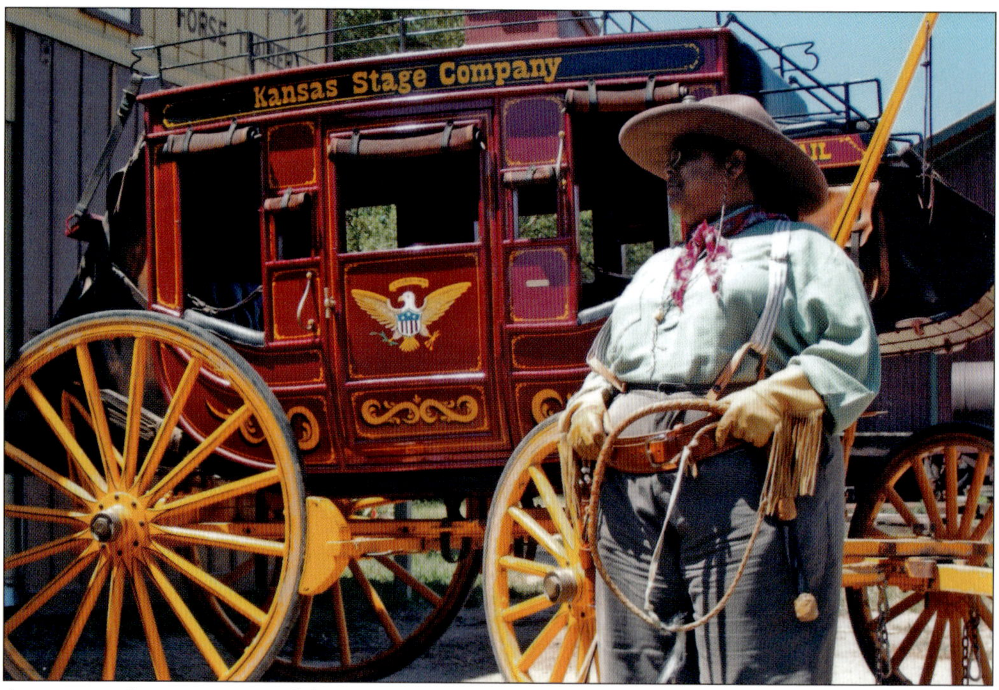

As a way to honor women of the pioneer era and the Old West, Old Cowtown Museum created the Women of the West Fest in 2003. The event coincided with the Wichita River Festival and featured reenactors portraying famous women from Wichita's history, including Annie Oakley and Mary Fields. Here, Angela Bates portrays Fields, an African American stagecoach driver. The event ended in 2009.

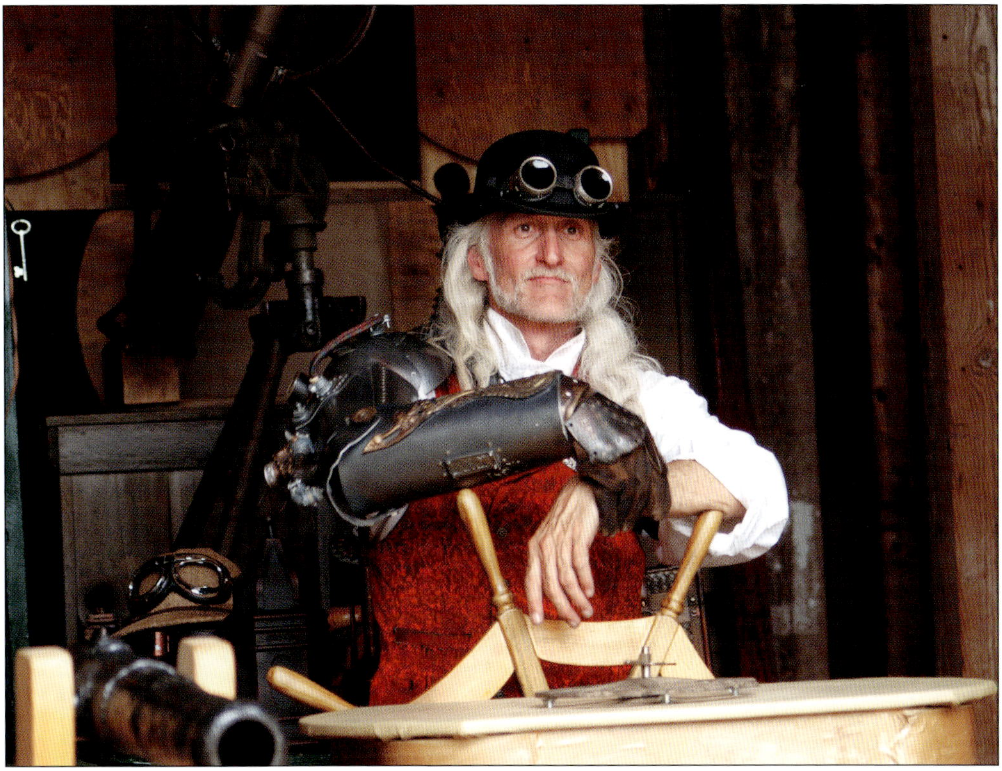

In November 2010, Old Cowtown Museum hosted Wichita's first Steampunk Day. The event was part of the growing Steampunk movement, which is best described as Victorian science fiction akin to Jules Verne or H.G. Wells novels. The event allows Cowtown to reach out to a younger audience, a goal that it might not achieve if it stuck to the Hollywood version of cowboy and western history. With most Steampunk conventions held in hotels, Cowtown's event became the first local Steampunk gathering held outdoors. The affair featured machines such as an anti-airship gun, pictured above. As the popularity of the event grew, staff and volunteers added penny farthing bicycle races, seen below. (Both, courtesy Keith Wondra.)

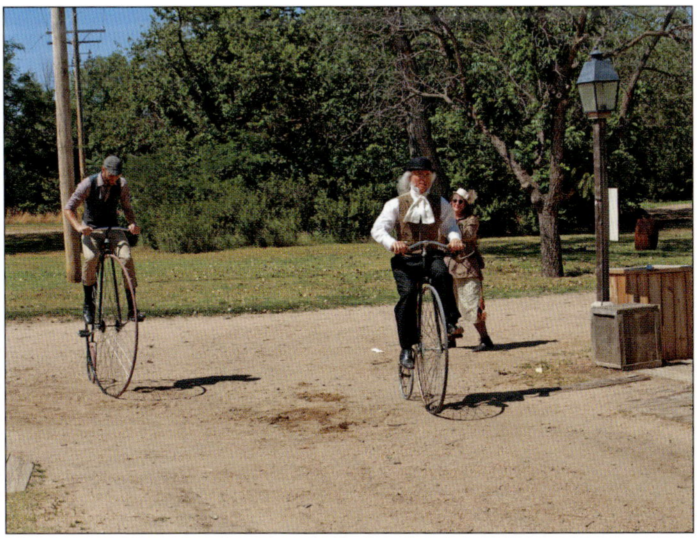

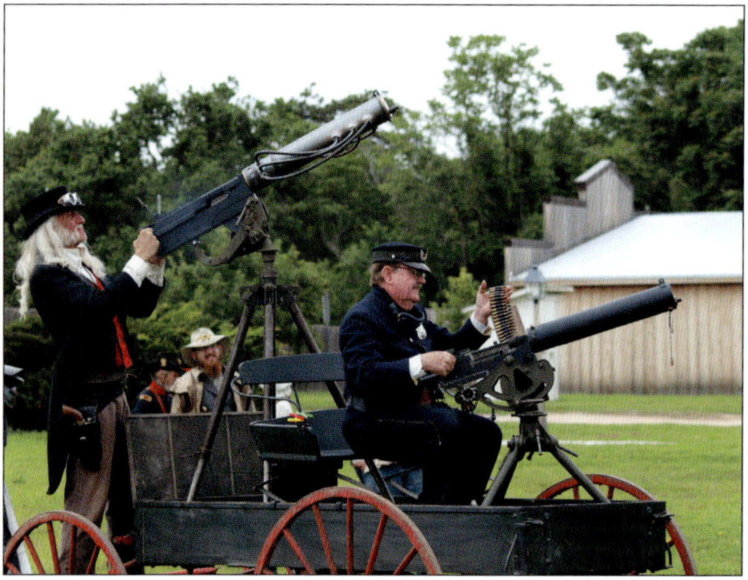

In 2012, Old Cowtown Museum's Steampunk Day made *True West* magazine's "Best of the West" list. As the event continued to grow, staff and volunteers added dueling cannons and extra anti-airship guns, as seen here. The event continues to be one of the museum's most anticipated events every year. (Courtesy Keith Wondra.)

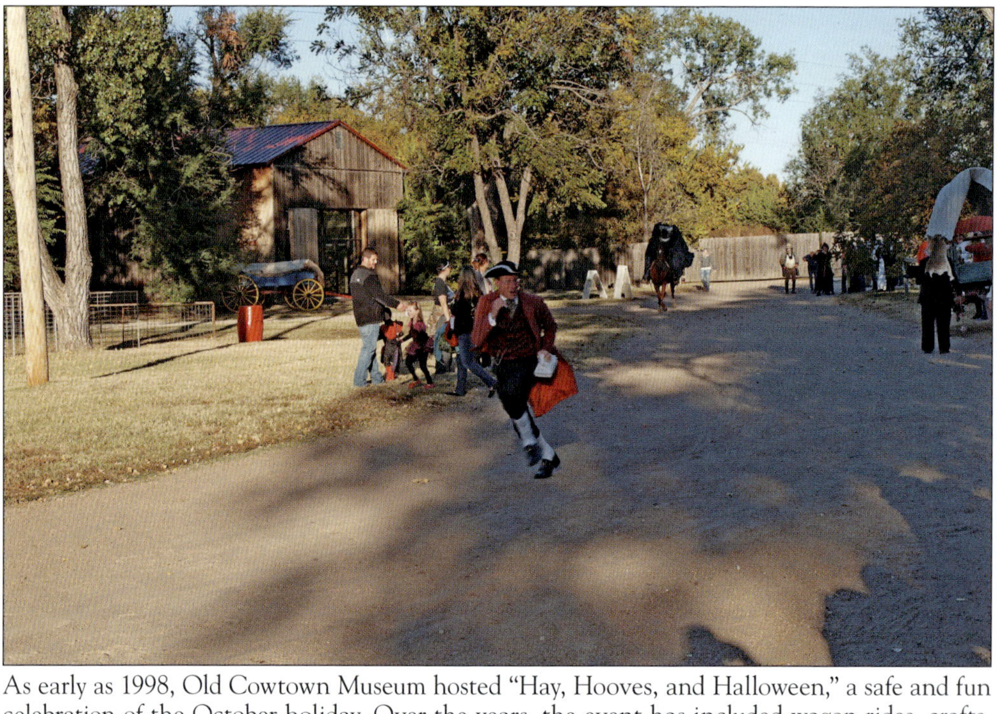

As early as 1998, Old Cowtown Museum hosted "Hay, Hooves, and Halloween," a safe and fun celebration of the October holiday. Over the years, the event has included wagon rides, crafts, pumpkin bowling, and the Headless Horseman chasing Ichabod Crane. In 2013, the event time was moved to the evening as a possible way to increase attendance. Since then, it has been the museum's most-attended event. (Courtesy Keith Wondra.)

To portray activities of Victorian society, longtime Cowtown volunteers Roselyn and Phil Hoch started the Entre Nous group, with the Hochs training the new dancers in several popular 19th-century dances, including the waltz and the grand march. As the group grew, it began to perform programs outside of Cowtown.

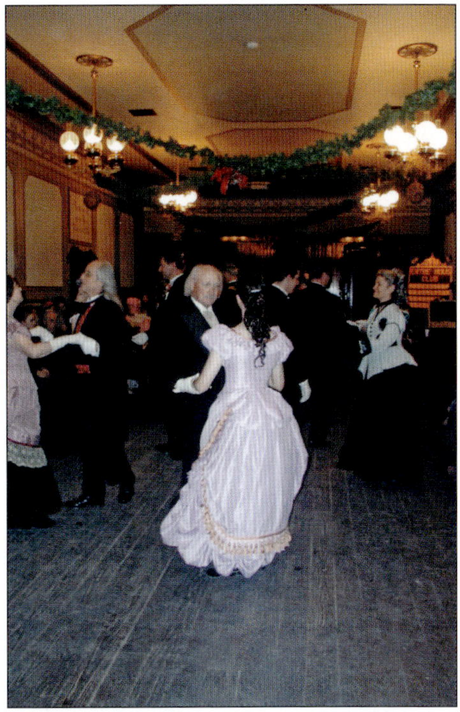

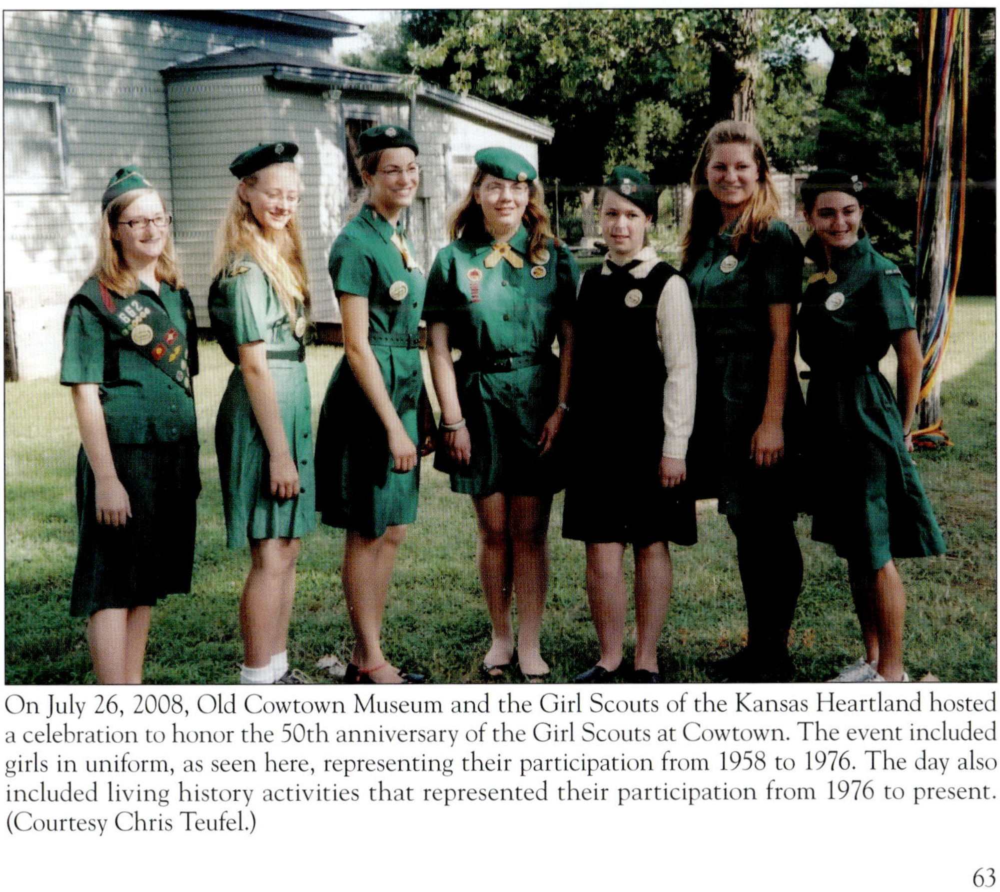

On July 26, 2008, Old Cowtown Museum and the Girl Scouts of the Kansas Heartland hosted a celebration to honor the 50th anniversary of the Girl Scouts at Cowtown. The event included girls in uniform, as seen here, representing their participation from 1958 to 1976. The day also included living history activities that represented their participation from 1976 to present. (Courtesy Chris Teufel.)

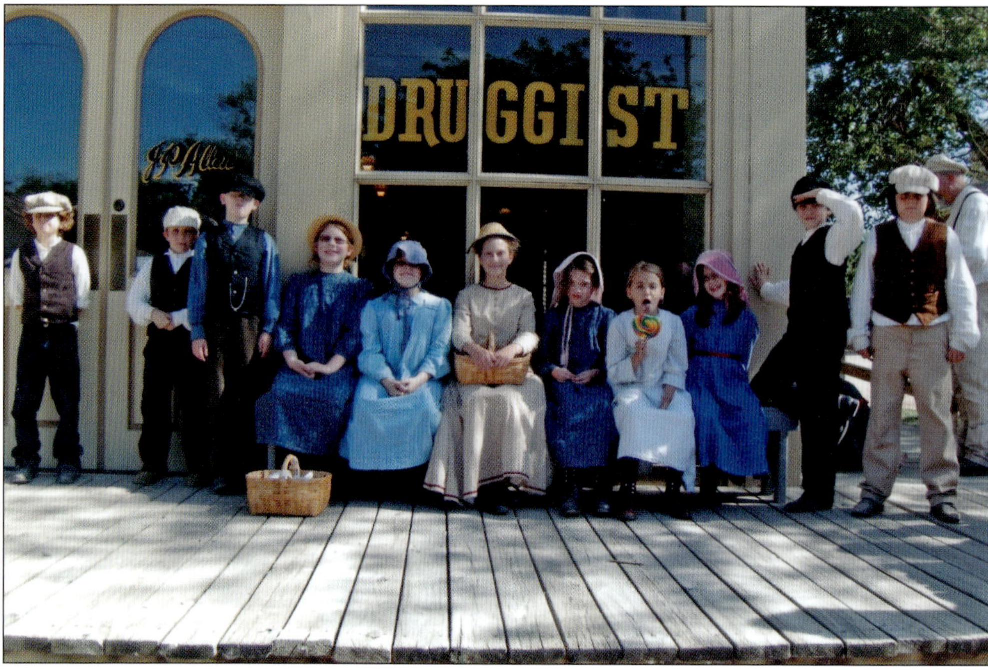

One of the newest groups was formed in 2013 by volunteer coordinator Jacky Goerzen as a needed direction and purpose for kids that came with the adults. Participants in the Kids of Cowtown group learn how to dance with Entre Nous, and girls learn how to sew while the boys apprentice in the Blacksmith Shop. The group fills in the gaps in the summer months left by the Girl Scouts.

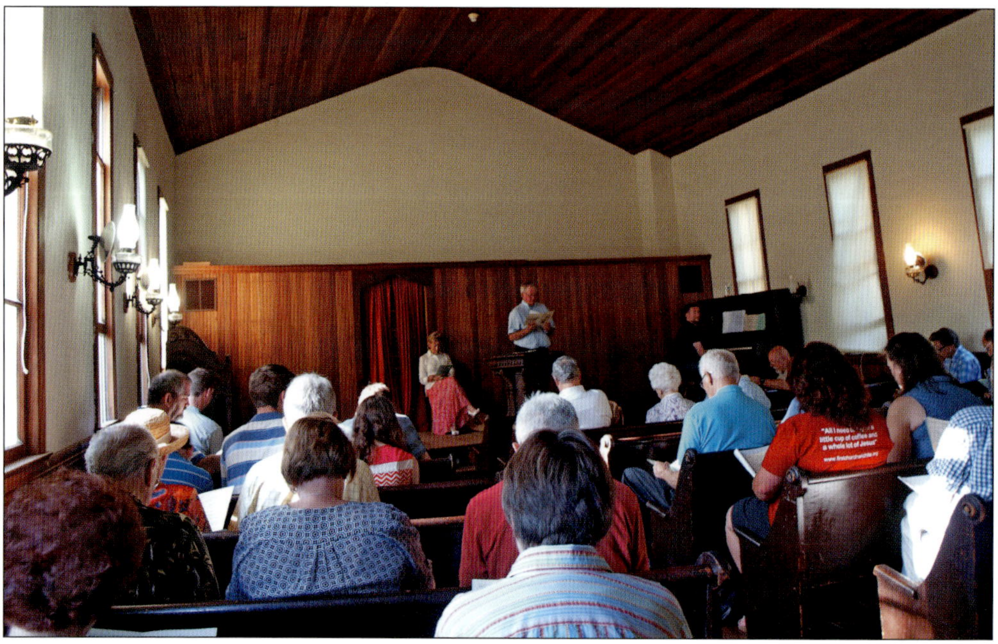

A service by Wichita's First Presbyterian Church was first held in the church at Old Cowtown Museum in the early 1960. Starting in 1975, on the first Sunday in June, the congregation began holding two services in the first permanent church building in Wichita. The tradition continues to this day at Old Cowtown Museum. (Courtesy Keith Wondra.)

Four

Myth and Reality

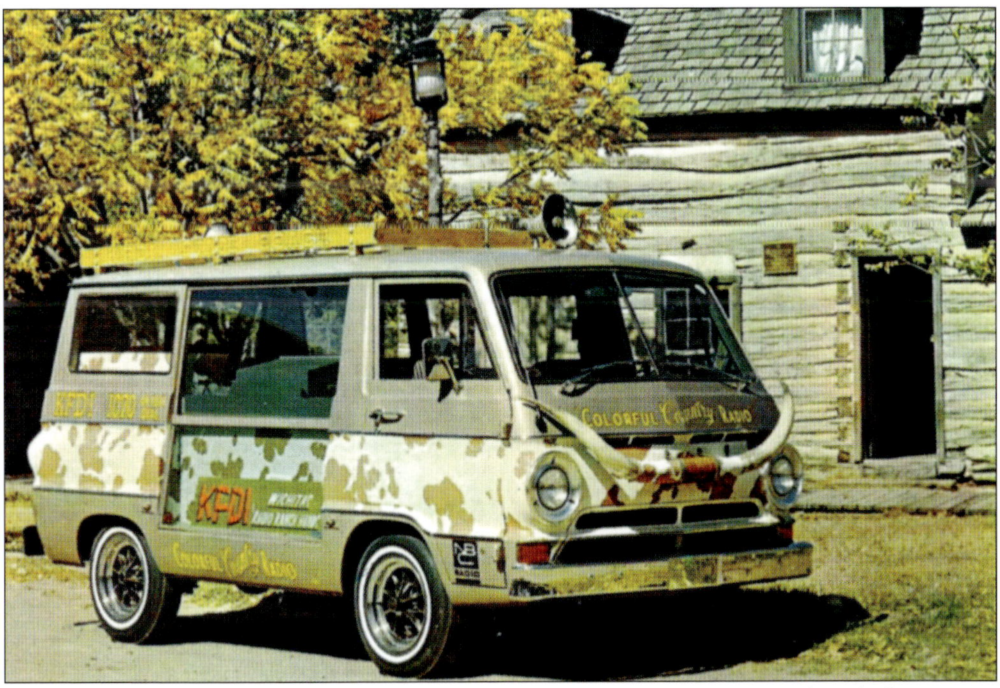

During the 1960s, Wichita started to promote the lore of the Old West, even though the city was proclaiming itself as the "Air Capital of the World." Along with attractions such as Old Cowtown Museum, local businesses—such as the newly formed KFDI country music radio station—embraced the western image, as shown here with the original KFDI "stagecoach" parked in front of the Munger House. (Courtesy Orin Friesen.)

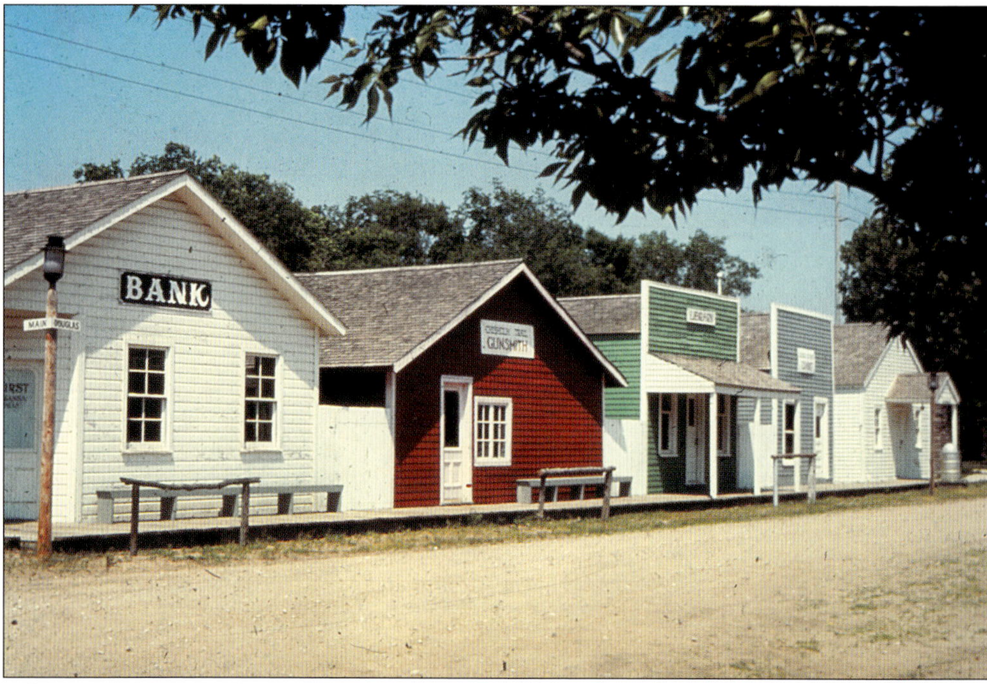

When Cowtown was first envisioned, founders had the original buildings of Wichita in mind. When original buildings were not available, replicas were built. Those built in 1961 include the First Arkansas Valley Bank, originally founded by W.C. Woodman, and the Dress Making and Millinery building, which formerly held the Gunsmith exhibit and the Marshal's Office. Other buildings were refurbished for different uses, such as Baldwin's Old Time Photos, which was built around 1910 and moved to Cowtown in 1954; and the Harness and Saddlery, also built around 1910 and moved to Cowtown in 1961, which was formerly the Lawrence Thompson exhibit and the Harry Shepler Saddle Shop. (Below, courtesy Keith Wondra.)

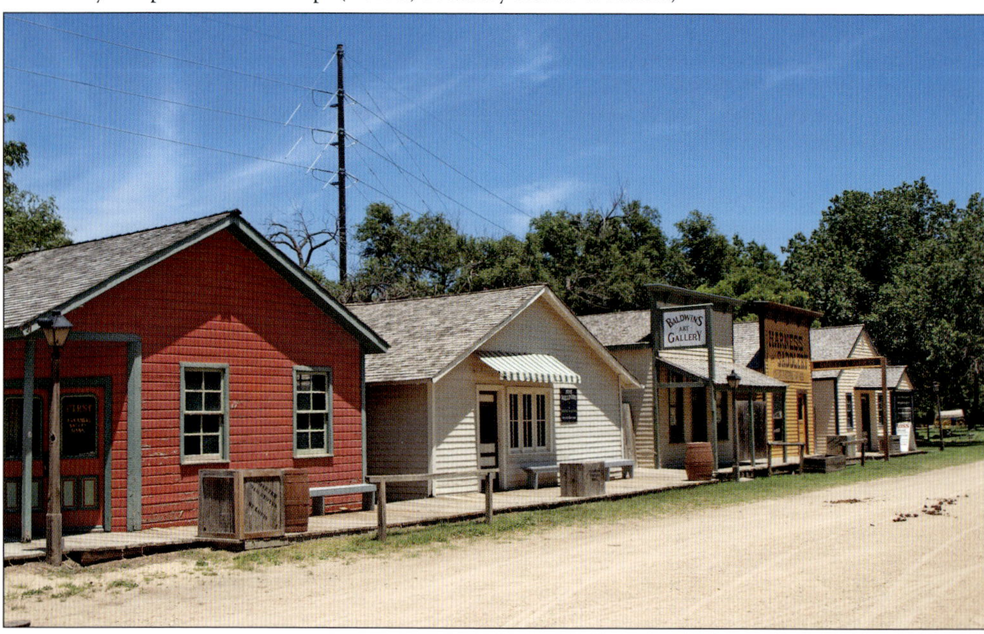

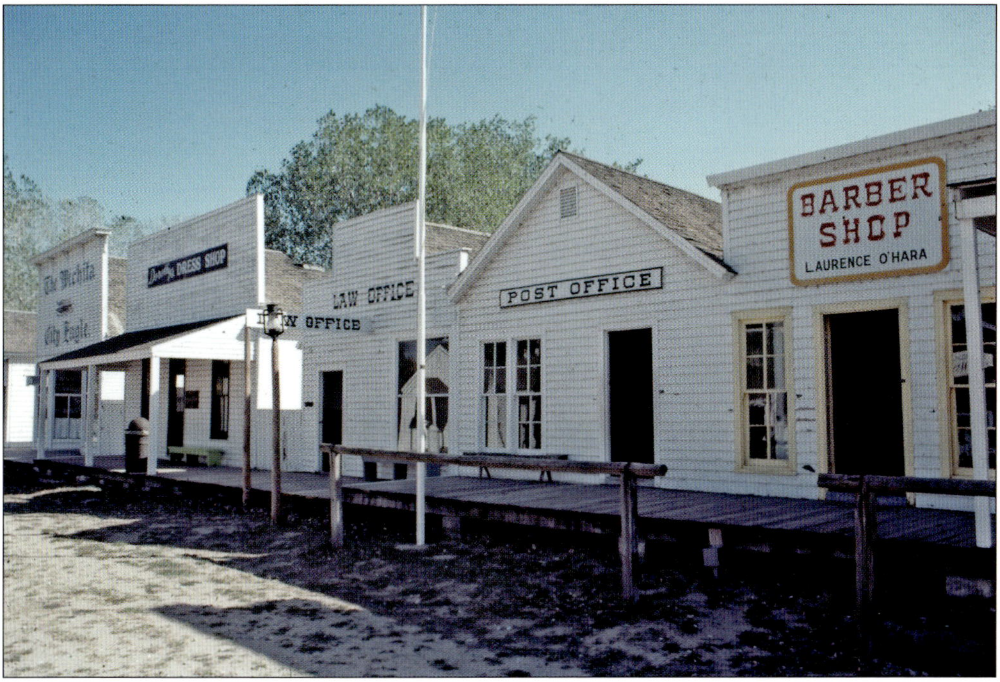

In the 1970s and 1980s, the look of buildings changed from a whitewashed storefront to more colorful painted appearances. Many of the buildings' uses were also changed, such as the Land Office, which was originally O'Hara's Barber; the structure that is now O'Hara's Barber, which was formerly the Post Office; and a re-creation of Fecheimer's Dry Goods and Clothing, which was built in 1880, moved to Cowtown around 1961, and known as Dorrthea's Dress Shop. Other businesses such as the Law Office and the Wichita City Eagle Print Shop only had cosmetic changes but have kept their original uses since 1960. (Below, courtesy Keith Wondra.)

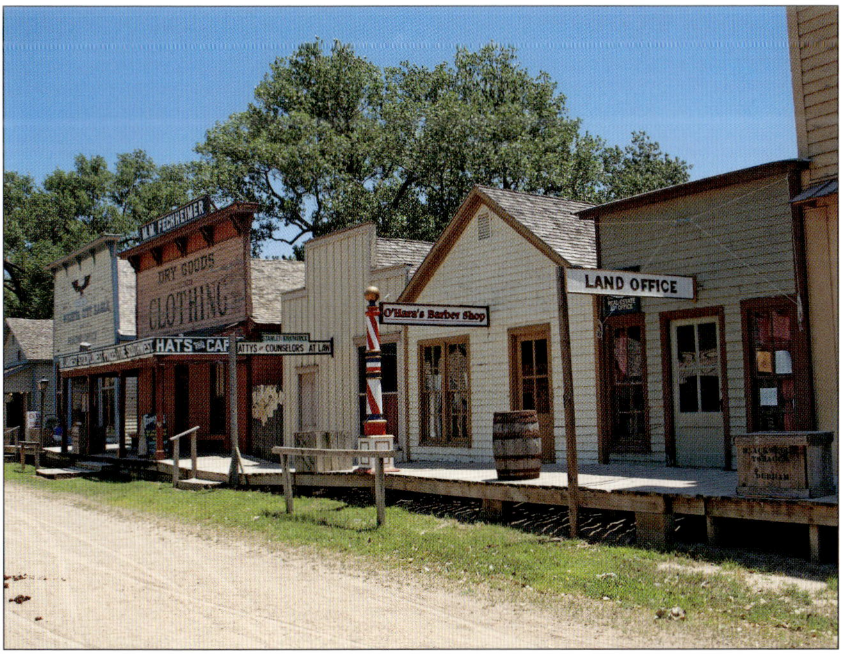

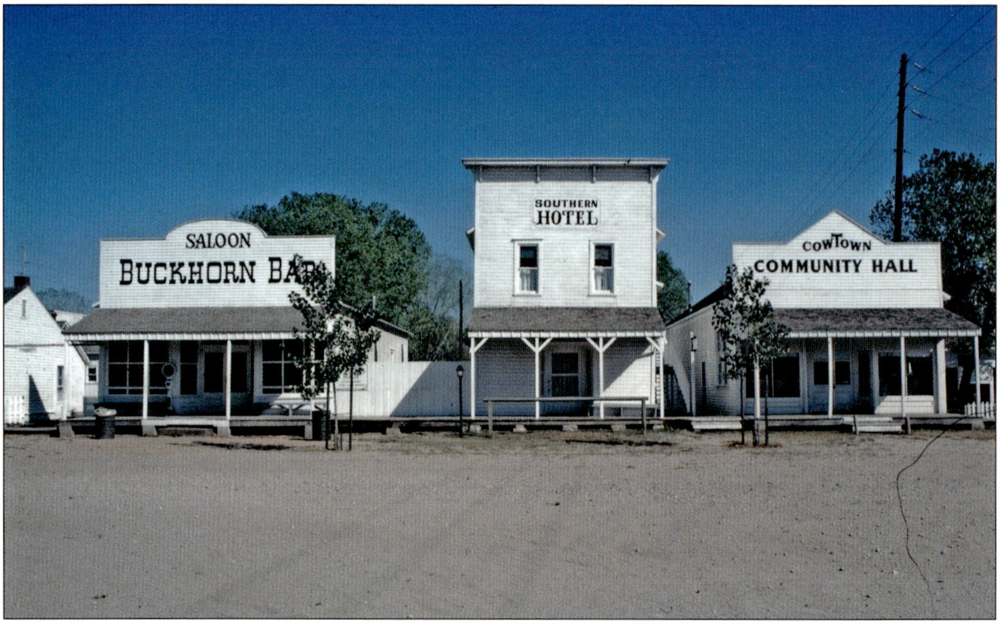

Many of Wichita's original businesses have been replicated and renovated in recent years to look exactly as they originally did in the 19th century. Henry Vigus's Buckhorn Saloon became Fritz Snitzler's Saloon, with Snitzler's distinctive portrait above the entrance of a reclaimed building from 1885 from Derby, Kansas. The Southern Hotel reuses a building from 1887 originally located at 1117 West Douglas Avenue. The Turnverein Hall, which was once known as Cow Town Community Hall and Keno Corner, uses an 1880 building from Derby, Kansas. To the left, the one-story drugstore was moved to make room for a two-story structure in the 1990s. (Below, courtesy Keith Wondra.)

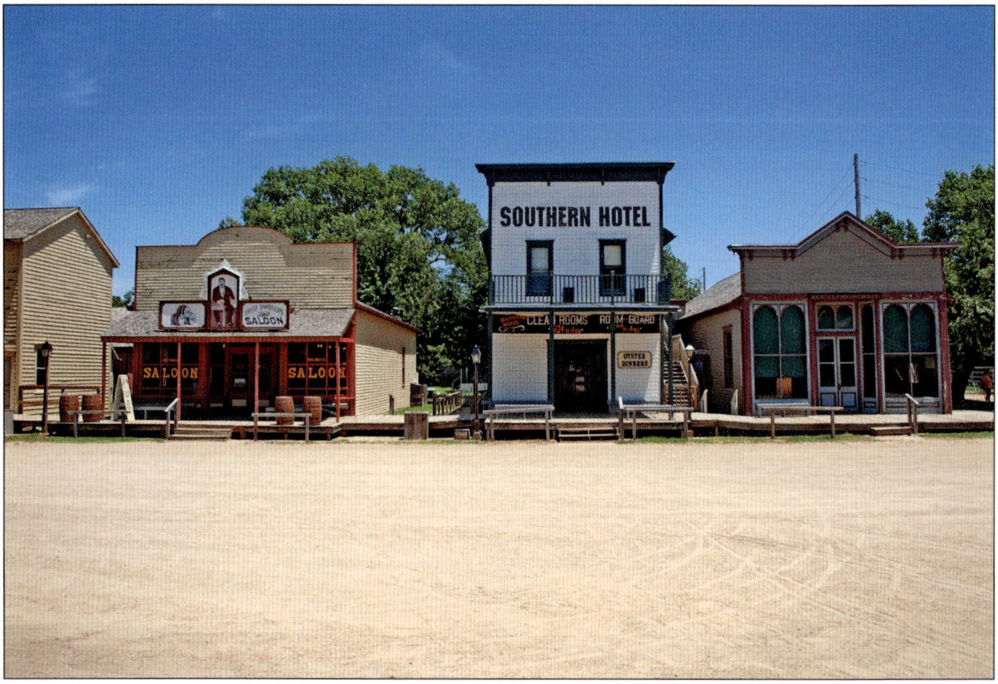

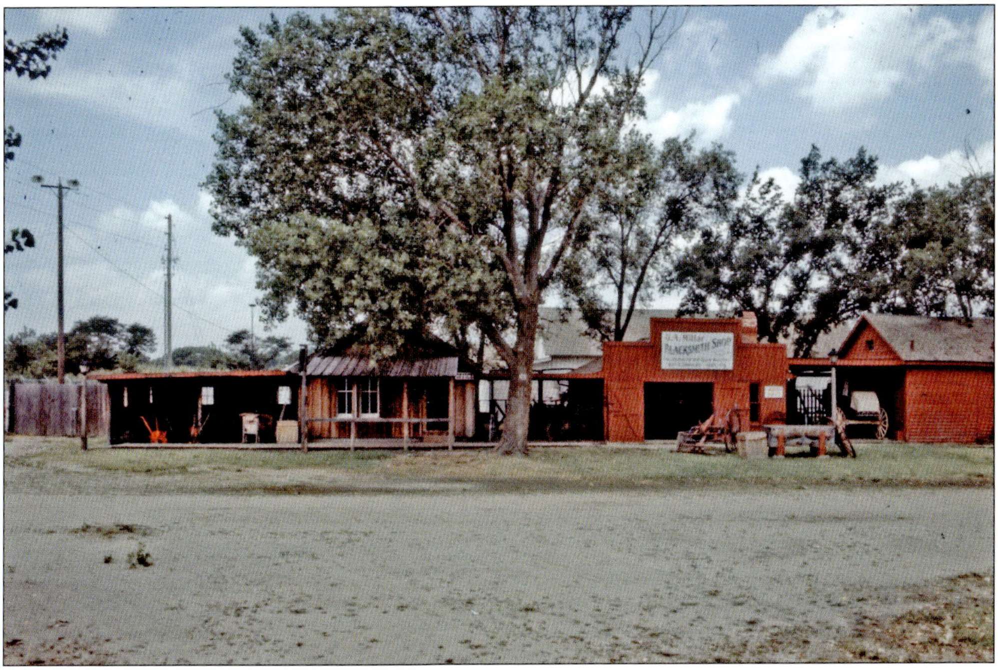

Across the road from the saloon, hotel, and Turnverein Hall, visitors to Cowtown will find businesses most likely found in Wichita in 1870. The Blacksmith, Marshal's Office, and the Children's Corner Creative Emporium were all built at Cowtown. However, the Breising Meat Market was built in 1890 in Whitewater, Kansas, and moved to Cowtown in 1986, replacing the one-story lean-to on the left. The road that would eventually lead out to the DeVore Farm would be built in the area seen to the left in the above image. The buildings were painted more vibrant colors in the 1980s and 1990s. (Below, courtesy Keith Wondra.)

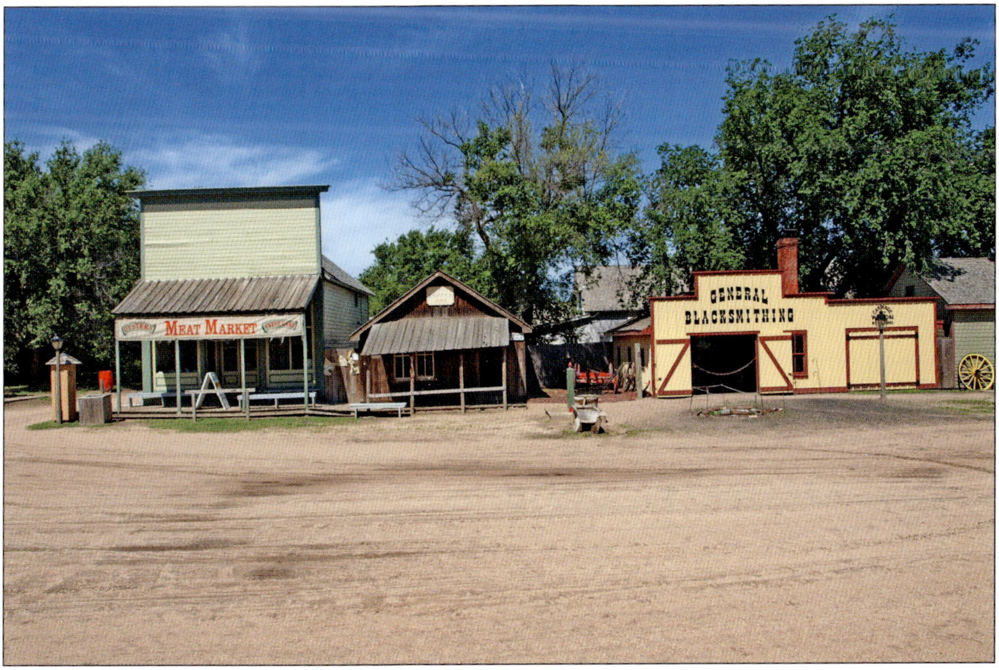

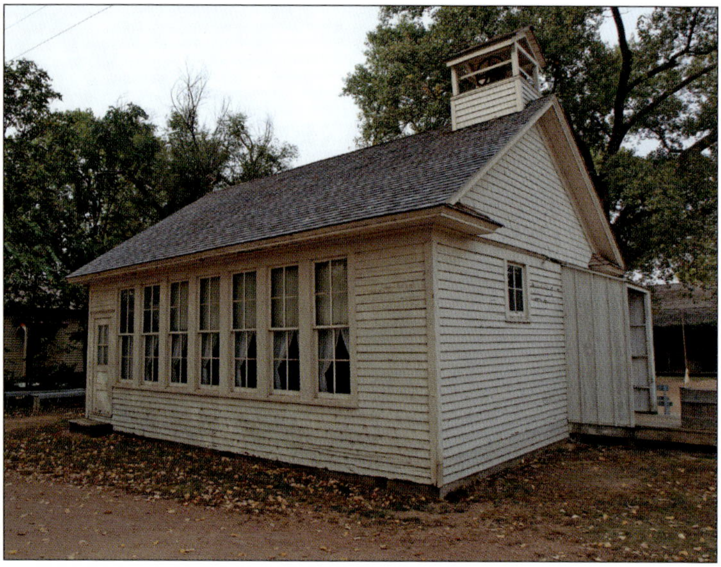

The One-Room School was built in 1910 and moved around as an additional classroom. Its final location was besides the Meridian School at 301 South Meridian Street. During the Kansas Centennial, antique desks, maps, equipment, and supplies were displayed in the building. It was then moved to Cowtown in 1962 so more people could see it. (Courtesy Keith Wondra.)

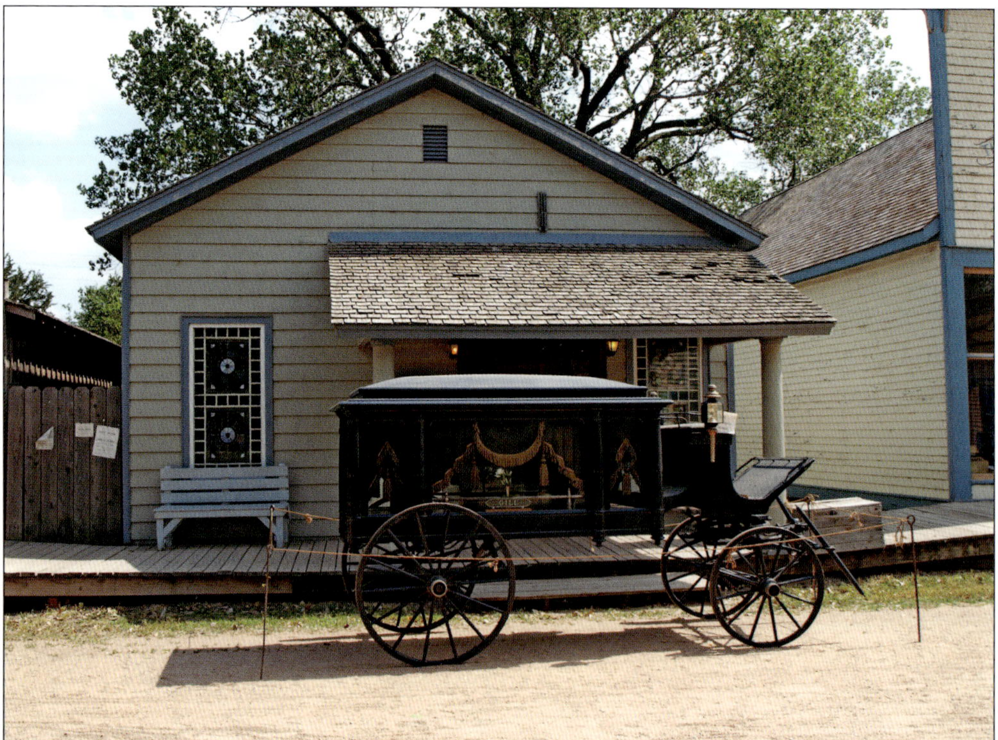

Gill Mortuary is a replica of one of Wichita's first funeral homes, owned and operated by I.W. Gill. The structure at Cowtown was erected in 1964 and was formerly known as the Undertaker's building. The exhibit includes coffins and a horse-drawn hearse. (Both, courtesy Keith Wondra.)

Trapper's Cabin started its existence as a shack located south of the Ninnescah River, near the Chisholm Trail, in 1865. It was moved to Cowtown in 1969 and has had many names: the Horse Thief Cabin, the Settler's Cabin, Sauffer Cabin, and the Trader's Cabin. (Courtesy Keith Wondra.)

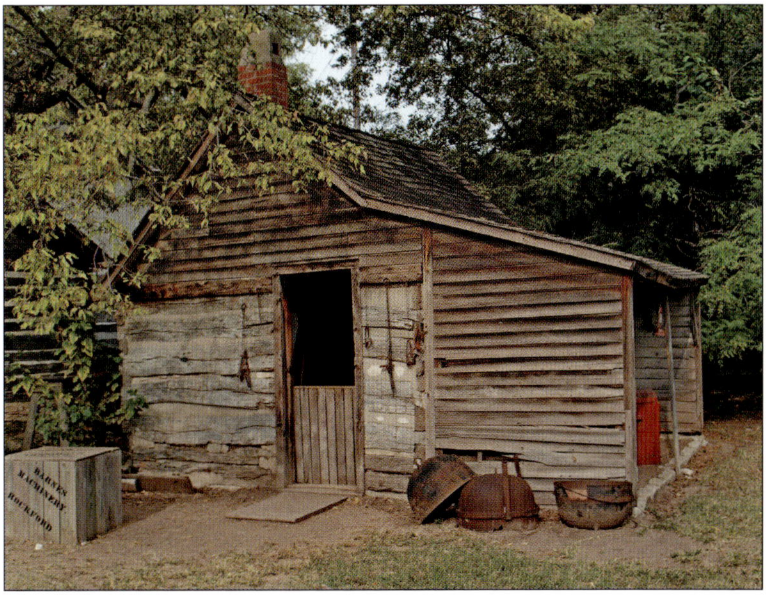

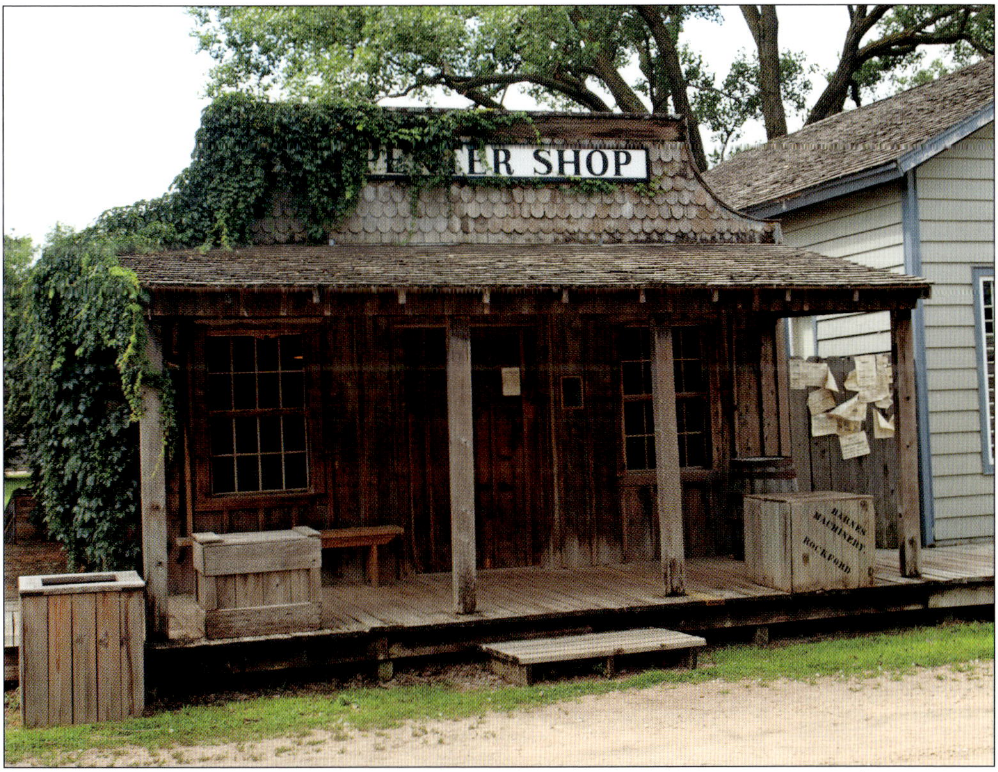

The Carpenter's Shop was built by the Women in Construction of Greater Wichita, Kansas, Chapter 120 in 1970. The chapter heard that the museum could not accept donations of tools since it had no building to house them. Thus, the women took on the task of erecting a shop to house the museum's collection of tools. (Courtesy Keith Wondra.)

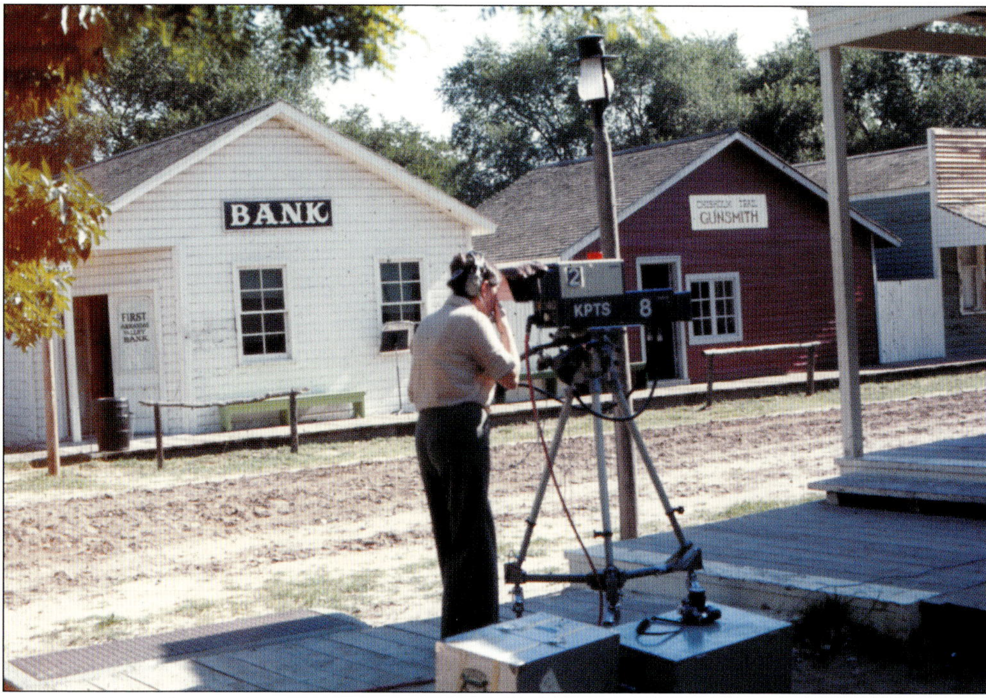

Above, KPTS films at Cowtown in the 1980s. The Arkansas Valley Bank and the Gunsmith Shop can be seen in the background on the left and right, respectively. The one-story buildings and ambiance of Cowtown lend to its desirability for the many local and national film, television, and news crews that have filmed at Cowtown over the years. Below, many local bands have also performed at Cowtown, such as Prairie Grass in the early 1970s and, later, the Diamond W Wranglers. Cliff Major, Charlie Castleberry, Tom Coleman, and Orin Friesen are shown from left to right in the c. 1972 photograph below. The Buckhorn Bar is now Fritz Snitzler's Saloon.

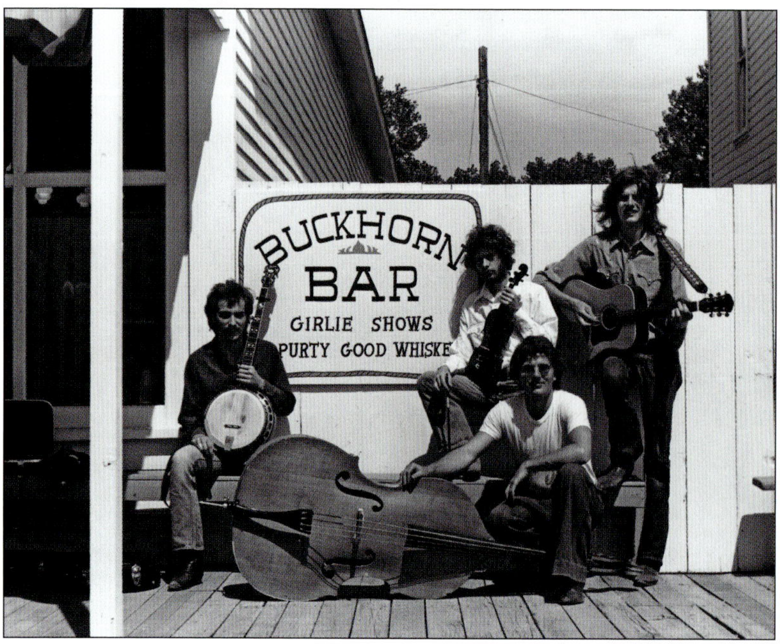

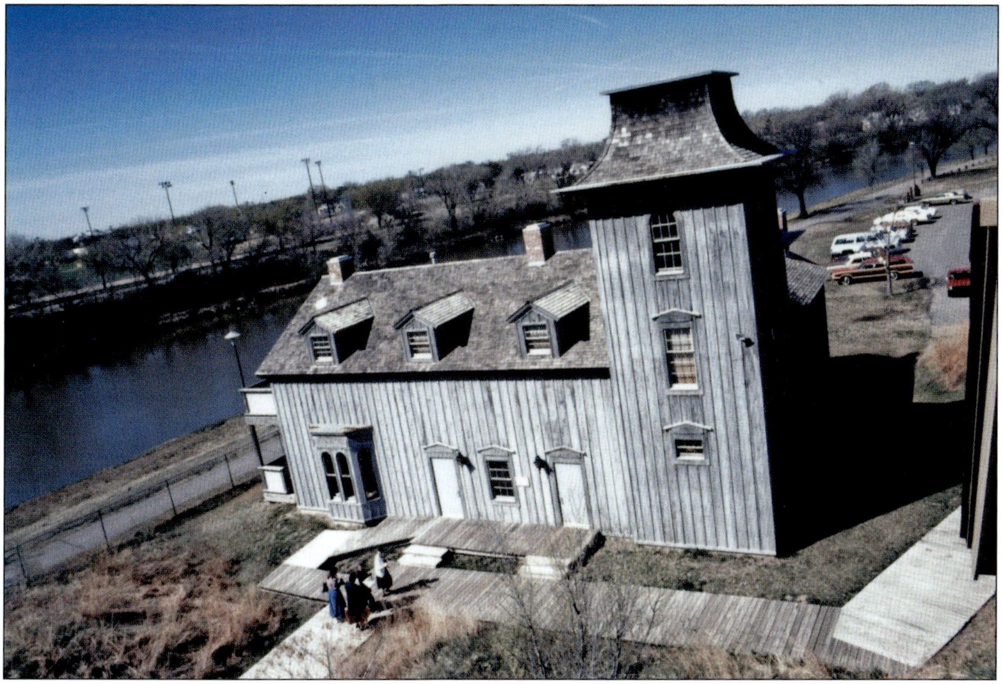

In 1978, a replica of W.C. Woodman's Lakeside Manor was built as a visitors center and administrative offices. Its construction on the southwest side of the museum forced the main entrance and parking lot to the west. This entrance stood until the opening of the Visitors Center in 2005 on the museum's east side. This building is now used mainly as administrative offices.

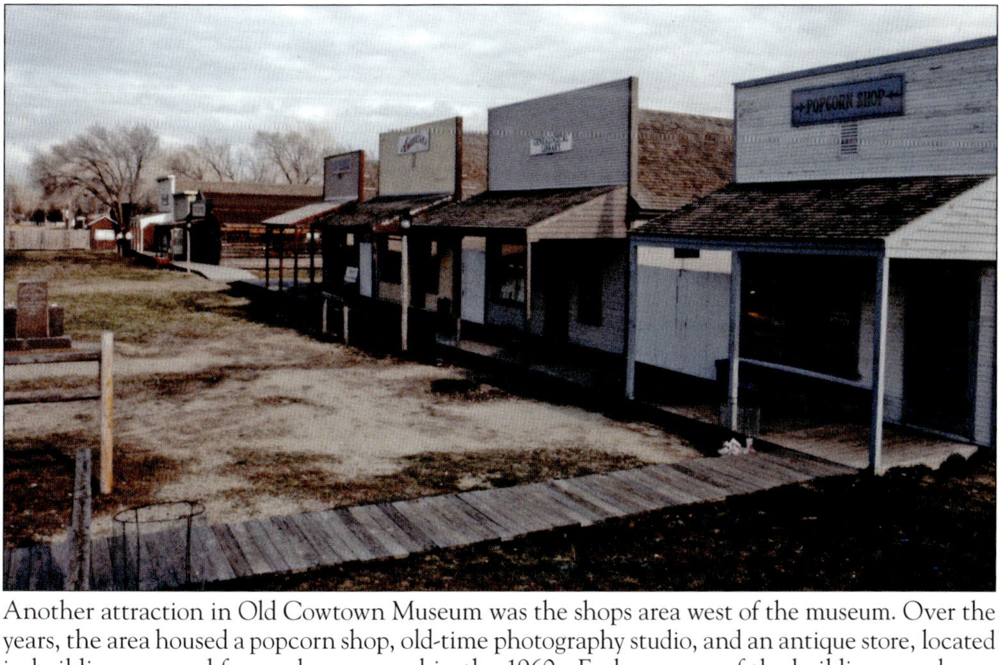

Another attraction in Old Cowtown Museum was the shops area west of the museum. Over the years, the area housed a popcorn shop, old-time photography studio, and an antique store, located in buildings rescued from urban renewal in the 1960s. Early on, one of the buildings was home to the Midwest Genealogical Society. The addition of the DeVore Farm in the 1990s forced the removal of the shops.

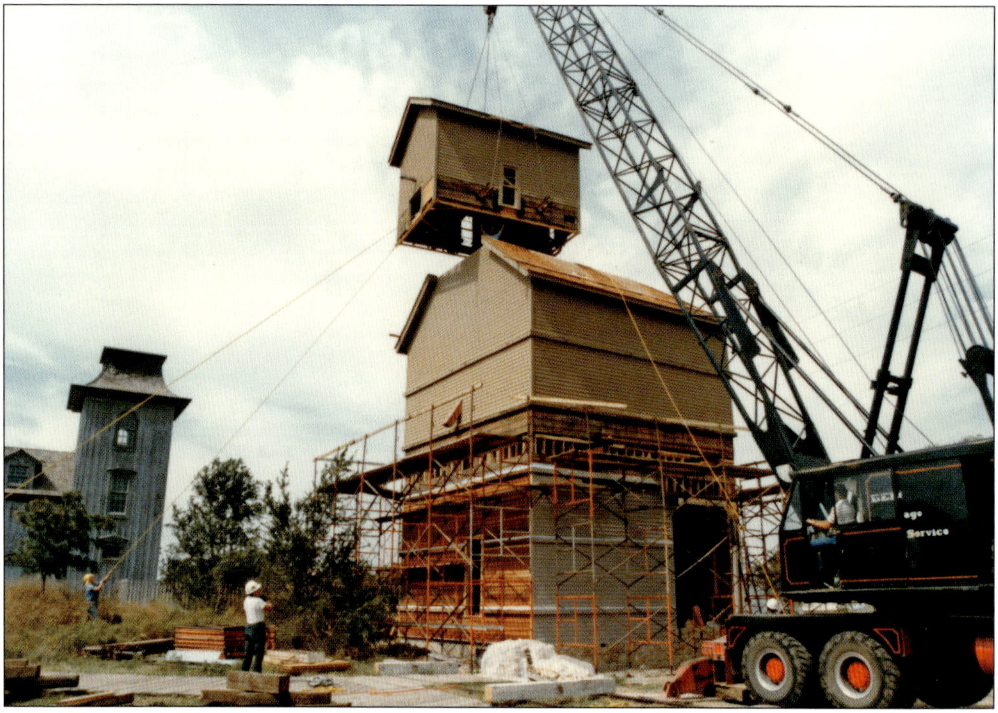

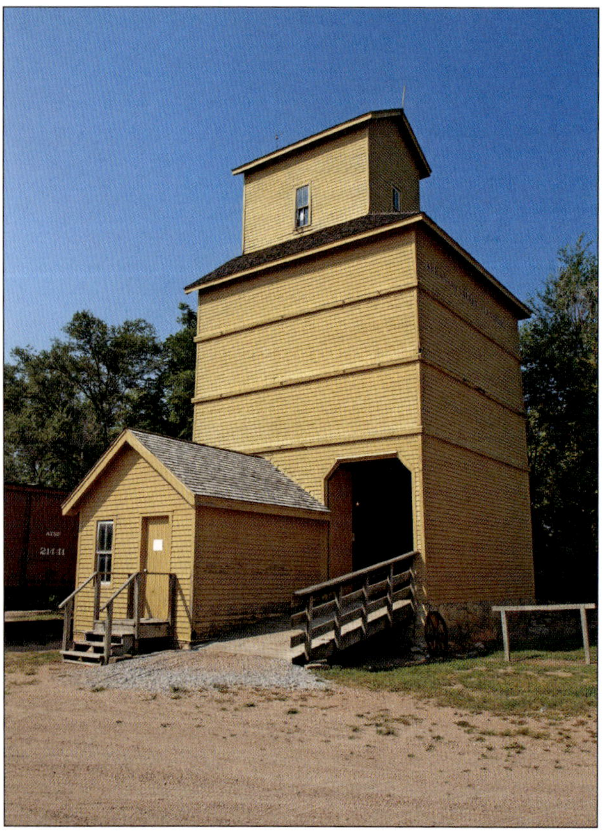

In 1986, to help represent the agricultural history of Wichita and Sedgwick County, Old Cowtown Museum, under the direction of Michael Husband, oversaw a donation from the Burlington Northern Railroad of an 1870- or 1880-era grain elevator located in Bentley, Kansas. In preparation for the move, the museum building was torn down, and the elevator was reconstructed in its place. The grain elevator gave the museum its third multistory building, which stands out next to the many one-story buildings on the grounds. Lakeside Manor is on the left of the above image. The second phase of the project involved the construction of a scale house north of the elevator and an engine room on the elevator's east side. (Left, courtesy Keith Wondra.)

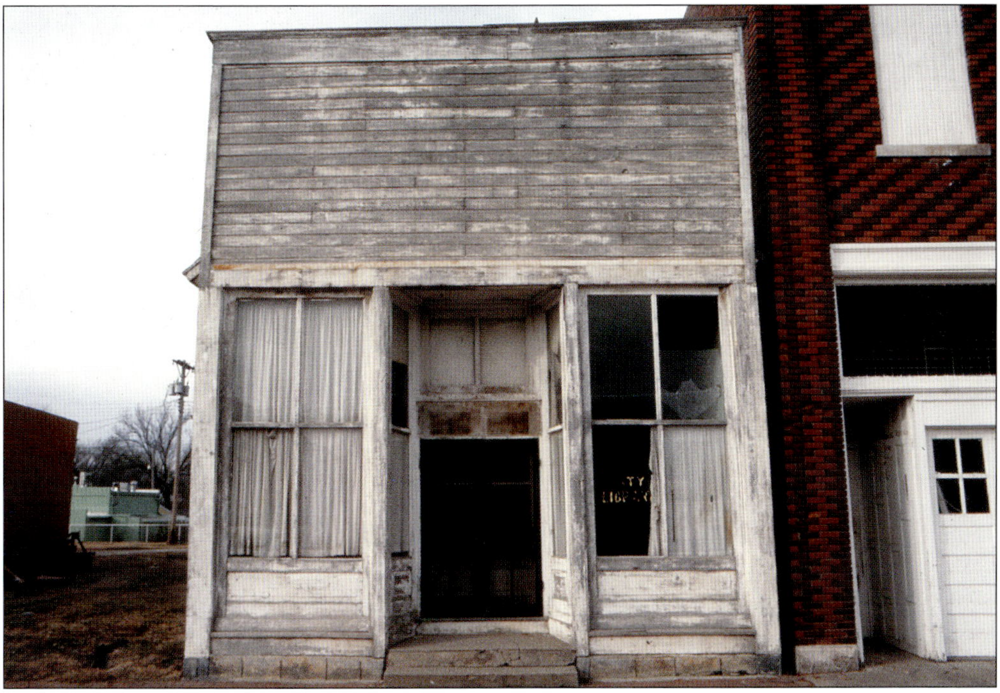

Originally located in Whitewater, Kansas, the 1890 Meat Market continued Old Cowtown Museum's mission of saving and restoring orphan buildings. After $4,000 was raised to move the building to the museum, it was relocated to its current site in 1987. Frank Breising Sr. operated a meat market in the building from 1890 until the 1920s. Frank Breising Jr. acquired the building in 1935. Later on, it had several uses, including as the Whitewater Public Library. After its move to the museum, work started on the exterior and interior. The grand opening of the Meat Market occurred in 1988. (Below, courtesy Keith Wondra.)

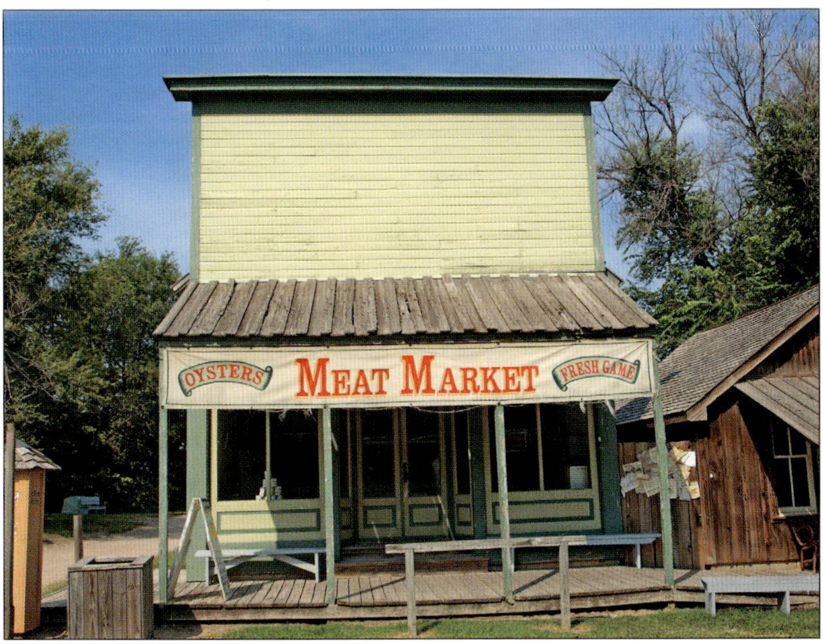

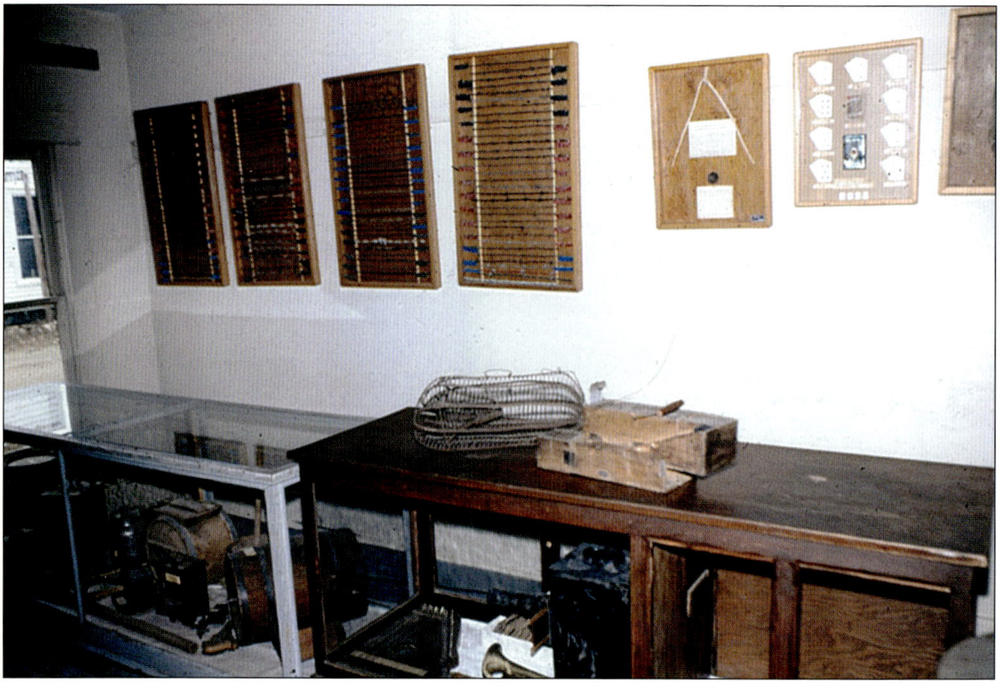

Just like the exteriors of buildings, the interiors have changed over the years, housing different types of artifacts, such as the ones inside the Lawrence Thompson exhibit. The structure is now known as the Harness and Saddlery building. The Harness and Saddlery exhibit opened in 1982 under the direction of museum curator Stan Harder.

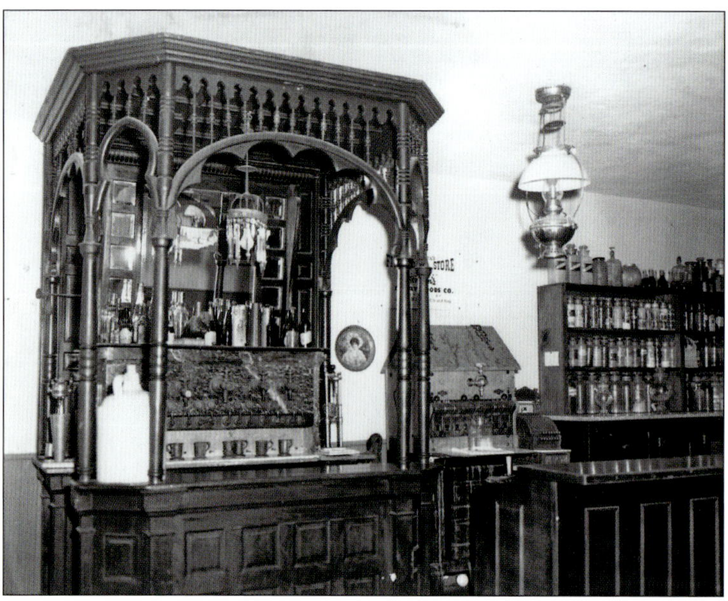

This view of the interior of the Drug Store shows one of Kansas's first soda fountains on the left. The fountain was built in Philadelphia and installed in Sargent's Drug Store in Junction City, Kansas, soon after the store opened in 1865. L.P. Phillipsen built the wooden canopy to protect the fountain. The whole design won special recognition at the 1893 Chicago World's Fair.

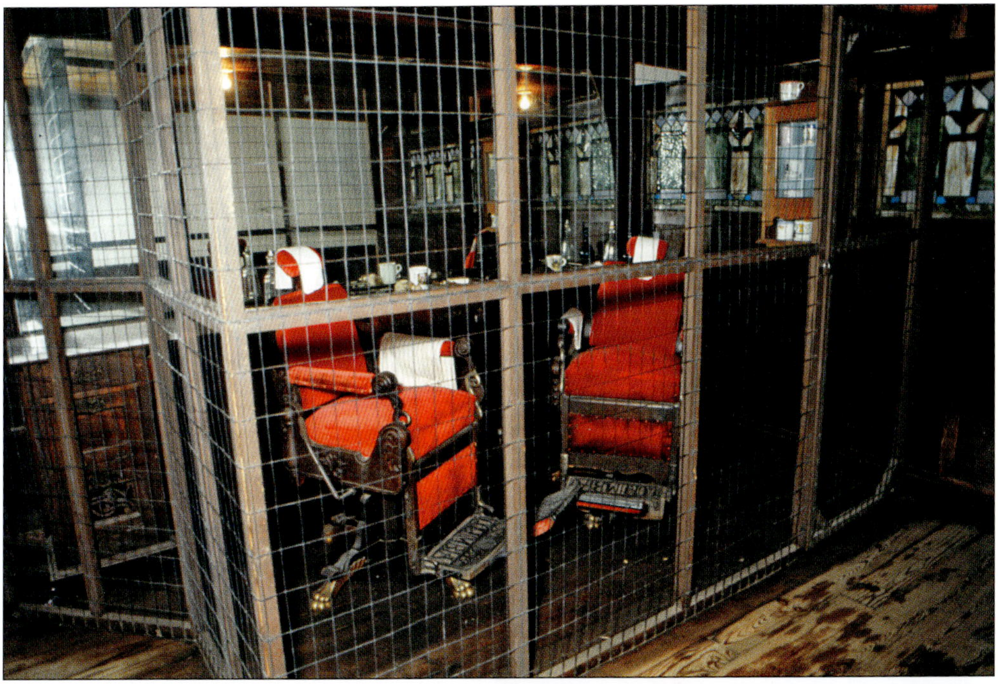

Visitors to Cowtown were once able to see what the exhibits would have looked like with "real" people in them or, in this case, mannequins. Wire fencing was extended from floor to ceiling, allowing visitors a close-up view of what was displayed in buildings such as the Barber Shop, seen above, built in 1955 on-site; and the General Store, pictured at right, built in 1884 and moved to Cowtown in 1965 from Garden Plain. In the 1980s, curator Stan Harder removed the wire and mannequins to give visitors a closer look at the artifacts. (Above, courtesy Wichita Festivals, Inc.)

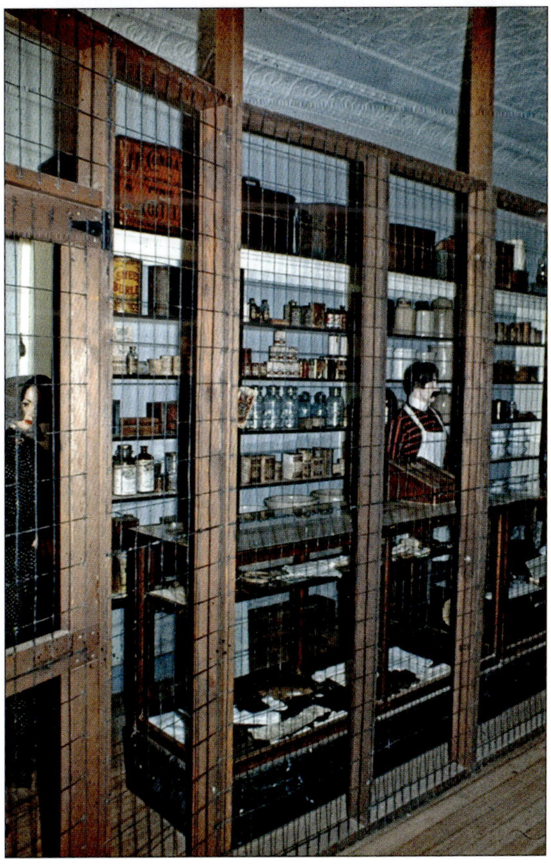

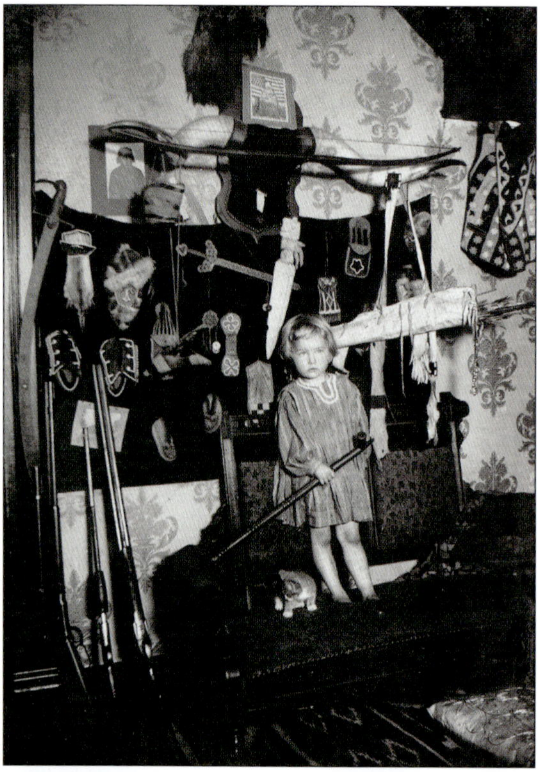

One such artifact that represents the history of Wichita is a divan once owned by James R. Mead, one of Wichita's founders. On the left is a well-known image of Ignace Mead Jones, at age 4, standing on the divan. Due to its condition, the divan is currently held in the archives of Cowtown, on the second floor of the Murdock House. Ignace Mead was the eldest of Mead's two daughters with his third wife, Fern. Ignace was also the mother of anthropologist Dr. Schuyler Jones. (Left, courtesy Wichita State University Libraries Special Collections and University Archives; below, courtesy Keith Wondra.)

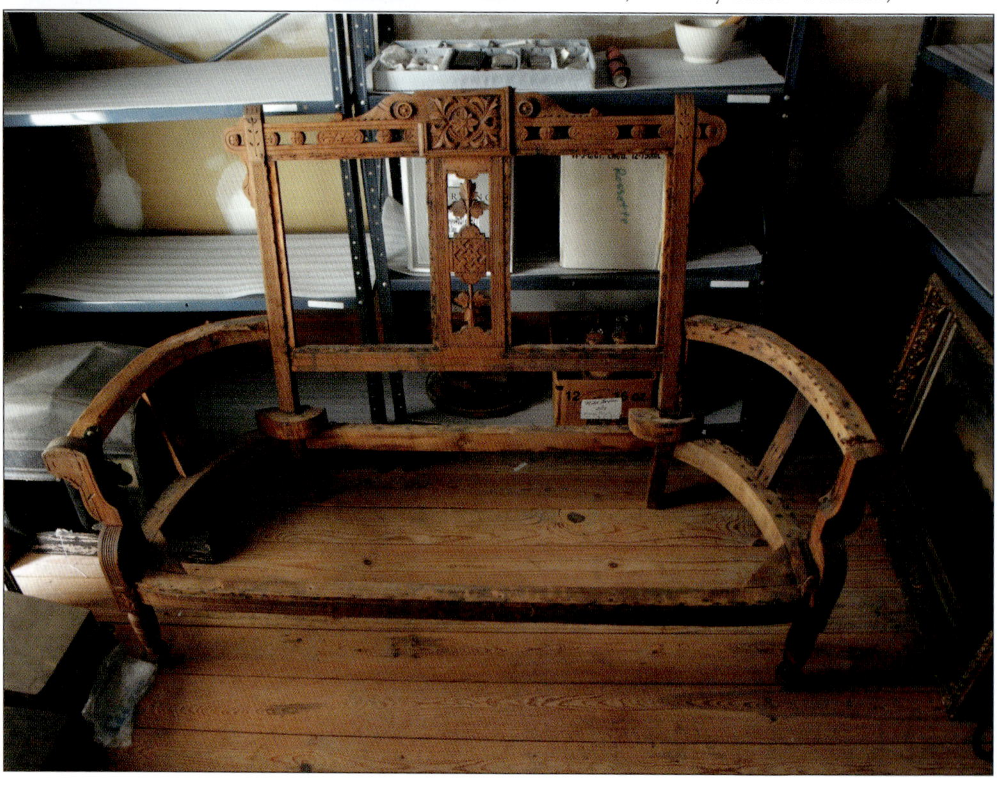

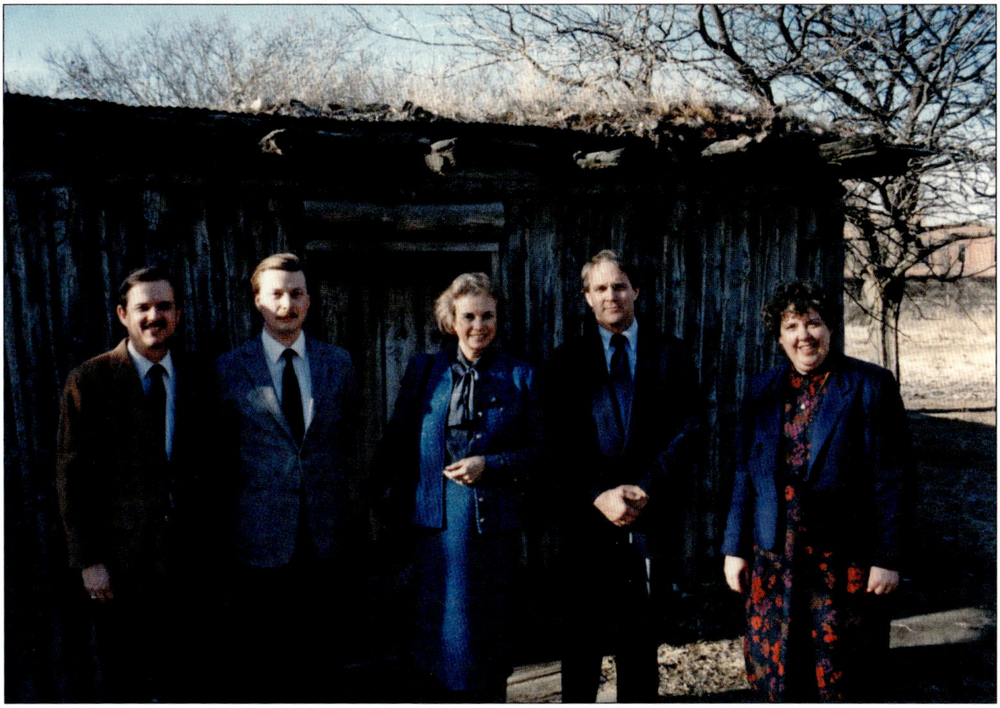

Cowtown has had many important visitors, such as then Supreme Court justice Sandra Day O'Connor; Kansas senator Bob Dole's wife and then president of the American Red Cross Elizabeth Dole; and then Russian president Boris Yeltsin's wife, Naina. Pictured above from left to right are Richard Basore, a longtime Old Cowtown Museum board member; Stan Harder, Old Cowtown Museum curator; Justice O'Connor; Michael Husband, Old Cowtown Museum director; and Elizabeth Kennedy, Old Cowtown Museum assistant director. Justice O'Connor's great-grandmother Eliza Flanders Day was from Wichita. Below, Elizabeth Dole (second from left) joins Naina Yeltsin (far right) and Girl Scouts during Yeltsin's visit to Old Cowtown Museum in 1992.

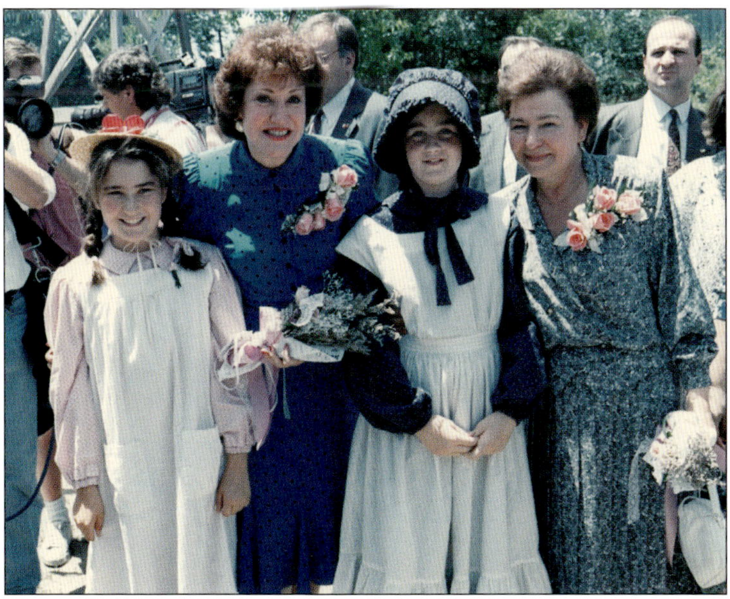

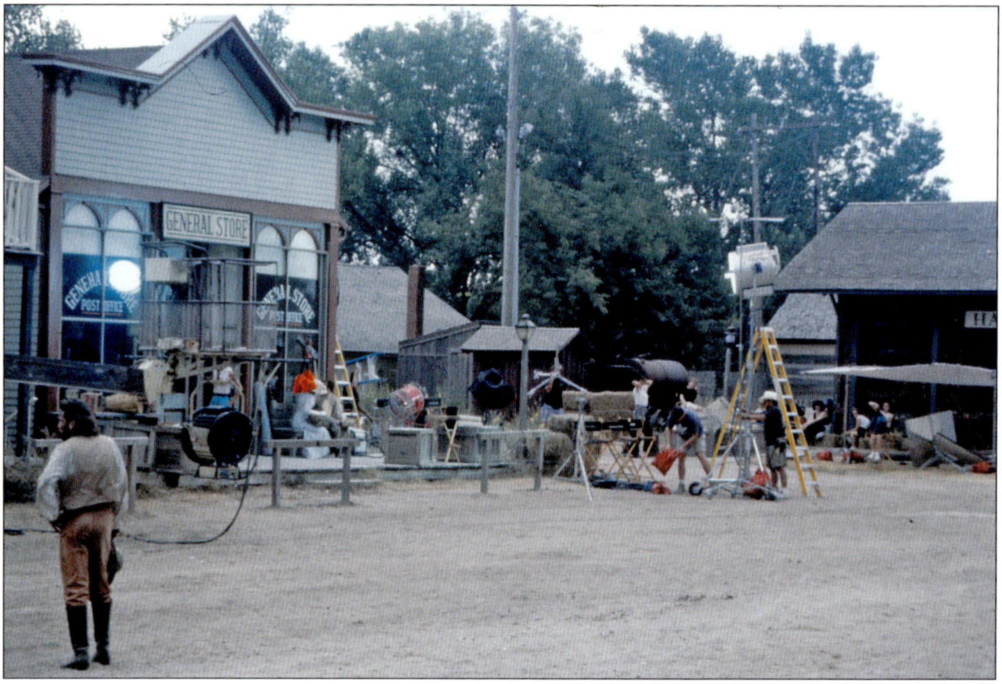

Over the years, Old Cowtown Museum has been a perfect setting for many movies, television shows, and documentaries. Filmmakers have used Cowtown as a backdrop for movies such as *Skylark*, starring Glenn Close and Christopher Walken, in 1993 (above) and *Sarah, Plain and Tall: Winter's End*, also starring Glenn Close and Christopher Walken, in 1999 (below). Other films and television shows filmed at the museum include *Stolen Women, Captured Hearts* in 1996, *The Only Good Indian* in 2007, and *Wichita* in 2013. The use of Old Cowtown Museum as a set for television and movies offers another source of revenue for the institution.

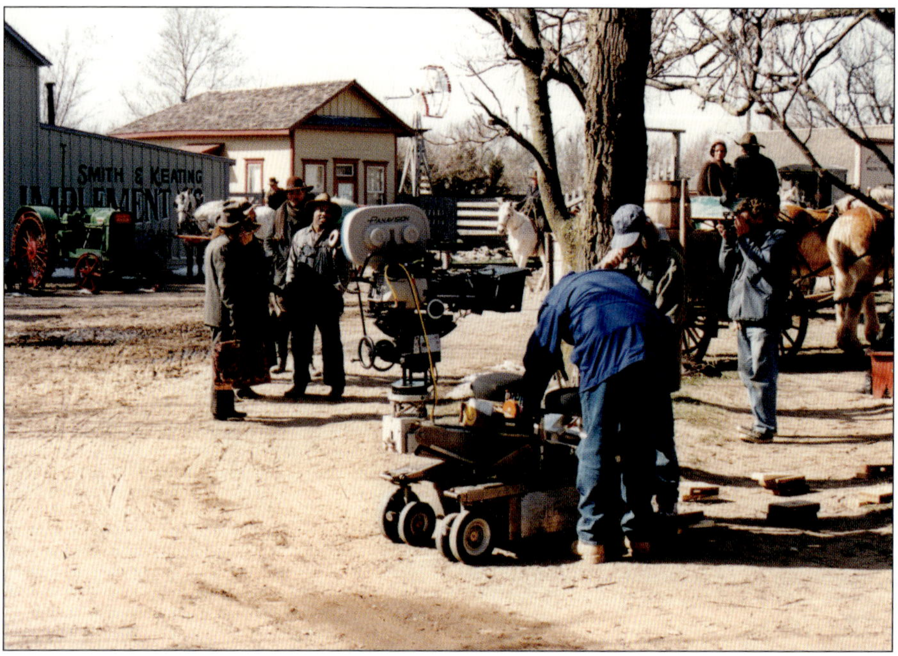

Throughout the 66 years of Old Cowtown Museum one of the most remembered people has been Galen Arnett, seen at right. Arnett has been influential in training animals and for the introduction of longhorn cattle drives during the Rails & Trails event in the 2000s. Below, as a reenactor, Duane Nelson represented the African American cowboys of the Old West era. It has been estimated that one in four cowboys of the time were African Americans, many of whom had been born into slavery. Nelson's reenacting of African American cowboys was part of the museum's effort to present the new history of women and minorities. This was a way to counter the fictionalized Old West version of history popular in the 1950s and 1960s.

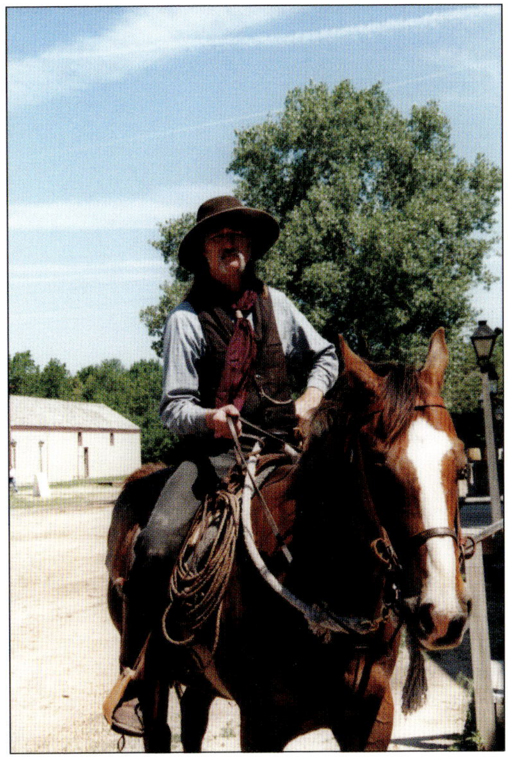

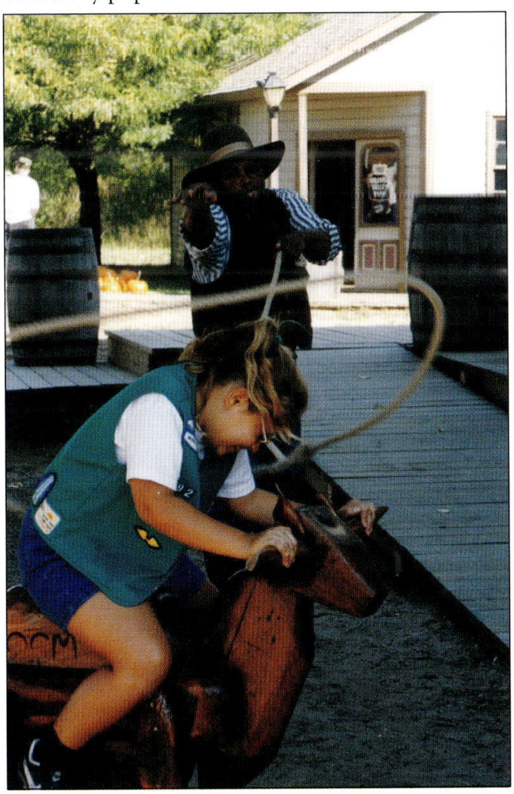

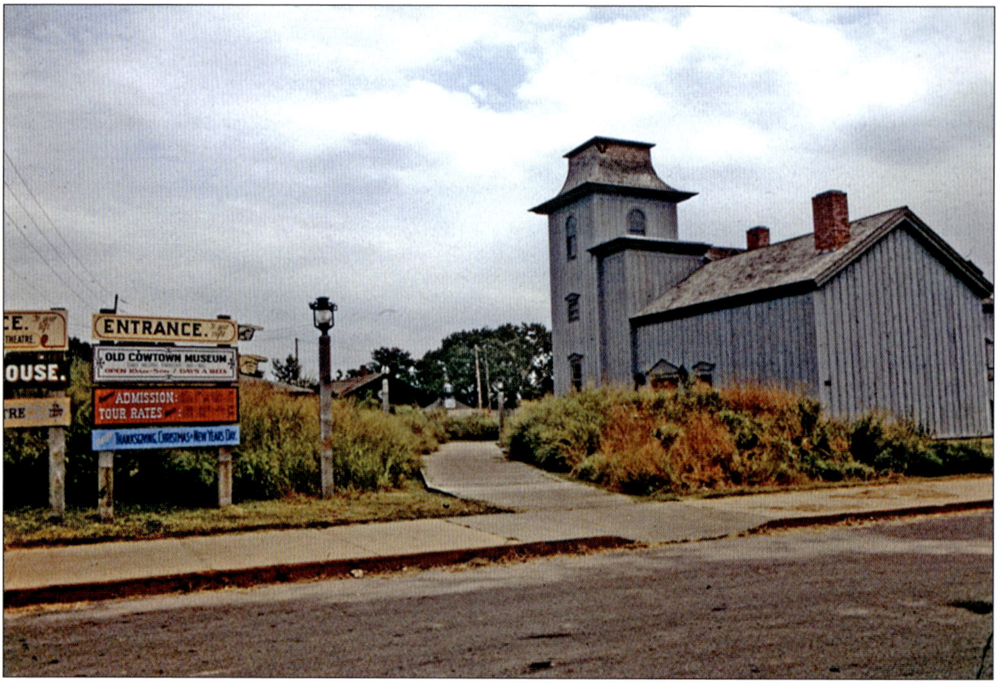

Many changes were made to Cowtown over the years, such as the location of the entrance, which has been moved from the east to the west side and back, at least twice, and the relocation of certain buildings. Additionally, there have been many new additions to the museum, such as the Smith Farm House in 1990, and the museum is still being added to. Now known as the DeVore Farm, the Smith Farm House was built in 1884 at 15428 East Central Avenue. It was moved to the museum in 1990 and sat on the east side until construction started on the Devore Farm in 1997.

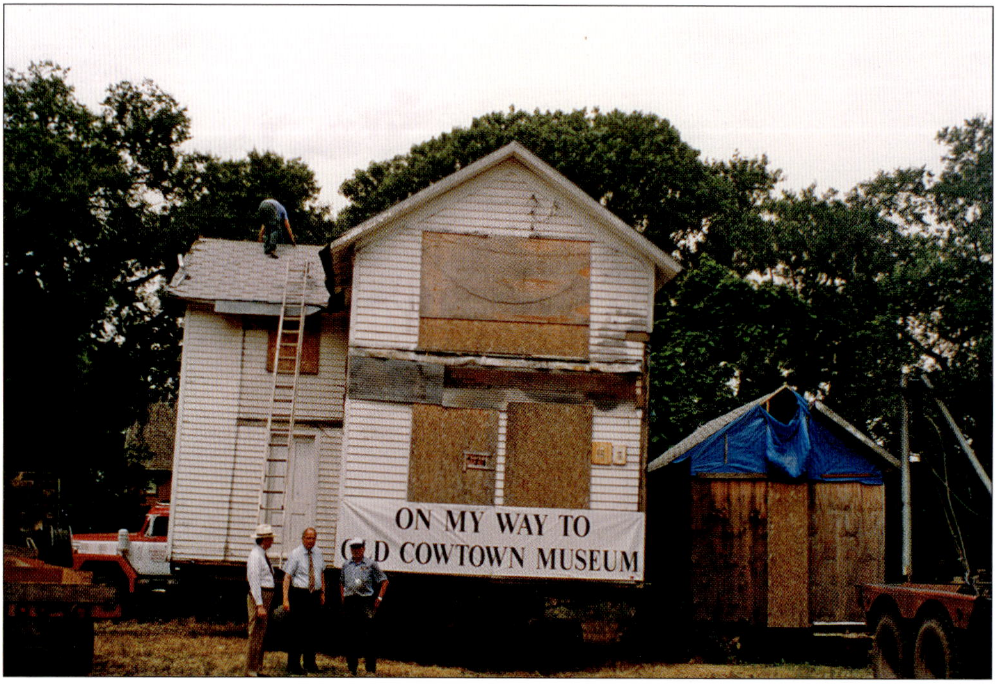

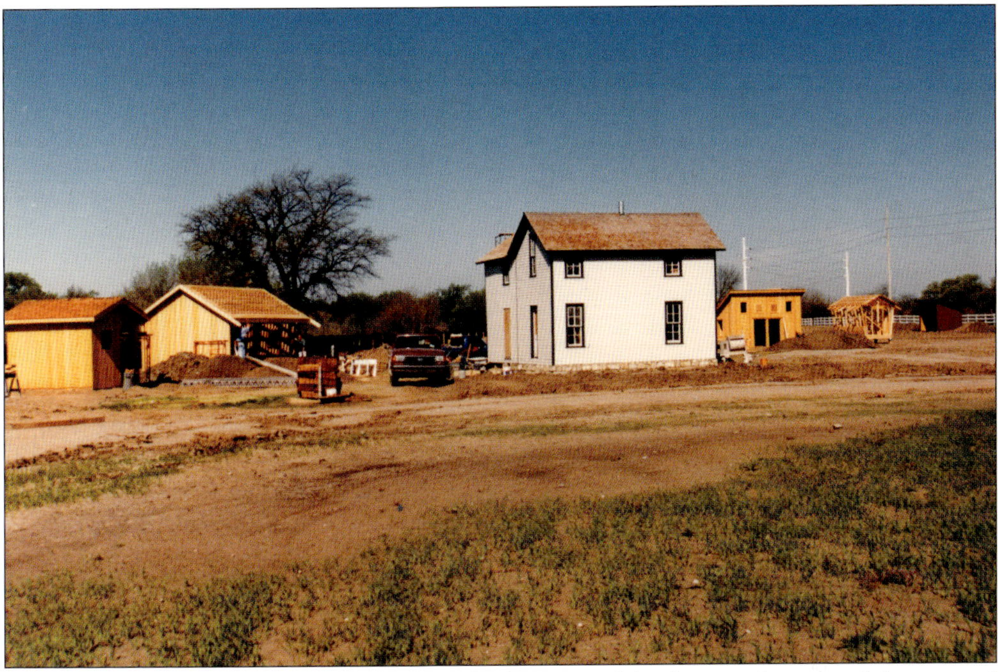

In 1997, construction started on the farm. The location of the farm to the west of the restored town necessitated the removal of the shops area west of the Variety Theater and the loss of 75 parking spaces. It also caused the closing of the Empire House Theatre, a melodrama theater run by longtime Wichitans John Boldenow and Michael Ballinger. As work continued, local lawyer Paul Dugan, in 1997, donated his family's 1882 barn for the farm project. After studying the barn to make sure it was safe to move, Cowtown staff made the decision to only use materials from the Dugan Barn to trim the interior of the farm's barn (Below, courtesy Keith Wondra.)

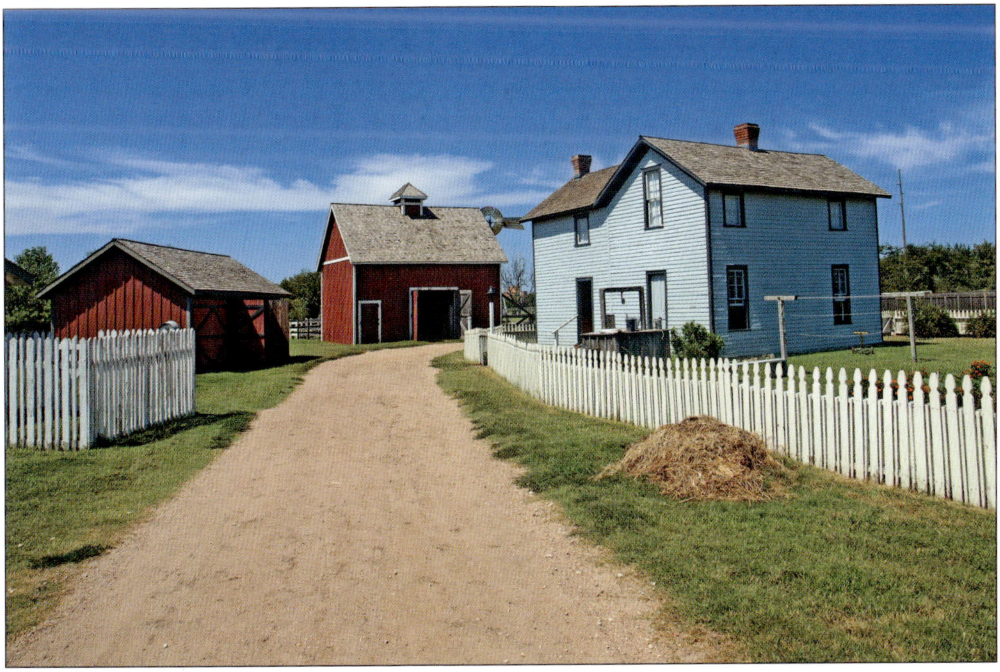

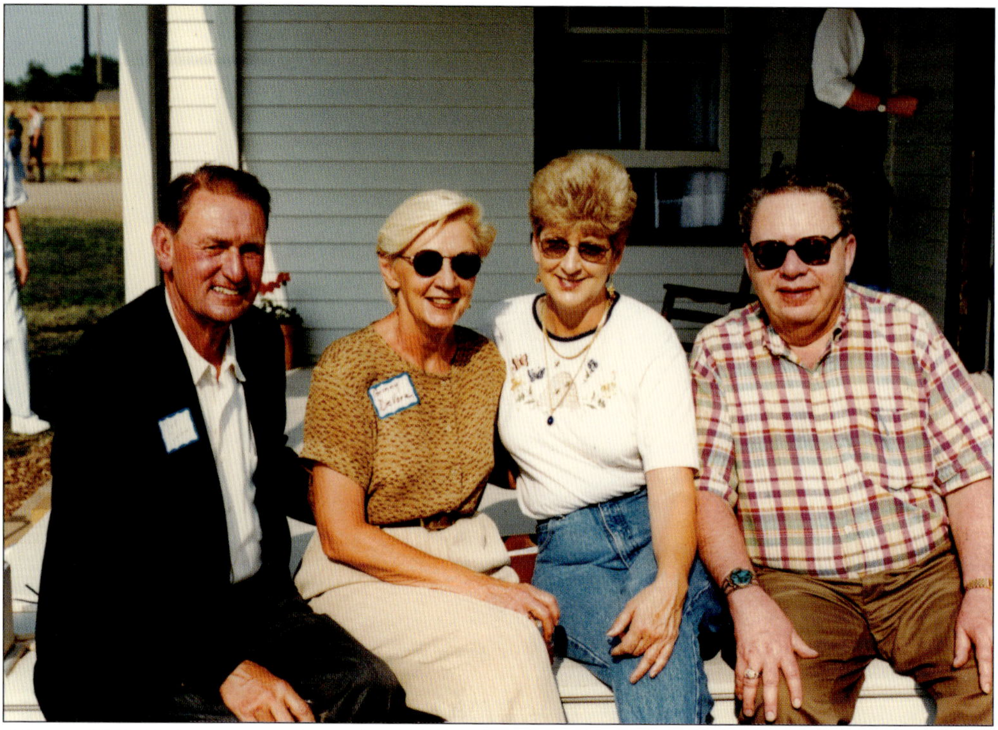

After a $150,000 donation from the DeVore Foundation, one of the largest in the museum's history, the 1870s farm was renamed the 1880 DeVore Farm. Taken during the DeVore Farm formal opening on May 22, 1998, this photograph shows, from left to right, Dick and Ginny DeVore and Alta and Bill DeVore on the front porch of the Smith Farm House.

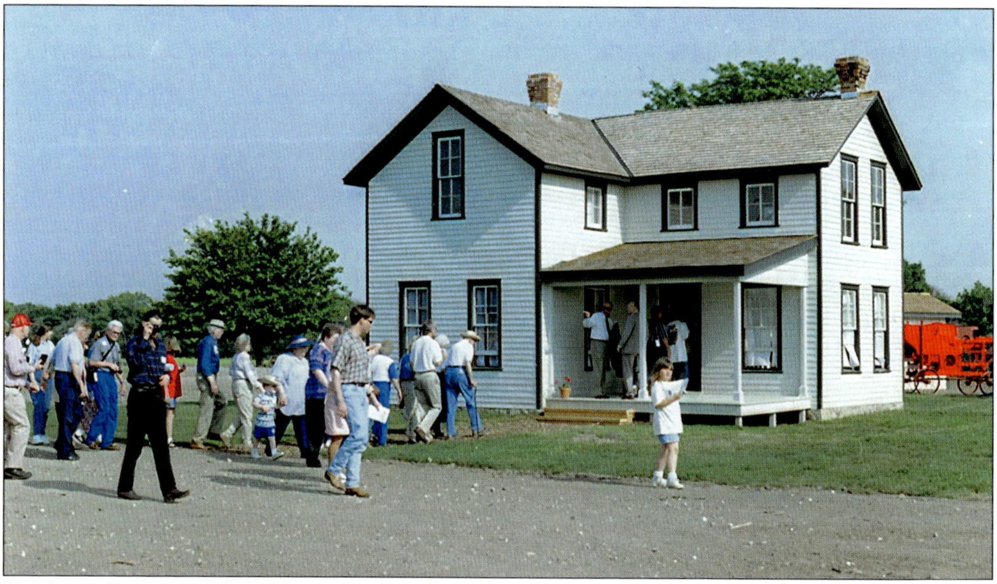

On May 22, 1998, Cowtown's newest exhibit opened to the public with over 750 people attending the opening, and 1,000 people came during the DeVore Farm opening weekend on May 23–25, 1998. The farm continues to be one of the biggest draws at the museum and is home to educational programs.

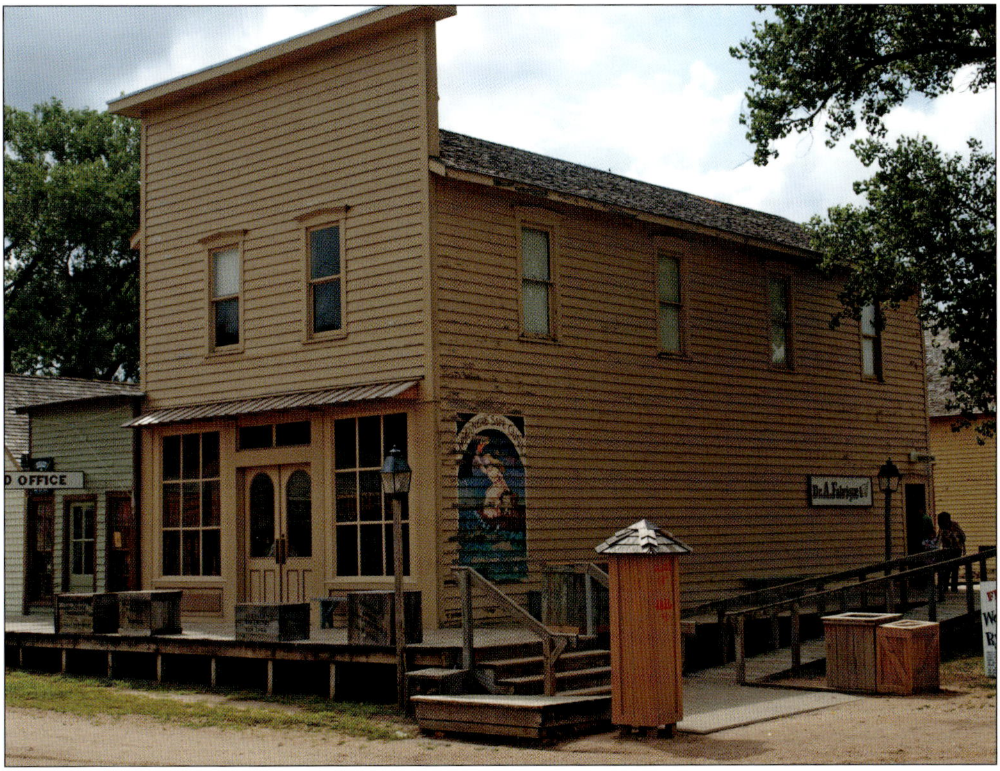

In 1995, with funding from the Kansas Department of Commerce and Housing, along with money from the local medical community, construction started on the new building. It housed the J.P. Allen Drug Store exhibit on the first floor, with Doctor and Dentist Office exhibits on the second floor. After months of construction and combing of antique stores for exhibit items by volunteers and staff, including Stan Harder and Roslyn Hoch, the J.P. Allen Drug Store was ready for its grand opening on May 9, 1996. Below, along with the addition of a new drugstore, Old Cowtown Museum saw the moving of its entrance from Lakeside Manor to the former Empire House. This was the entrance to the museum until the Visitors Center opened in 2005. (Above, courtesy Keith Wondra.)

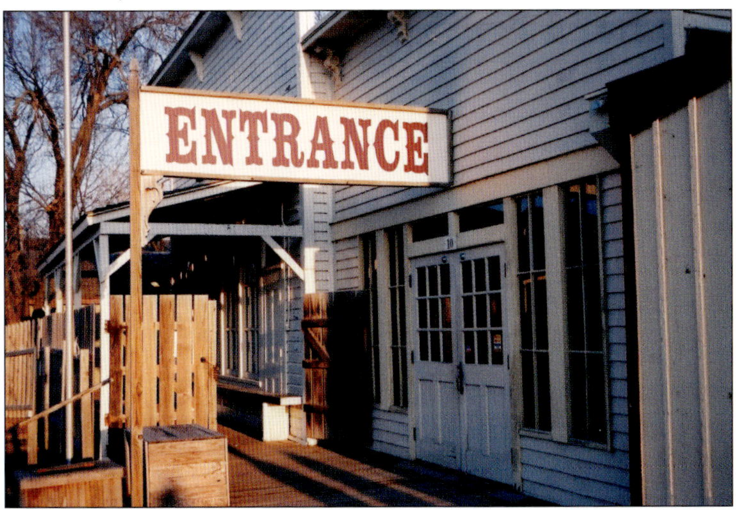

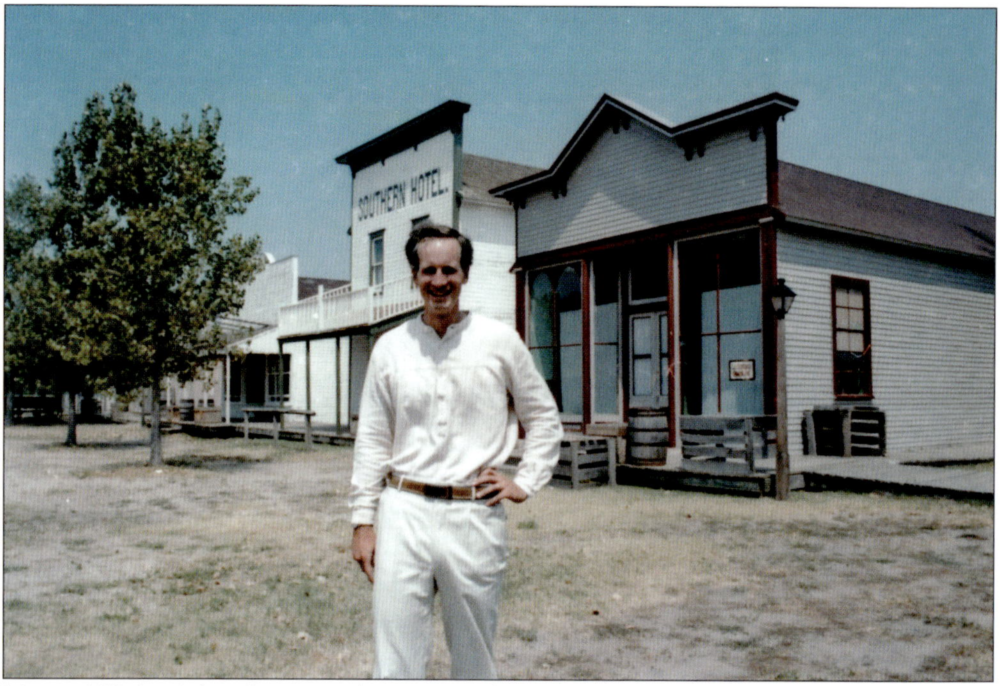

Many of Wichita's best historians have given their time and skills to Cowtown over the years, such as Bill Ellington, Dr. Craig Miner, Dr. Jay Price, Stan Harder, and Dr. Schuyler Jones. There have been many more, and without all of the people who have worked for, volunteered at, written about, or done research for Cowtown, much of Wichita's history would have been lost and forgotten to time. Dr. Craig Miner, pictured above, wrote one of the influential books on early Wichita history, *Wichita: The Early Years,* as a fundraiser for the museum. Along with writing about Wichita history, Dr. Jay Price, seen below, also served on Old Cowtown Museum's board and its collection committee.

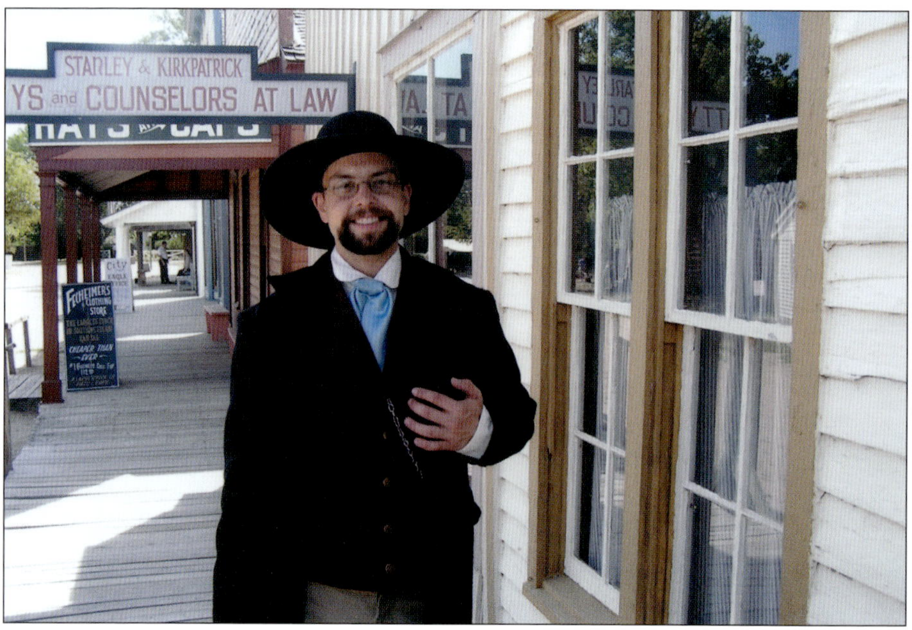

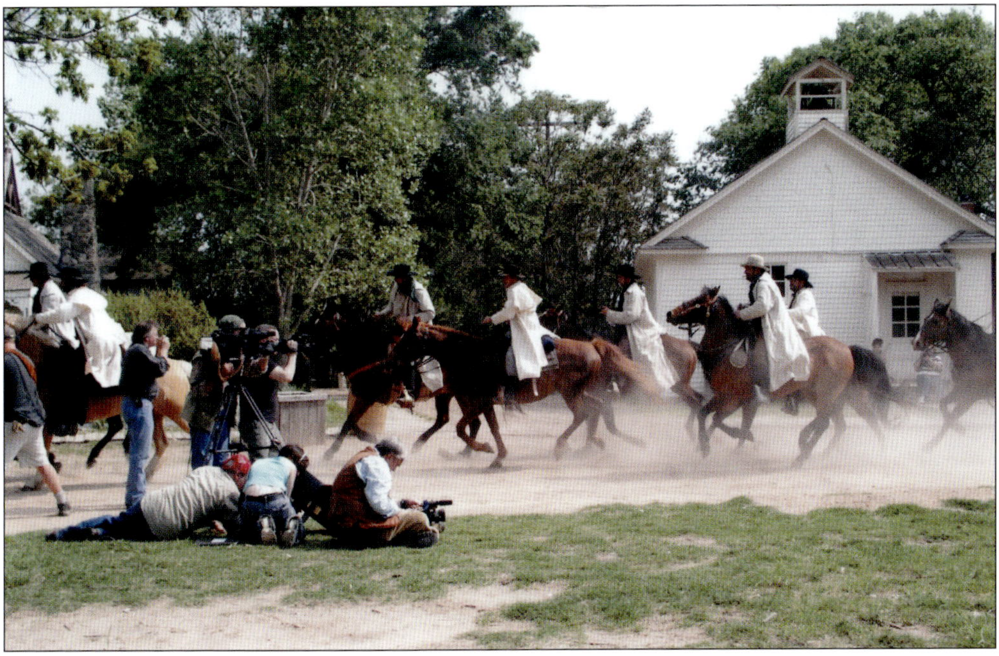

Just like movies, Old Cowtown Museum has been an ideal place to film television shows such as *Investigating History: The Mystery of Jesse James* in 2003. The one-story buildings provide a perfect backdrop that lets viewers go back in time in any region, not just Wichita and Kansas.

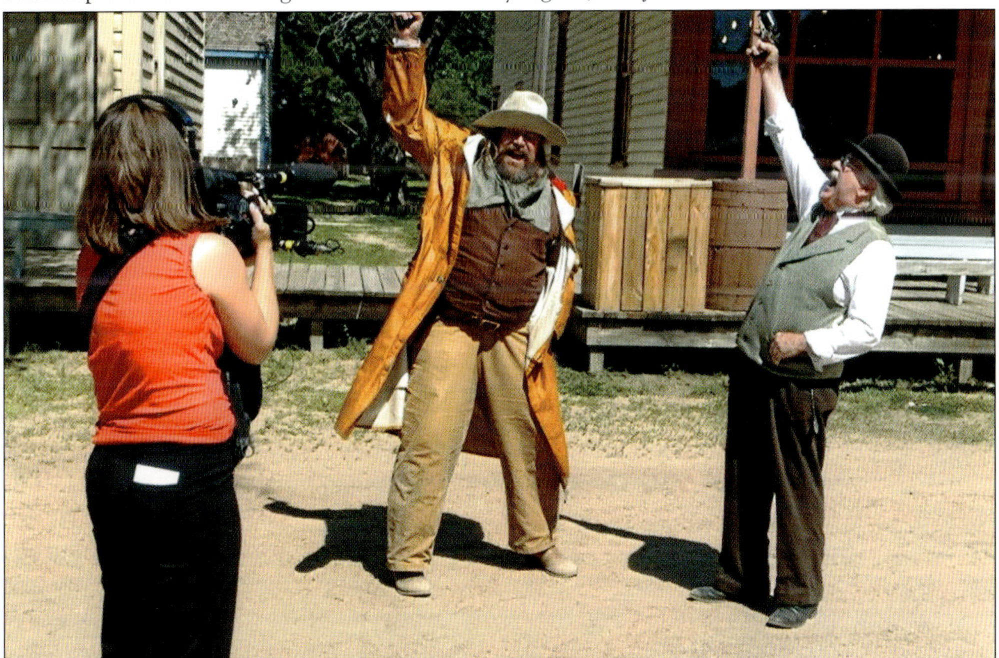

In 2012, Old Cowtown Museum was part of the Wichita Weekend Episodes on C-SPAN's *American History TV* series that feature the history and literary life of Wichita. The nationally broadcast programs showcase the museum and many of its volunteers and staff. They also provide an avenue to promote Old Cowtown Museum's role in telling the history of Wichita and Sedgwick County.

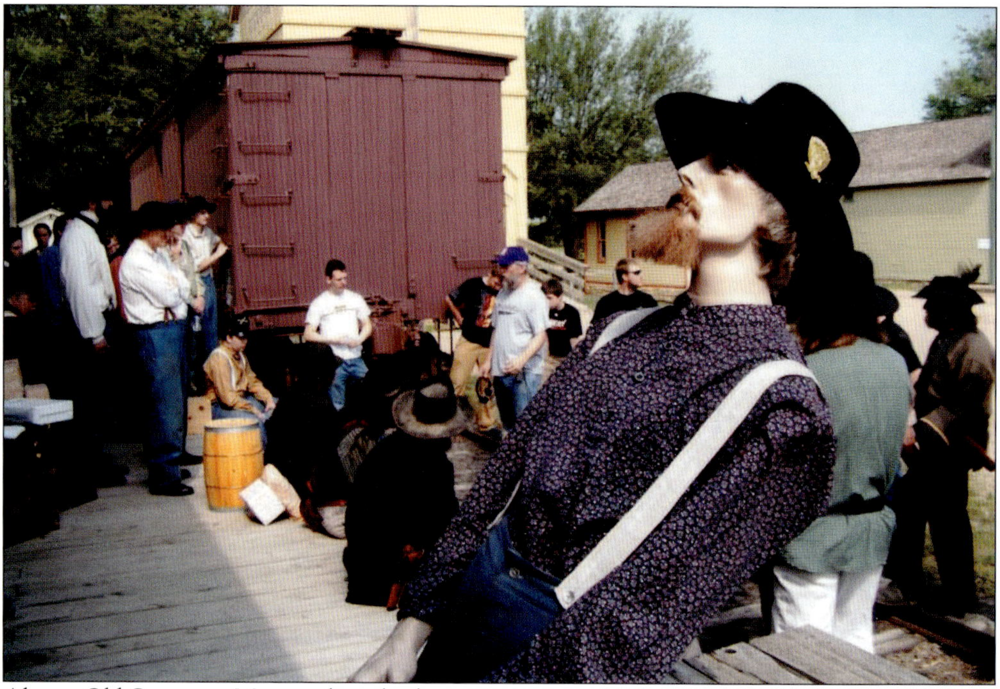

Above, Old Cowtown Museum has also been instrumental in helping with Ken Spurgeon's Lone Chimney Films' filming of its Civil War documentaries, including *Touched by Fire* in 2004 and *The Road to Valhalla* in 2013, at Cowtown. Ken Spurgeon is in the middle wearing the blue hat, T-shirt, and jeans. Below, the museum has also been the setting for locally produced commercials and trailers such as the one for the 2014 Tallgrass Film Festival. Locally, the museum has been the setting for hundreds of movies, documentaries, and commercials. (Above, photograph by Lauren Pope, courtesy Lone Chimney Films; below, courtesy Tallgrass Film Festival.)

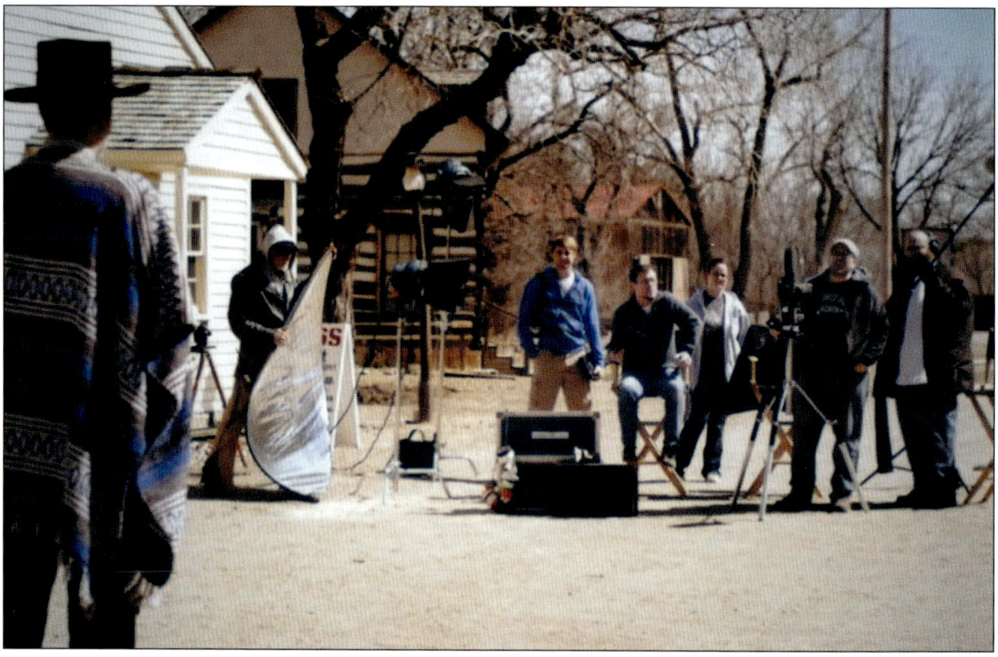

Five

Decline and Resurgence

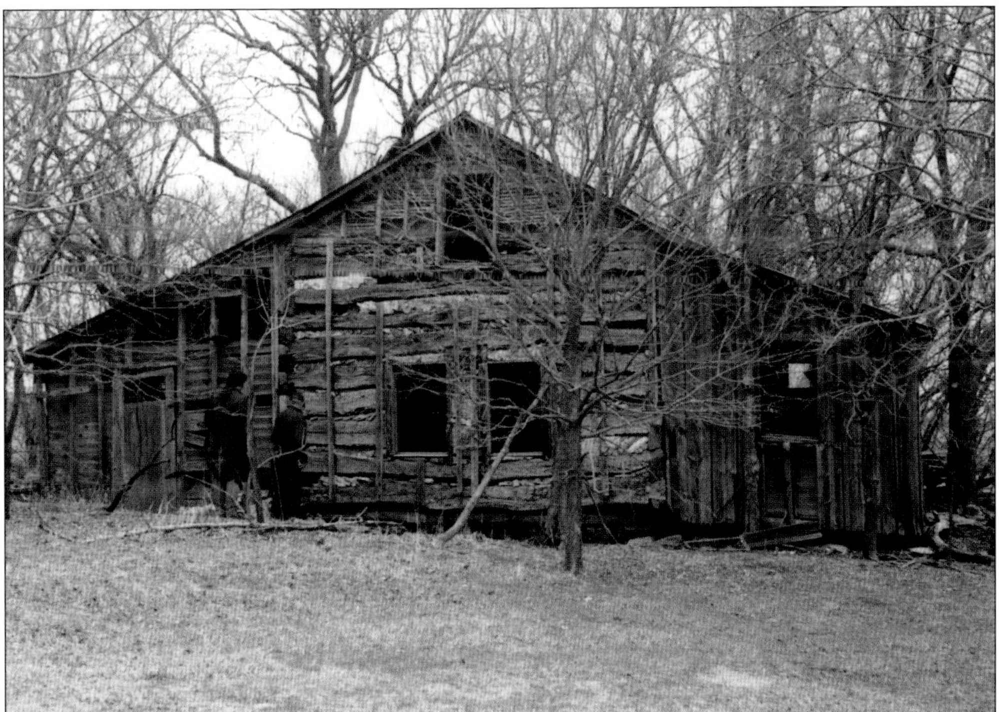

In 2000, the museum board received a donation of the Heller Cabin from Dickinson County, Kansas. The cabin was originally built by Leonard Hoffman in the 1870s in Elmo, near Abilene, Kansas. Later, the Heller family purchased the land and cabin. The cabin was moved to the west end of the museum on the road to the DeVore Farm in 2002 while the location of a permanent home was decided.

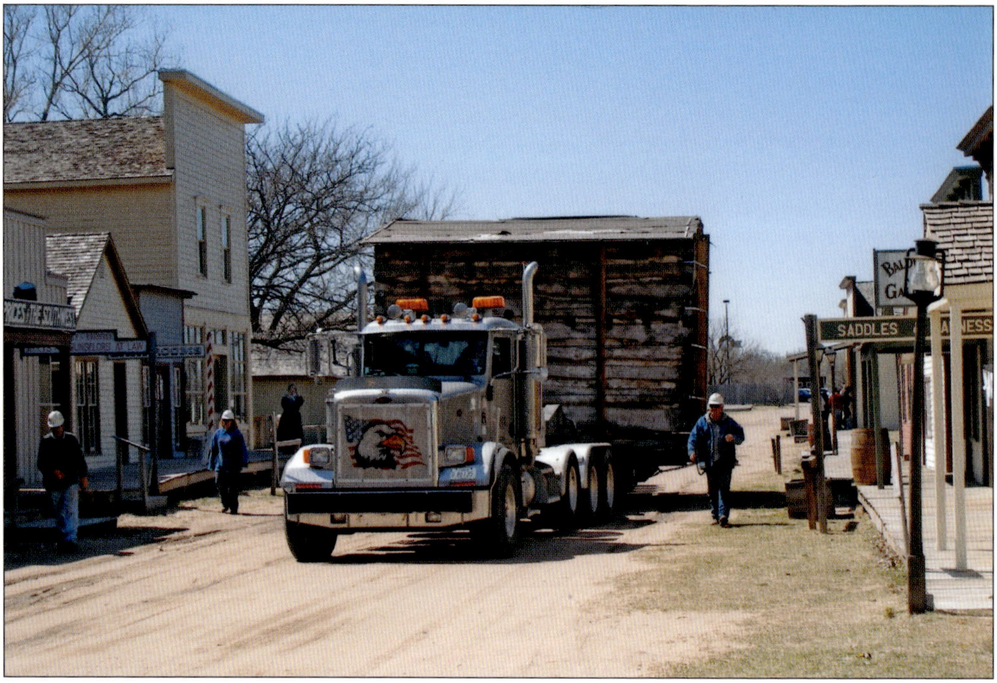

The opening of the Visitors Center on the east side of the museum put to rest where the Heller Cabin was finally going to be placed. The final move of the cabin occurred in 2009 when it was transported from the west side of the museum, barely passing the Meat Market en route to its present site east of the Visitors Center. Nine years and five months after its acquisition and three directors later, the cabin opened to the public. The interpretation of not just the Heller Cabin, but also of other buildings at Old Cowtown Museum, away from their original use is unique to Old Cowtown Museum. (Below, courtesy Keith Wondra.)

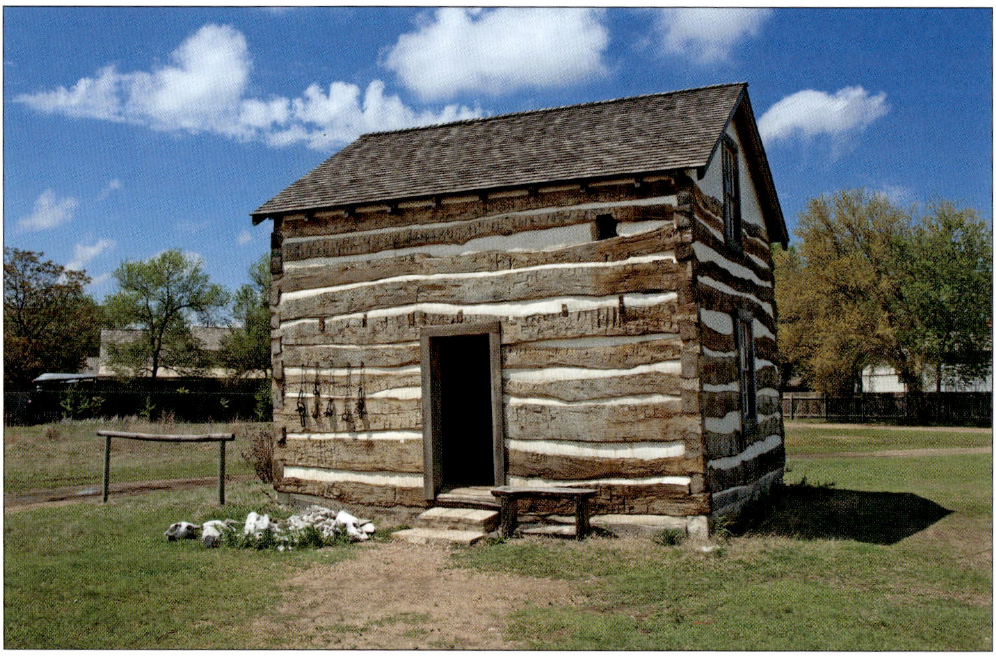

One of the museum's longtime volunteers is Bob Garrett. He started out by making a precise and detailed inventory of the collections. Over the years, he has been a board member, interim director, and curator. In the 1970s, Garrett came up with the idea that Cowtown should become the "Williamsburg of the West." It is an idea that still awaits a major financial benefactor to become reality. (Courtesy Keith Wondra.)

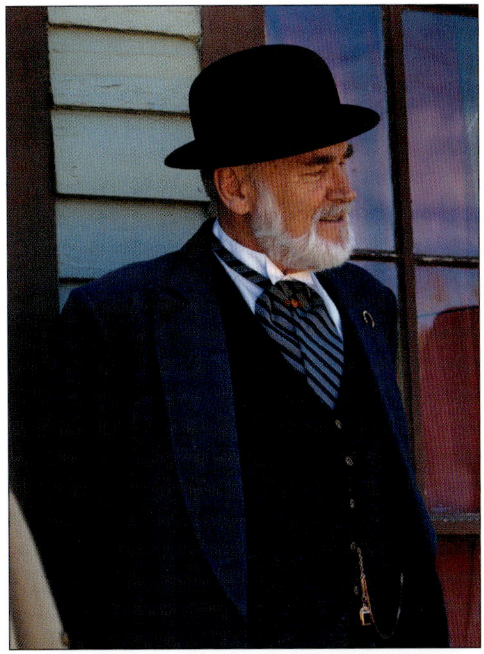

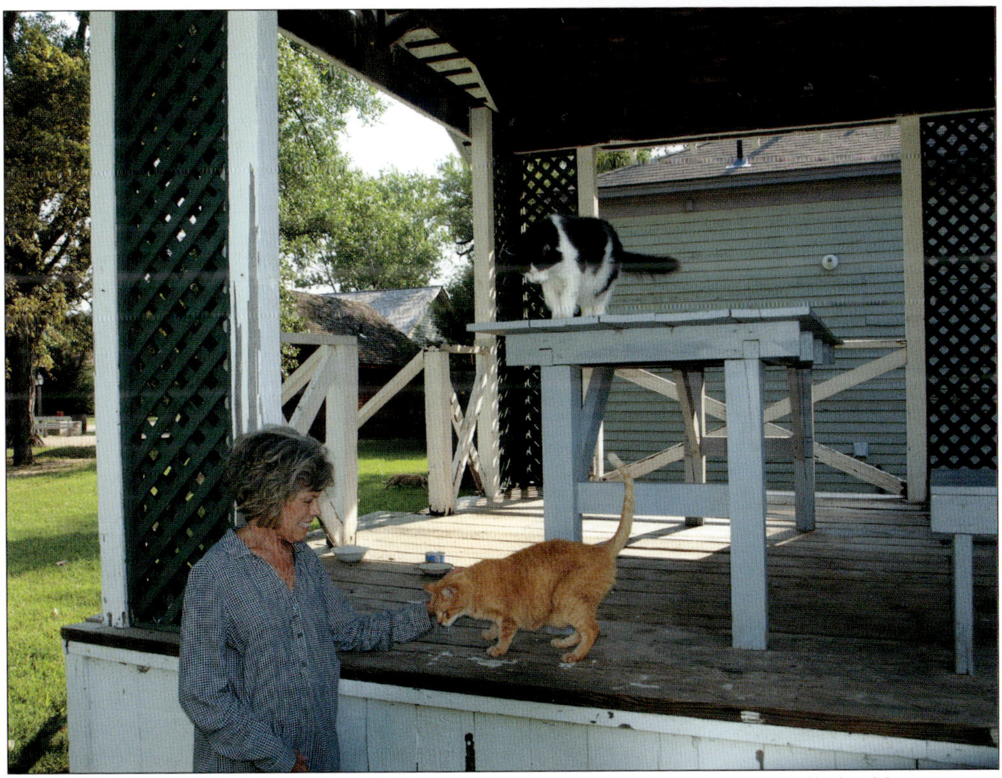

Beginning in 1976, Shirley Hutchison started to feed the stray cats that called Old Cowtown Museum home. She started feeding them out of her own pocket, but donations came in from individuals and local pet stores in the years that followed. Due to her daily care for the museum's cats, Hutchison has the most volunteer hours at the museum. (Courtesy Keith Wondra.)

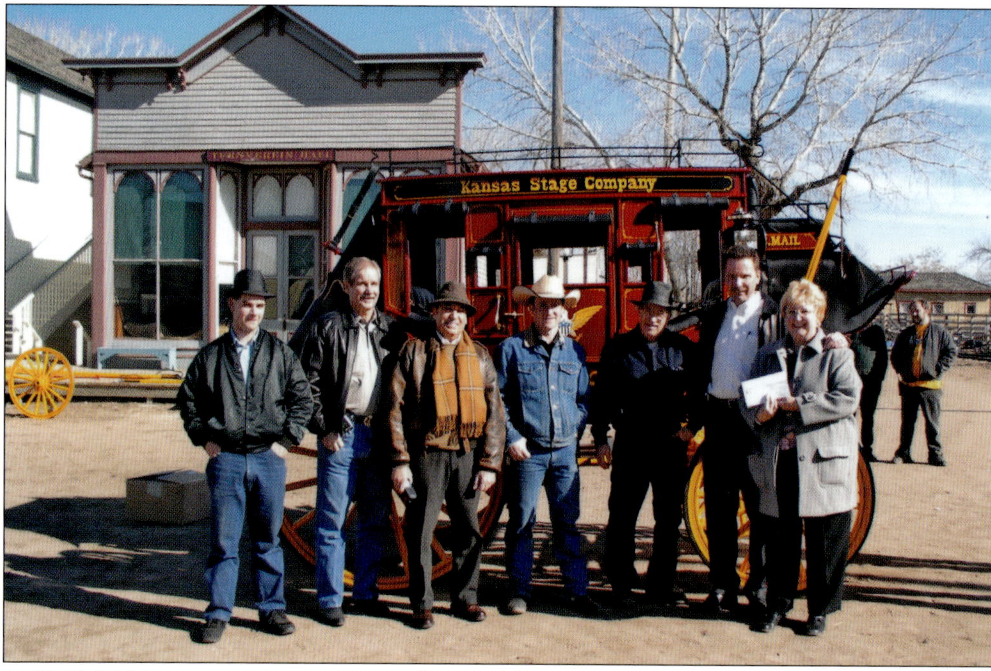

In 2005, Old Cowtown Museum received a reproduction Concord stagecoach provided by three key donors: Terry Newman of Papa John's Pizza, Terry Cole of KAKE-TV, and Dawson Grimsley of Davis-Moore Auto Group. The 8.5-foot wooden coach, made by Latham Coach Works of Fortuna, Missouri, arrived at the museum on January 28, 2005.

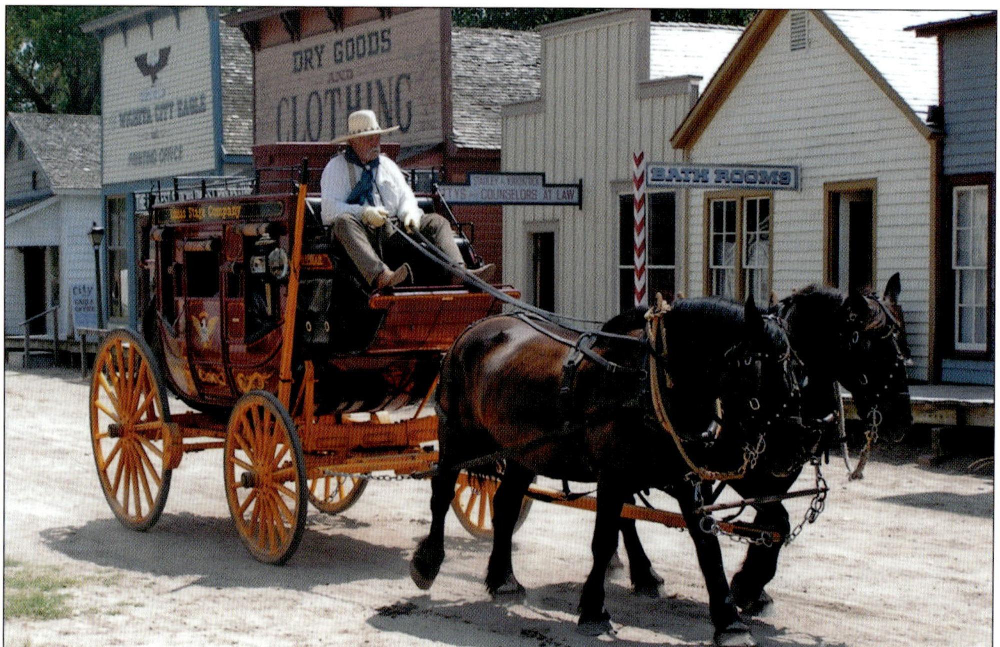

For 17 years, Old Cowtown Museum's Percheron horses Tim (right) and Barney pulled the wagon and stagecoach, much to the delight of visitors and staff. On July 29, 2014, Tim passed away at the age of 23 from cancer of the spleen, while Barney was retired at the end of 2014.

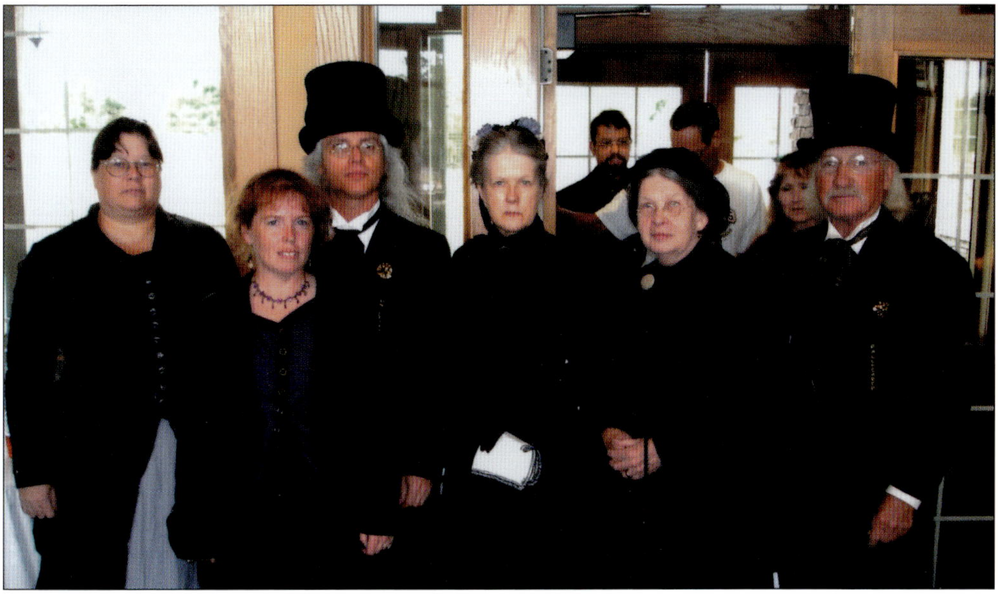

Old Cowtown Museum's financial problems in 2005 and 2006 prompted the involvement of Sedgwick County and the City of Wichita for financial help. The meetings between the city, Historic Wichita-Sedgwick County, Inc., and the county became contentious. Museum supporters picketed along Sim Park Drive, while volunteers dressed in black during the Historic Wichita-Sedgwick County, Inc. board meeting on September 11, 2006.

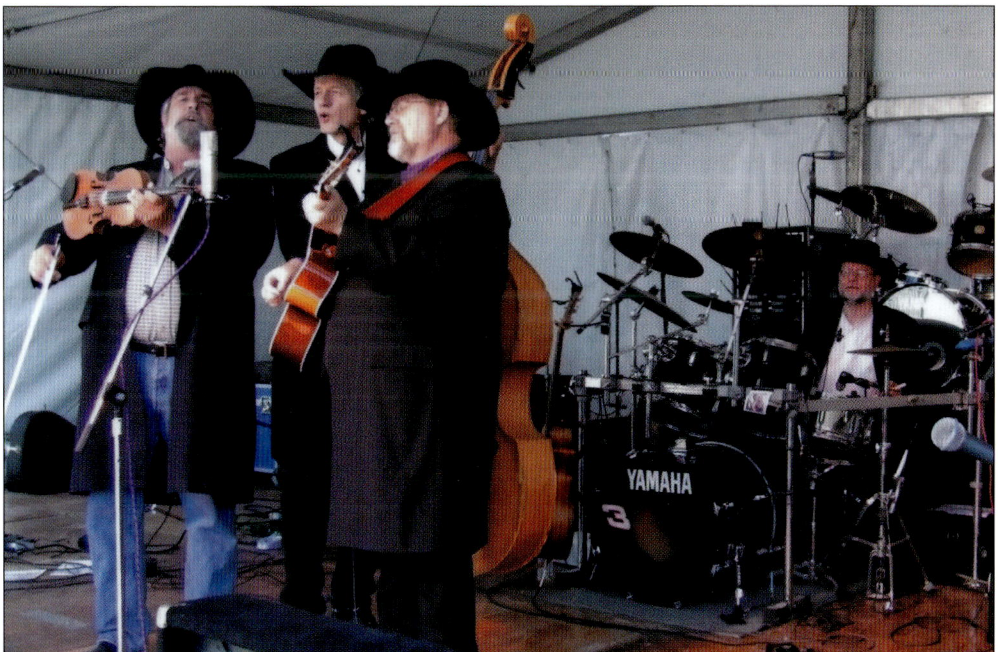

In 2007, Thomas Etheridge's Wild West World and Prairie Rose Chuckwagon Supper went bankrupt, and the famous Prairie Rose Wranglers needed a place to perform. The City of Wichita needed a draw for its newly acquired attraction, and the renamed Diamond W. Wranglers played to sold out crowds in the Visitors Center.

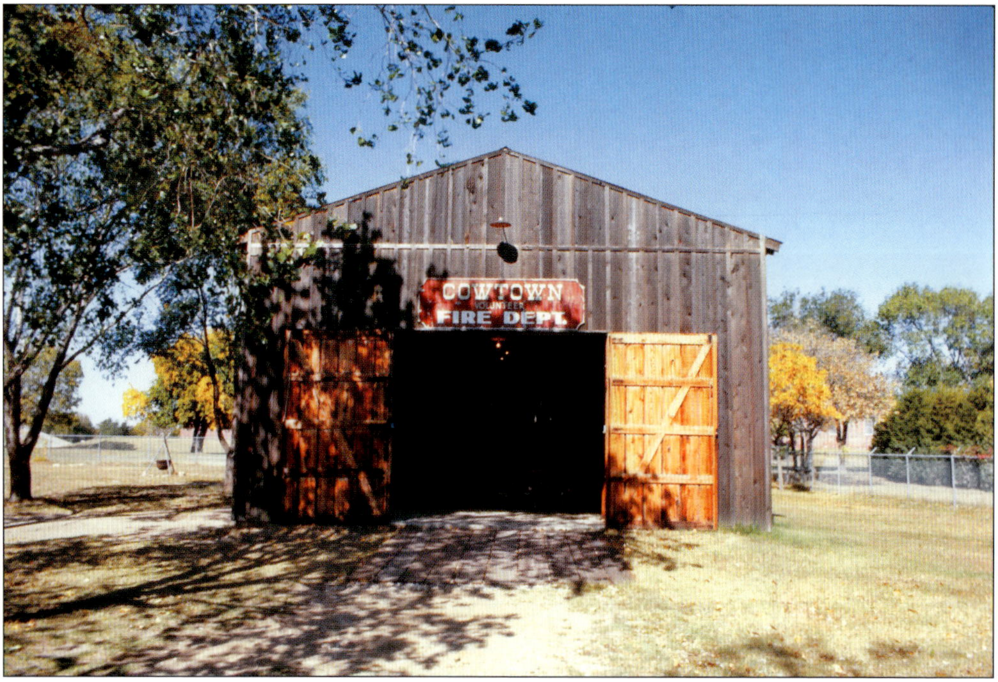

The Orientation Building was originally built around 1969 to house Old Cowtown Museum's volunteer fire department. In the 1980s, when all of the fire equipment was moved out to the Kansas Firefighters Museum on South Broadway, the structure became a storage building. In 2013, museum staff remodeled the first story of the brown storage barn with financial help from Historic Wichita, Inc. to become home to the new Orientation Building, a structure scrapped from the Visitors Center plans due to the financial issues. The new building was home to information on the history of the museum as well as a scale model of the grounds so visitors could orient themselves. (Below, courtesy Keith Wondra.)

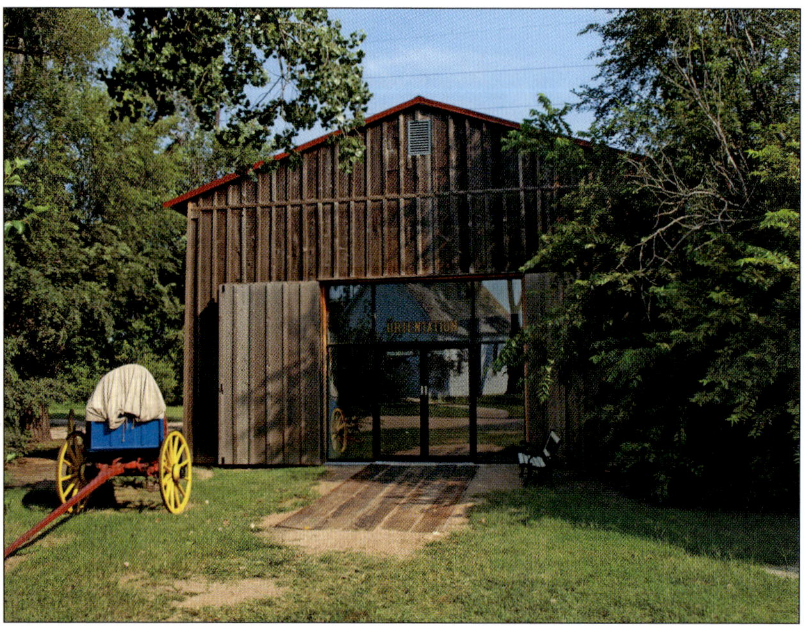

Bibliography

Girl Scouts of the Golden Plains Council. *Reflections 50 Years: Girl Scouts at Old Cowtown Museum, 1958–2008*. Wichita: Girl Scouts of the Golden Plains Council, 2007.

Historic Wichita, Inc. *Guide Book of Wichita Cowtown, 1869–1872*. Wichita: Historic Wichita, Inc., n.d.

———. *Historic Wichita Cow Town*. Wichita: Historic Wichita, n.d.

———. *Historic Wichita Cow Town: A Walk Down the Wooden Sidewalks of the Old West*. Wichita: Historic Wichita, Inc., n.d.

Levin, Amy K., ed. *Defining Memory: Local Museums and the Construction of History in America's Changing Communities*. Lanham, MD: Rowman & Littlefield Publishers, 2007.

Midtown Citizens Association. *10 Years Old and Growing Strong, 1972–1982*. Wichita: Midtown Citizens Association, 1982.

Miner, H. Craig. *Wichita: The Magic City*. Wichita: Wichita-Sedgwick County Historical Museum Association, 1988.

Old Cowtown Museum. *An Illustrated Walking Tour Guide to Historic Wichita Cowtown*. Wichita: Old Cowtown Museum, c. 1980.

———. *Wichita's Historic Cowtown*. Wichita: Old Cowtown Museum, c. 1980.

Price, Jay. "Cowboy Boosterism: Old Cowtown Museum and the Image of Wichita, Kansas." *Kansas History: A Journal of the Central Plains* 24 (Winter 2001/2002): 301–317.

Relive Yesterday at Historic Cowtown. Wichita: Historic Wichita, Inc., 1960s.

Unrau, William E., H. Craig Miner, Patricia Christgau, Stan Harder, and Elizabeth D. Kennedy. "Old Cowtown Museum Story Line and Planning Recommendations." Wichita: Historic Wichita-Sedgwick County, Inc., 1984.

Wondra, Keith. "'Where The Old West Comes to Life': The Story of Old Cowtown Museum." Master's thesis, Wichita State University, 2014.